D0914031

Legislators and Interpreters

Legislators and Interpreters

On modernity, post-modernity and intellectuals

ZYGMUNT BAUMAN

Polity Press

Copyright © Zygmunt Bauman, 1987

First published 1987 by Polity Press in association with
Basil Blackwell.
First published in paperback 1989.

Editorial office:
Polity Press, 65 Bridge Street,
Cambridge CB2 1UR, UK

Marketing and production:
Basil Blackwell Ltd
108 Cowley Road, Oxford OX4 1JF, UK

British Library Cataloguing in Publication Data

Bauman, Zygmunt
Legislators and interpreters: on
modernity, post-modernity and intellectuals.
1. Intellectuals   2. Culture
I. Title
306   HM213
ISBN 0-7456-0136-7
ISBN 0-7456-0790-X (pbk)

Typeset in 11 on 12½ Baskerville
by DMB (Typesetting), Oxford

Contents

Introduction

INTELLECTUALS: FROM MODERN LEGISLATORS TO POST-MODERN INTERPRETERS

When it was coined in the early years of the present century, the word 'intellectuals' was an attempt to recapture and reassert that societal centrality and those global concerns which had been associated with the production and dissemination of knowledge during the age of Enlightenment. The word was addressed to a motley collection of novelists, poets, artists, journalists, scientists and other public figures who felt it their moral responsibility, and their collective right, to interfere directly with the political process through influencing the minds of the nation and moulding the actions of its political leaders. By the time the word was coined, the descendants of *les philosophes* or *la république des lettres* had already been divided into specialized enclaves with their partial interests and localized concerns. The word was hence a rallying call, sounded over the closely guarded frontiers of professions and artistic *genres*; a call to resuscitate the tradition (or materialize the collective memory) of 'men of knowledge' embodying and practising the unity of truth, moral values and aesthetic judgement.

Like *la république des lettres*, integrated by the shared activity of discussion and commonality of its topics, the collectivity of the intellectuals was to be united by the response to the call, by the acceptance of the rights and responsibilities the call implied. Only ostensibly, if at all, was the category of 'intellectuals' intended as a descriptive category. It did not draw an objective boundary of the area it denoted, neither did it assume the pre-existence of such a boundary (though it did indicate the pool from which the volunteers might be sought and recruited). The category was rather expected to create its own referent through arousing concerns, mobilizing loyalties and prompting self-definitions, and thus deploying partial authorities of experts and artists in a collective political, moral and aesthetic authority of men of knowledge. The category was, so to speak, a widely opened invitation to join in a certain kind of practice of a global-societal import. And so it remained to this day. It makes little sense therefore to ask the question 'who are the intellectuals?' and expect in reply a set of objective measurements or even a finger-pointing exercise. It makes no sense to compose a list of professions whose members are intellectuals, or draw a line inside professional hierarchy above which the intellectuals are located. In any place and at any time 'the intellectuals' are constituted as a combined effect of mobilization and self-recruitment. The intentional meaning of 'being an intellectual' is to rise above the partial preoccupation of one's own profession or artistic *genre* and engage with the global issues of truth, judgement and taste of the time. The line dividing 'intellectuals' and 'non-intellectuals' is drawn and redrawn by decisions to join in a particular mode of activity.

At the time it entered the west European vocabulary, the concept of 'the intellectuals' drew its meaning from the collective memory of the Enlightenment era. It was in that era that the power/knowledge syndrome, a most conspicuous attribute of modernity, had been set. The syndrome was a joint product of two novel developments which took place at the beginning of the modern times: the emergence of a new type of state power with resources and will necessary to shape and administer the social system according to a preconceived model of order; and the establishment of a relatively autonomous, self-managing discourse able to generate such a model complete with the practices its implementation required. This book explores the hypothesis that the combination of those two developments created the kind of experience which was articulated in the particular world-view and associated intellectual strategies to be given the name of 'modernity'. This book also explores the hypothesis that the subsequent divorce between the state and intellectual discourse, together with the inner transformations of both spheres, has led to an experience articulated today in a world-view and associated strategies often referred to under the name of 'post-modernity'.

It ought to be clear from what has been said so far that the concepts of modernity and post-modernity are not used in this book as equivalents of the apparently similar oppositions with which they are frequently confused – like 'industrial' and 'post-industrial' society, or 'capitalist' and 'post-capitalist' society. Neither are they employed as synonyms for 'modernism' and 'post-modernism', the terms used to describe self-constituted, in large measure self-conscious, cultural and artistic styles. In the sense they are used in this book, the concepts of modernity and post-modernity stand for two sharply different contexts in which the 'intellectual role' is performed; and two distinct strategies which develop in response to them. The opposition between modernity and post-modernity has been employed here in the service of theorizing the last three centuries of West European history (or West European dominated history) from the perspective of intellectual praxis. It is this practice that can be modern or post-modern; the dominance of one or other of the two modes (not necessarily without exceptions) distinguishes modernity and post-modernity as periods in intellectual history. Even if the idea of modernity and post-modernity as *successive* historical periods is viewed as contentious (when it is justly pointed out that modern and post-modern practices coexist, though in varying proportion, within each of the two eras, and that one can speak of the domination of one or the other pattern only relatively, as of tendencies), the distinction between the two practices remains useful, if only as 'ideal types'; it does go some way towards revealing the essence of the current intellectual controversies and the range of the intellectual strategies available.

In referring to intellectual practices, the opposition between the terms modern and post-modern stands for differences in understanding the nature of the world, and the social world in particular, and in understanding the related nature, and purpose, of intellectual work.

The typically modern view of the world is one of an essentially orderly totality; the presence of a pattern of uneven distribution of probabilities allows a sort of explanation of the events which – if correct – is simultaneously a tool of prediction and (if required resources are available) of control. Control ('mastery over nature', 'planning' or 'designing' of society) is well nigh synonymously associated with ordering action, understood as the manipulation of probabilities (rendering some events more likely, others less likely). Effectivity of control depends on the adequacy of knowledge of the 'natural' order. Such adequate knowledge is, in principle, attainable. Effectivity of control and correctness of knowledge are tightly related (the second explains the first, the first corroborates the second), whether in laboratory experiment or societal practice. Between themselves, they supply criteria to classify existing practices as superior or inferior. Such classification is – again in principle – objective, that is, publicly testable and demonstrable each time the above-mentioned criteria are applied. Practices which cannot be objectively justified (for example, practices which legitimize themselves by reference to habits or opinions binding in a particular locality or particular time) are inferior as they distort knowledge and limit effectivity of control. Moving up the hierarchy of practices measured by the control/knowledge syndrome, means also moving toward universality and away from 'parochial', 'particularistic', 'localized' practices.

The typically post-modern view of the world is, in principle, one of an unlimited number of models of order, each one generated by a relatively autonomous set of practices. Order does not precede practices and hence cannot serve as an outside measure of their validity. Each of the many models of order makes sense solely in terms of the practices which validate it. In each case, validation brings in criteria which are developed within a particular tradition; they are upheld by the habits and beliefs of a 'community of meanings' and admit of no other tests of legitimacy. Criteria described above as 'typically modern' are no exception to this general rule; they are ultimately validated by one of the many possible 'local traditions', and their historical fate depends on the fortunes of the tradition in which they reside. There are no criteria for evaluating local practices which are situated outside traditions, outside 'localities'. Systems of knowledge may only be evaluated from 'inside' their respective traditions. If, from the modern point of view, relativism of knowledge was a problem to be struggled against and eventually overcome in theory and in practice, from the post-modern point of view relativity of knowledge (that is, its 'embeddedness' in its own communally supported tradition) is a lasting feature of the world.

The typically modern strategy of intellectual work is one best characterized by the metaphor of the 'legislator' role. It consists of making authoritative statements which arbitrate in controversies of opinions and which select those opinions which, having been selected, become correct and binding. The authority to arbitrate is in this case legitimized by superior (objective) knowledge to which intellectuals have a better access than the non-intellectual part of society. Access to such knowledge is better thanks to procedural rules which assure the attainment of truth, the arrival at valid moral judgement, and the selection of proper artistic taste. Such procedural rules have a universal validity, as do the products of their application. The employment of such procedural rules makes the intellectual professions (scientists, moral philosphers, aesthetes) collective owners of knowledge of direct and crucial relevance to the maintenance and perfection of the social order. The condition of this being so is the work of the 'intellectuals proper' – meta-professionals, so to speak – to be responsible for the formulation of procedural rules and to control their correct application. Like the knowledge they produce, intellectuals are not bound by localized, communal traditions. They are, together with their knowledge, extra-territorial. This gives them the right and the duty to validate (or invalidate) beliefs which may be held in various sections of society. Indeed, as Popper observed, falsifying poorly founded, or unfounded views is what the procedural rules are best at.

The typically post-modern strategy of intellectual work is one best characterized by the metaphor of the 'interpreter' role. It consists of translating statements, made within one communally based tradition, so that they can be understood within the system of knowledge based on another tradition. Instead of being orientated towards selecting the best social order, this strategy is aimed at facilitating communication between autonomous (sovereign) participants. It is concerned with preventing the distortion of meaning in the process of communication. For this purpose, it promotes the need to penetrate deeply the alien system of knowledge from which the translation is to be made (for example, Geertz's 'thick description'), and the need to maintain the delicate balance between the two conversing traditions necessary for the message to be both undistorted (regarding the meaning invested by the sender) and understood (by the recipient). It is vitally important to note that the post-modern strategy does not imply the elimination of the modern one; on the contrary, it cannot be conceived without the continuation of the latter. While the post-modern strategy entails the abandonment of the universalistic ambitions of the intellectuals' own tradition, it does not abandon the universalistic ambitions of the intellectuals towards their own tradition; here, they retain their meta-professional authority, legislating about the procedural rules which allow them to arbitrate controversies of opinion and make statements intended as binding. The novel difficulty, however, is how to draw the boundaries of such community as may serve as the territory for legislative practices.

This is a minor irritant for the numerous specialized offshoots of intellectual practices served by 'partial' intellectuals. The contemporary 'general' intellectuals find, however, their territorial claims contested. And with the post-modern strategy around, such territorial claims become inherently problematic and difficult to legitimize.

It is the purpose of this book to explore the historical conditions under which the modern world-view and intellectual strategy were formed; and the conditions under which they were challenged and partly supplanted, or at least complemented, by an alternative, post-modern world-view and strategy. It is the assumption of this book that the emergence and the influence of the two distinct varieties of intellectual practice can be best understood when considered against the changes in the relations between the industrialized West and the rest of the world, in the internal organization of Western societies, in the location of knowledge and knowledge-producers within that organization, and in the mode of life of the intellectuals themselves. The book is, in other words, an attempt to apply sociological hermeneutics to understand the successive tendencies in the meta-narrative of Western intellectuals. In this meta-narrative its producers, the intellectuals, remain invisible – 'transparent'. The ambition of this exercise in sociological hermeneutics is to make this transparency opaque and hence visible and open to scrutiny.

One last remark is in order. In no way am I implying that the post-modern mode constitutes an advance over the modern one, that the two may be arranged in a progressive sequence in any of the possible meanings of the notoriously confusing idea of 'progress'. Moreover, I do not believe that modernity, as a type of intellectual mode, has been conclusively superseded by the advent of post-modernity, or that the latter has refuted the validity of the first (if one can refute anything taking a consistently post-modern stance). I am merely interested in understanding the social conditions under which the appearance of the two modes has been possible; and the factors responsible for their changing fortunes.

This study has been completed thanks to a research leave generously granted by the University of Leeds.

In the course of writing, I have been enormously helped by the interest, critique and ideas offered by Judith Adler, Rick Johnston, Volker Meja, Barbara Neiss, Robert Paine, Paul Piccone, Peter Sinclair, Victor Zaslavsky and other friends and colleagues at the Memorial University, St John's, Newfoundland.

Tony Giddens' stimulation and encouragement assisted this project from its inception.

To all of them I owe my gratitude.

Z.B.

Leeds-St Johns

1

Paul Radin, or an aetiology of the intellectuals

Definitions of the intellectual are many and diverse. They have, however, one trait in common, which makes them also different from all other definitions: they are all self-definitions. Indeed, their authors are the members of the same rare species they attempt to define. Hence every definition they propose is an attempt to draw a boundary of their own identity. Each boundary splits the territory into two sides: here and there, in and out, us and them. Each self-definition is in the end a pronouncement of an opposition marked by the presence of a distinction on one side of the boundary and its absence on the other.

Most definitions, however, refrain from admitting the true nature of their accomplishment: by defining two social spaces they assume they have the right to draw the boundary. Instead, they focus ostensibly on only one side of the boundary; they pretend to confine themselves to the articulation of the attributes uniquely present on one side; and they are silent about the necessarily divisive effects of the operation. What most definitions refuse to admit is that the separation of the two spaces (and the legislating of a specific relationship between them) is the purpose and the *raison d'être* of the definitional exercise, not its side-effect.

Thus the authors of most known definitions attempt to list the properties of the intellectuals before any reference is made to the extant or postulated social relationship which sets off the defined group from the rest of society. What is overlooked in the process is that this relationship itself, rather than any special qualities and possessions of the intellectuals as a group, constitutes them as a separate entity. Being intellectuals, they subsequently seek to reforge their separatedness into a self-identity. The specifically intellectual form of the operation – self-definition – masks its universal content, which is the reproduction and reinforcement of a given social config- uration, and – within it – a given (or claimed) status for the group.

The relatively rare exceptions to this rule come from those cases where the intellectuals focus their attention on another society, starkly different from their own; the more different, as it were, the better. Configurations salient in their own practice, but seldom brought to the surface when dealing with their own society, provide a frame of reference in which knowledge of the other society is ordered and interpreted. Self-delusion, indispensable for pragmatic reasons whenever the defence or enhancement of the group's own status is involved, becomes superfluous (indeed, counter-productive) when it is necessary to come to grips with alien experience. As both Levi-Strauss and Gadamer would say, only when confronting another culture, or another text (confronting them, let us clarify, in a purely cognitive, theoretical mode), can the intellectual 'under- stand oneself'. Indeed, the confrontation with the other is first and foremost the recognition of oneself; an objectification, in terms of a theory, of what would otherwise remain pre-theoretical, subcon- scious, inarticulate.

Nowhere perhaps has this self-revelatory character of cross- cultural hermeneutic exercise found a better illustration than in the work of the eminent American anthropologist Paul Radin. This comes as no surprise, as Radin's life-long preoccupation was the 'primitive world-view', the ideas held by primitive societies; their religious views, moral systems, philosophy. One can legitimately expect such a topic to set in operations precisely those constituents of the researcher's perspective which bear direct relation to under- standing his own role within the world of ideas. He can hardly come to grips with 'primitive religion' without scanning the field in search of 'primitive theologians'; his effort to understand primitive phil- osophy would require him to locate (or at least construe) primitive philosophers. The way he goes about this task will be found illumin- ating by anyone wishing to comprehend the processes by which intellectuals are self-constituted in the society of the researcher.

What Radin first found in primitive societies was 'the existence of two general types of temperament among primitive peoples, that of the priest-thinker and that of the layman; the one only secondarily identified with action, the other primarily so; the one interested in the analysis of the religious phenomena, the other in their effect'.[1] In the beginning, there is an opposition between the great majority of ordinary people, preoccupied with their daily business of survival, 'action' in the sense of the routine reproduction of their conditions of existence, and a small group of those who could not but reflect upon 'action': 'truly religious people . . . have always been few in number'. The opposition is at the same time a relation: the smaller group comes into existence only for some features (or, rather, the absence of some features) in the 'unmarked' majority; it has been, so to speak, 'called into existence' by a certain insufficiency or incompleteness in the larger group's equipment; thus the smaller group is in one sense a necessary complement of the 'unmarked' majority; in another sense, however, it exists in a derivative, perhaps even parasitic, mode in relation to the larger group.

This interplay between the two aspects of this complex relationship comes out clearly in Radin's description. 'Primitive man is afraid of one thing, of the uncertainties of the struggle of life.'[2] Uncertainty has always been the paramount source of fear. The random behaviour of factors crucial for the success or failure of one's life struggle, the stubborn unpredictability of outcome, lack of control over so many unknowns within the life equation, these have always generated acute spiritual discomfort and made the sufferers crave for the security which only the practical control, or intellectual awareness, of probabilities may bring. This urge has been the prime yarn of which the roles of magicians, priests, scientific experts, political prophets or professionals are spun.

> The religious formulator, at first unconsciously if you will, capitalised on the sense of insecurity of the ordinary man . . . The religious formulator developed the theory that everything of value, even everything unchangeable and predictable about man and the world around him, was surrounded and immersed in danger, that these dangers could be overcome only in a specific fashion and according to a prescription devised and perfected by him.[3]

Capitalising 'on the sense of insecurity' expressed itself in the postulation of a special vantage point, accessible only to special people and on special condition, from which a logic could be discerned beneath superficial randomness, so that the random could be made predictable. The control over fate proposed by the religious formulators was thus mediated by knowledge from the very start; a crucial element of the operation, as Radin insists, was 'the transference of the coercive power from the subject to the object'. (As Francis Bacon would say in a society separated from that described by Radin by millenia of *Naturgeschichte* time, 'one can master Nature by surrendering to its laws'.) Once the determinants of fate have been objectified, once the subject's will has been denied the power of forcing, coaxing or enticing the external objects into submission, the only power of relevance to the primeval urge for certainty is knowledge. By proxy, it is the power of the knowledge-holders. The specific way in which the sense of insecurity was capitalized upon by religious formulators and their later equivalents elevated the attribute of 'being in the know' as, simultaneously, its premise and inevitable effect.

But there is still more light in Radin's analysis. The kind of knowledge the religious formulators claimed was in no way predetermined by, or confined to, the concrete fears which had always haunted 'ordinary people'. The remarkable feature of the knowledge-attaining process was that it spawned as many new mysteries as it solved among the old ones; and generated as many new fears as it assuaged among the old. The way in which the uncertainty was originally capitalized upon triggered off an unending, self-propelled and self-reinforcing process, in which the very possibility of ever bringing the effort to an end and replacing the situation of uncertainty (within given parameters of the life-process) with one of spiritual balance and practical control was excluded. Once this process had been set in motion, it became apparent that even things seemingly 'unchangeable and predictable' were in fact 'surrounded and immersed in danger'. Power/knowledge denotes a self-perpetuating mechanism, which at a relatively early stage stops being dependent on the original impetus, as it creates conditions for its own continuous and ever more vigorous operation. More fear-generating uncertainties are introduced into the life-world of the 'laymen'. Many of them are so remote from the daily practice of the latter, that neither their gravity nor their declared cure may be checked against subjectively evident effects. This circumstance, of course, further enhances the power of knowledge and of the knowledge-guardians. Moreover, it renders this power virtually invulnerable to contest.

The relatively innocuous distinction drawn between 'religious formulators' and 'ordinary people', between 'being interested in the ideas' and 'being interested in their effects', leads to altogether formidable consequences. It engenders an acute asymmetry in the deployment of social power. Not only does it promote sharp polarization of status, influence, and access to the socially produced surplus, but it also (and perhaps most importantly) builds upon the opposition of temperaments a relationship of dependency. The doers now become dependent upon the thinkers; the ordinary people cannot conduct their life business without asking for, and receiving, the religious formulators' assistance. As members of society, the ordinary people are now incomplete, imperfect, wanting. There is no clear way in which their morbid flaws can be permanently repaired. Burdened with their flaws forever, they need the constant presence and ongoing intervention of the shamans, magicians, priests, theologians.

The intensity of this need (and hence the strength of dependence) grows with the number of uncertainties built into the existence of ordinary people, and the degree to which the shamans, magicians, etc., enjoy a monopoly in handling them. If, therefore, as Radin suggests, the religious formulators are motivated by the intention to 'strengthen their authority', or even, more cynically, by the wish to 'attain and enhance' their 'economic security',[4] the most rational strategy open to them will be to manipulate the beliefs of the ordinary people in such a way as to increase their experience of uncertainty, and of their personal inability to ward off its potentially deleterious effects. (This strategy would be a case application of the general cybernetic rule, according to which in every complex system the subsystem 'nearest to instability rules'.)[5] The latter condition can be best achieved if the knowledge indispensable for handling the uncertainty is esoteric (or better still, held secret), if handling the uncertainty demands implements the ordinary people do not possess, or if the participation of the shaman, priest, etc., is recognized as an irreplaceable ingredient of the procedure. One can easily observe the application of all these tactical principles in the history of expert–layman relations.

One of the most intriguing of Radin's insights into the pragmatics of the intellectual role can be found in his attempt to trace back the model of the primitive philosopher to a pattern first introduced by shamans.

> The basic qualification for the shaman and medicine-man in the more simply organised groups like the Eskimo and the Arunta is that he belong to the neurotic-epileptoid type. It is likewise clear that, as we approach tribes with a more complex form of economic organisation,

these qualifications, while still present, become secondary to new ones. For this we have already given explanation, namely, that, as the emoluments of office increased, many people who were quite normal were attracted to the priesthood. The pattern of behaviour, however, had by that time become fixed and the non-neurotic shaman had to accept the formulation which owed its origin and its initial development to his neurotic predecessors and colleagues. This formulation . . . consisted of three parts: first, the description of his neurotic temperament and of his actual suffering and trance; second, the description of his enforced isolation, physical and spiritual, from the rest of the group; and, third, the detailed description of what might best be called an obsessive identification with his goal. From the first arose the theory of the nature of the ordeal through which he must pass; from the second the insistence upon taboos and purifications; and from the third the theory either that he was possessed of the goal or that he was possessed by the goal, in other words, all that is connected by the concept of spirit-possession.[6]

The accuracy of the reconstructed history of succession does not interest us here; it may merely be observed as an essentially untestable 'myth of origin'. What is of more direct relevance to our topic is the striking parallelity revealed by Radin between some all-too-contemporary elements of the legitimation of the intellectual role and those qualities of the shamans widely described in ethnological literature. If seen against the latter, the most vital characteristics of the first come fully into view; normally hidden beneath the diverse wrappings of many colours and designs in which they are presented at different times by different varieties of intellectuals, they may now be examined in their essential shape.

Ordeal, purification and possession; these three seminal and, arguably, permanent constituents of the legitimation of priestly authority have one feature in common. They all proclaim, and explain, the separation of the priesthood from the laity. They put whatever wisdom or skill the priests may own beyond the reach of all those who are not priests. They elevate the priestly ways, by the same token downgrading the paths of the laity. And they present the resultant relationship of domination as one of service and self-sacrifice.

All three have been met throughout history (and are still being met) in many guises. We can recognize the 'theory of the ordeal', depending on the leading fashion of the era, in references to physical asceticism and self-immolation, monastic humility, the protracted miseries of student life, an existence devoid of leisure and short on the joys the consumer society may offer. The 'taboo and purification' aspect has been elaborated upon with particular zeal: its endless inventory extends from the sexual abstinence of the ancient authors, through the bohemianism of romantic artists to the 'value-neutrality' and non-commitment of modern scientists or the auto-violence of 'transcendental reduction' of the Husserlian seekers of certainty. In all epochs (though in none as much as in the modern world) this aspect spawned some degree of institutionalized isolation for men of knowledge, in which outside instrusions were seen as impure and potentially contaminating, and elaborate practical measures were taken to keep intruders away. The aspect of 'possession' was perhaps that most resistant to institutionalization. It was, however, never abandoned as a professional myth. At the start of their professional careers men of knowledge, sacred or secular, take an oath of utter and sole dedication to the pursuit of wisdom and the disposition of their resulting skills; while professions defend their standing by insisting that this is exactly where they stand and that they cannot but stand there.

The glory and nobility of sacrifice rub off on the knowledge to which it leads. Tools and products ennoble each other, and, once started, reinforce each other's authority and supply reciprocal justification. The result is that both acquire a degree of independence from the social demand which they invoke as their validity test. 'Formulations' enjoy an untarnished reputation because they have been authored by the 'formulators' who followed a life which, from their lack of ability and will, ordinary people would not follow. The formulators, on the other hand, retain the esteem they once acquired through putting out a regular supply of highly reputable formulations. The formulators and the formulations now need only each other to substantiate their claim to high status.

We have drawn so far (in a somewhat free fashion, to be fair) on Paul Radin's *Primitive Religion* – a study published in 1937. Even allowing for the fact that some of the more radical interpretations in the above analysis go beyond the letter (if not the spirit) of that study, there is little doubt that *Primitive Religion* was a product of Radin's intense effort to break through the self-spun, but firmly institutionalized mythology of 'thinkers', sacred or secular, 'primitive' or modern (the first confronted by him as the object, the second as the subject of his study). He wished to disclose the social relationship which alone underwrites the rationality of the thinkers' action but which is all but decreed out of existence by the literal message of the myth. How great the effort must have been becomes apparent once *Primitive Religion* is compared with *Primitive Man as Philosopher*, a study published by Radin ten years earlier. Radin was already in possession of most of the material used for his later book when the first was published; and yet the conclusions drawn in the two books bear virtually no resemblance to each other.

The following extended quotation conveys the interpretative tenor of *Primitive Man:*

> The man of action, broadly characterised, is oriented toward the object, interested primarily in practical results, and indifferent to the claims and stirrings of his inner self. He recognises them but he dismisses them shortly, granting them no validity either in influencing his actions or in explaining them. The Thinker, on the other hand, although he, too, is definitely desirous of practical results . . . is nevertheless impelled by his whole nature to spend a considerable time in analysing his subjective states and attaches great importance both to their influence upon his actions and to the explanations he has developed.
>
> The first is satisfied that the world exists and that things happen. Explanations are of secondary consequence. He is ready to accept the first one that comes to hand. At bottom it is a matter of utter indifference. He does, however, show a predilection for one type of explanation as opposed to another. He prefers an explanation in which the purely mechanical relation between a series of events is specifically stressed. His mental rhythm . . . is characterised by a demand for endless repetition of the same event . . . Monotony holds no terror for him . . .
>
> Now the rhythm of the thinker is quite different.[7]

In this interpretation, thinkers and non-thinkers ('men of action') are set apart by a difference in their mental proclivities and aptitudes. This difference neither generates, nor stands, for a relationship between the two groups. If a relationship may be deduced from a difference so described, it may be only one postulated in the commentary of the distinguished American psychiatrist Kurt Goldstein:

> One can only distinguish in all primitive societies two types of people, those who live strictly in accord with the rules of the society, whom

[Radin] calls the 'nonthinkers', and those who think, the 'thinkers'.
The number of thinkers may be small but they play a great role in the
tribe; they are the people who formulate the concepts and organise
them in systems, which are then taken over – generally without criticism – by the nonthinkers.[8]

The distinction which ten years later Radin was to conceive of as a
product and a factor of the historical process, of social struggle and
the complex relation of dependence, here nests still in its mythological, 'naturalized' shell. People cannot help being what they are.
Some are born to think, others – to labour. The latter are well
satisfied with their lot; indeed, the very repetitiveness of their daily
chores suits them well and provides for a life free of anxiety. The
thinkers, however, cannot help but ponder, doubt, invent. Theirs is,
by necessity, a very different life – one which non-thinkers would
rather not emulate. The thinkers are cultural heroes to be admired
and respected, but not imitated. One would assume that the same
Nature which had made people so sharply different linked the special
qualities of the thinkers to their special position among the others.

Radin suggests that what anthropologists consider the primitive
culture is in fact the expression of the 'mental rhythm' of the non-
thinkers. He implies that primitivity is self-defining and hermeneutically self-contained and self-sufficient: that the concept is fully
explicable only in reference to the attributes of the entities it denotes.
We confront here another mystification causally related to the
'mythological' definition of the intellectual. Not only does this latter
occlude the historical character and the conflicts inherent in the
separation and the salience of the intellectuals as indicated above,
but it reverses the direction in which the resulting opposition
operates. It presents the primitivity as the unmarked side of the
opposition, and hence the other side (allegedly coined as a negation
of some features of the first, that is, non-primitive) as the marked
one. This is a reversal, both sociologically (it is the non-primitives,
to wit the intellectuals, who define their opposite as their negation
not vice versa) and semantically (the meaning of primitivity is the
absence of some attributes which characterize the other side; the
meaning of whatever stands against the primitive is positive –
construed of traits later to be declared lacking on the other side). It is
the constitution of the intellectuals as a distinct social formation with
at least a degree of self-consciousness and some joint strategy

designed for the status-game, that casts the rest of the society, kept outside the closing ranks, as an entity in its own right, possessed of its own characteristics (even if such characteristics are entirely composed of 'absences'). It is the primitivity that is the marked side of the opposition; and the primitive is constituted as a by-product of the self-constitution of the intellectuals.

The primitive is therefore a relative (or, rather, relational) notion coined by those who are, and see themselves as being, outside the space it denotes. The baseline against which the concept is construed is the self-image of those outside; it is constructed to denote 'the rest of the world'.

Let us note that what has been said above about the derivative and relational character of the concept of the primitive applies to a whole family of notions born within the context of asymmetry of power, as factors in the reproduction of a structure of domination. Different concepts are employed depending on what particular domination, or dimension in the distribution of social power, is at stake. The primitive as used by Radin betrays the kinship ties within the family: a concept usually only employed in terms of the division between the Western (developed, advanced, complex, civilized, etc.) society and the rest of the world, as scanned from the Western vantage point, here collapsed into the 'non-intellectual' part of the world, and is thus used in the context of another structure of domination. It is because of their shared features that the concepts belonging to the family under discussion are, at least to some extent, mutually exchangeable. What makes the exchange possible without defying the sense of semantic clarity is, of course, the essential isomorphism of all asymmetrical distributions of power. More interestingly, however, at least a part of the explanation may be found in the fact that whatever structure of domination is reflected in, and served by, a given concept, all such concepts are coined, or refined, or logically polished, not by the dominating side of the structure as a whole, but by the intellectual part of it. No wonder the intellectual self-image (or, more fundamentally, the cognitive predisposition shaped up by the specifically intellectual mode of praxis) colours the articulation of all aspects of power asymmetry.

Such a colouring is particularly recognizable in almost ubiquitous references to certain mental deficiencies in the definitions of otherwise quite different dominated groups and categories. Whether the dominated are construed as primitive, traditional, or uncivilized;

whether the category construed is that of non-European cultures, non-white races, the lower classes, women, the insane, the sick, or the criminal – inferiority of mental capability in general, and inferior grasp of moral principles or the absence of self-reflection and rational self-analysis in particular, are almost invariably salient in the definition. The overall effect of such a universality is the enthrone-ment of knowledge, the feature pertaining particularly strongly to the intellectual mode of praxis, in the very heart of the legitimation of any form of social superiority. By the same token, any claim for domination and superiority must, if only obliquely, pay tribute to the very factors on which the intellectuals ground their power claims.

We have now collected all the elements necessary to construct the meaning in which the concept of the intellectual will be employed in the present study; and to describe the strategy which will be applied to the analysis of the past and present of the social category of the intellectuals.

First of all, the concept of the intellectual does not refer in this study to any real or postulated characteristics which can be ascribed or imputed to a specific category of people within society – such as its native qualities, attained attributes or acquired possessions. It is assumed that the category of the intellectuals never has been and never can be 'definitionally self-sufficient'; and that no current definition which proposes to focus on the features of the category itself in order to explain its position and role within a larger society, can break through the level of legitimations to the social configuration they legitimize. As they draw heavily on the power rhetoric the category itself develops; such current definitions, so to speak, 'take the topic for the resource'.

Secondly, we refrain here from any attempt to build up a collec-tive definition of the intellectual by a 'finger pointing' method – by enumerating skills, occupations, attitudes, biographical types, etc., which at a given time or in a given society may claim to belong, or are thought of as belonging, to the category. Even more radically, we refrain from participating in the (politically crucial, but sociologically secondary) debate aimed at deciding which individuals or groups 'still are', and which 'just miss' parts of the intellectual category. In our view, this debate is either an element of power rhetoric devel-oped by some sectors of the category to serve the 'closure' struggles, or the result of the outsiders confusing power rhetoric with sociological analysis. Again in this case, the topic is mistaken for a resource. What lies behind the debate in which we refuse to participate is a hope to prefigure theoretically what can only be a shifting manifestation of the ongoing political struggles, if not an attempt to interfere with the outcome of such a struggle while accepting the weapon its participants tend to use – that of representing political solutions as decisions about the truth of the matter. Instead, we will confine our search to the task of locating the category of the intellectual within the structure of the larger society as a 'spot', a 'territory' within such a structure; a territory inhabited by a shifting population, and open to invasions, conquests and legal claims as all ordinary territories are.

We will treat the category of the intellectual as a structural element within the societal figuration, an element defined not by its intrinsic qualities, but by the place it occupies within the system of dependencies which such a figuration represents, and by the role it performs in the reproduction and development of the figuration. We assume that the sociological meaning of the category can be obtained only through the study of the figuration as a totality. But we assume as well that the fact that the category of the intellectuals does appear as a structural element of a figuration is in its turn crucial for the understanding of the figuration in question – of the nature of dependencies which hold it together and the mechanism of its reproduction, in both its conservative and innovative aspects. Analyses of the intellectual category and of the figurations in which it appears are inseparably bound together in a hermeneutic circle.

Figurations which do have the intellectual category as their structural element are certain to possess a number of characteristics.

First, a major dependency among those which weave together into the figuration in question is grounded in the socially produced incapacity of individuals (singly or in the groups they form) to conduct their life business on their own. Some stages of their life activity, material or spiritual, in their practical or ideational aspects, must be beyond their control, and hence they need the advice, assistance or active interference of someone else.

Secondly, this insufficiency makes for a genuine dependency, as it casts the 'helpers' close to the sources of uncertainty, and thus into a position of domination. What emerges is power of the 'pastoral' kind, which – in the description given to it by Michel Foucault – means domination exercised 'for the benefit of' the dominated, in their interest, for the sake of the proper and complete conduct of their life business.

Thirdly, what the dominated are lacking (thereby rendering the power a pastoral one) is knowledge or the resources to apply knowledge in their acts. By the same token, the dominating possess the missing knowledge, or mediate and control its distribution, or have at their disposal the resources needed to apply the knowledge they possess and to share the products of such application. The dominating are therefore sages, teachers, or experts.

Fourthly, the intensity and the scope of their domination depends on how acute is the sense of uncertainty or deprivation caused by the absence of knowledge in an area serviced by a given group of sages, teachers or experts. More importantly still, it depends on the latter's ability to create or intensify such a sense of uncertainty or deprivation; to produce, in other words, the social indispensability of the kind of knowledge they control.

Two further comments are necessary, however. First, what we have described above is seldom the only type of dependence and domination which binds a figuration together and presides over its reproduction. Lack of control over life business gives rise to other kinds of domination than the power of knowledge (power over means of production or over access to the means of consumption being the most obvious and notorious examples). Hence an analysis of the intellectual category calls not only for the study of the relationship between the intellectuals on the one hand and the 'clients of knowledge services' on the other, but also for the study of the complex web of competitive relations between several, mutually autonomous, dimensions of domination and the social categories they generate. And secondly, we have outlined above the 'figurational method' of analysing the category of the intellectuals in terms general enough not to limit its application to the problems related to the so-called 'global society'. This method seems to be equally useful for studying smaller sections of the category which might be located within a figuration of a single class, organized group or functional area of social life.

2

Les philosophes: the archetype and the utopia

The collective noun 'intellectuals' is of relatively recent origin. It is credited sometimes to Clemenceau, sometimes to the signatories of a public protest against the Dreyfus trial; in no case, however, has it been traced beyond the turn of the century. At its inception, the new term was an attempt to recapture the unity of men and women of many widely different occupations and social stations, otherwise unlikely to meet, still less to co-operate, in the pursuit of their professional tasks: scientists, politicians, writers, artists, philosophers, lawyers, architects, high-rank engineers. The uniting element, as the new term vaguely hinted, was the central role played by intellect in all these occupations. Shared intimacy with the intellect not only set such men and women apart from the rest of the population, but also determined a certain similarity in their rights and duties. Most importantly, it gave the incumbents of intellectual roles a right (and a duty) to address the nation on behalf of Reason, standing above partisan divisions and earth-bound sectarian interests. It also attached to their pronouncement the exclusive veracity and moral authority which only such a spokesmanship may bestow.

Of considerable sociological interest, and worthy of a separate study, is the fact that such a commonality of status and purpose was postulated at a time when the pristine unity of Reason was already in a state of advanced disintegration. Relentless separation of the scientific, moral and aesthetic discourses was one of the central features of modernity. By the time the concept of the intellectual was coined, their autonomy had reached a point of virtual non-translatability. In Habermas's words, 'pluralization of diverging universes of discourse belongs to specifically modern experience . . .

We cannot now simply wish this experience away; we can only
negate it . . .'[1] Negated it is, and repeatedly so, ostensibly in the
name of some common assumptions, processes or effects which must
be implicit in all rational thought. The coining (and the keen adop-
tion) of the common name for otherwise diverse and disparate discourses was a spectacular, yet not the only attempt to negate (if not
actually to wish away) a process well under way for more than a
century and apparently irreversible.

The three-way split of rational discourse does not exhaust the
whole story of disaggregation. The new discourses themselves have
come a long away from initial, true or imagined, unity. The times
when every 'intelligent person' could hope to master, with due dili-
gence, the totality of contemporary knowledge, and develop an
informed opinion on everything schools and books had to offer (or,
at least, everything worth having an informed opinion on) ended
early in the last century. Since then the sum of objectively extant
knowledge has been divorced from any subjectively assimilated
knowledge, actual or possible. The alleged unity of rational thought
ceased to be a matter of reciprocal co-ordination between the agents
of knowledge production; it could only be postulated, with no means
of practical control attached. The presence or absence of such a
unity could not be tested inductively. It could only be imputed, and
then only on limited authority.

Among many such imputations, the coining (and many a later
usage) of the collective noun 'intellectuals' occupies a special place.
Every naming divides, but the division implied by the separation of
the intellectuals as a group is one that cuts across the category of the
intelligent, thinking, educated, enlightened elite. Tacitly, it ac-
knowledges a century or more of relentless division of labour. Over
the fragmented field of specialists and experts it raises, however, the
phantom of 'thinkers as such', persons living for and by ideas untarnished by any preoccupation bound by function or interest; persons
who preserve the ability, and the right, to address the rest of their
society (other parts of the educated elite included), in the name of
Reason and universal moral principles. Each one of these persons
has a profession or an occupation, each one belongs to a functionally
specialized group. But beyond this each person lifts himself or
herself to another, more general level, where the voice of Reason and
morality is heard unjammed and undistorted. It is possible that such
a self-elevation is easier and more likely in the case of some profes-

sions rather than others. Yet, by and large, it is not fully determined by mundane functions. It remains in the end a question of decision and commitment. Accepting for oneself the label of 'intellectual', together with the obligations that other members of the group agree to carry, is in itself a factor of such a commitment. An attempt to set aside those who 'are intellectuals' from those who are not, to draw an 'objective' boundary for the group by listing the names of relevant professions, occupations or educational credits, makes no sense and is doomed from the start.

The concept of the intellectuals was coined as a rallying call, and as an attempt to resuscitate the unfulfilled claims of the past. As a rallying call, it was no different from those of all the previously unheard of nations which began to clamour for attention in the public vocabulary at the beginning of the twentieth century; messages were sent into a wide open social space, with broadcasting dishes pointed in a selected direction, but reception still dependent on the many individual decisions to switch the receivers on or off. It was intended, so to speak, as an act of propaganda. Ostensibly, it referred to qualities its intended recipient already possessed; in fact, it connoted motives and actions wished for the future. As an attempt to reclaim the frustrated hopes of the past, the new concept appealed to a century-old memory of those magnificent times of excitement and promise, when doctors, scientists, engineers, country squires, priests or writers belonged to one happy family of *les philosophes*, read each other's work, talked to each other, and shared the responsibilities of a collective judge, guide and conscience of human kind. In the second of its senses the freshly coined concept was also aimed at the future: the true message was the possibility of recapturing the spirit of bygone and fast receding times, or, rather, the spirit now projected, in retrospect, upon such times in a world changed beyond recognition. It was the possibility of piecing together the broken communication among the intelligent and educated; to recreate, or create anew, a shared discourse unifying the plethora of specialized discourses; and to mount on this foundation a shared purpose and common responsibility. Only when it is shared, will this responsibility become an entitlement to a position of social influence comparable to that enjoyed by *les philosophes*.

Whatever the historian may say about the convoluted path leading from the eighteenth-century philosophers to the twentieth-century educated experts, and whatever his or her informed verdict on the

continuity or discontinuity of the process, the fact most directly
relevant to our theme is the tangible presence of *les philosophes* in the
process of the self-constitution of modern intellectuals. Their
memory, their myth, their idealized image (seen as a reflection of
present dreams in the mirror of the past), is itself a most powerful
factor in that self-constitution. The remembered, or retrospectively
construed, mode and role of *les philosophes* serve as the 'active utopia',
the standard by which ambitions and performances are measured,
criticized and corrected. One may guess that if the original term, *les
philosophes*, has not been employed directly in the self-assembly of
modern intellectuals, it is only because philosophy itself has turned
meanwhile into a narrowly circumscribed, specialized occupation; a
call for unification launched from its territory would be inevitably
decoded as an exercise in imperialism, and accordingly resisted or
laughed off (as, indeed, has repeatedly been the case). The idea of
'the intellectuals' at least stood a chance of reviving the sense of a *jeu
sans frontiers* which seemed to come so naturally to the philosophers of
the Enlightenment era. To them we need to turn now, therefore, to
explore, and possibly reveal, this modality which stands behind the
idea of intellectuals in our own time.

   Les philosophes were not a 'school of thought'. For virtually every
proposition or positive observation one of the *philosophes* wrote down
there was another to contradict it -- to be found in the writings of
another *philosophe,* or in another work of the same author. One
would be hard put to spell out a 'paradigm' (in the Kuhnian sense)
which united the *philosophes* and enabled them both to communicate
with each other without difficulty and to contribute to a common
purpose. As to their commonality of experience and upbringing –
there was none. *Les philosophes* like the Russian *raznochintsy* a century
later, counted in their ranks people of practically all estates and
social stations (with the exception, perhaps, of the most humble).
Nor were they brought together by similarity of temperament or
taste; in this respect, as in all others, there was more to divide than
to unite them.

   And yet, there are few, if any, times and places in human history,
in which the educated and thinking crust of society was seen – by
others as much as by themselves – as a unified and compact group,
which could compare with that of *les philosophes* in France in the third
quarter of the eighteenth century. What was it that united them,
acknowledged at the time and of which they were aware, and which

was reinforced powerfully by the living memory of a later age? I suggest that the only, but powerful and decisive, unifying factor ought to be sought not in what, or even how, did the *philosophes* profess – but in the purpose and the importance of the very act of professing. Purpose and importance were imputed to this act by the *philosophes* themselves; but they were also, and more seminally, assigned to it by a brief, yet spectacular and unforgettable, encounter with political history. The persistent presence of *les philosophes* (rather than their philosophies) in the living historical memory – as an active utopia, a promise still awaiting fulfilment, a pattern for self-definition, a horizon for the blueprints of good society – is the product of unique circumstances; only partly has it been determined by what the *philosophes* did; to at least the same, if not a greater, extent, it has been decided by those conditions which, in a flash, short-circuited knowledge and power.

Among these conditions, one needs to name quite a few. None was unique to France; none was confined in its duration to that one momentous quarter of a century. But together they appeared only in one place and only for a short time. It was their coincidence which was unique – unprecedented, and so far unrepeated.

First, the absolutist monarchy was about to reach its maturity – to disclose its weakness as much as its strength, the yet unsatisfied prerequisites of its survival together with its still unexhausted revolutionary potential.

Secondly, there was the advanced demise of the old ruling class, the nobility, which left two yawning gaps among the factors deemed indispensable in the reproduction of social order: to fill them, a new concept of social control was needed together with a new formula for the legitimation of political authority.

Thirdly, the nobility lost its political significance well before a new social force, strong enough to claim the vacant political estate, appeared. The robe of the political class was, so to speak, put to auction, and open to competitive bids. The bids could be radical; they had no one's established interests to accommodate.

Fourthly, the French *philosophes* were distinguished 'by the absence of a traditional status or particular function specially appropriate to them in the society. In Germany, the representatives of the Enlightenment were often university professors or state officials. In Protestant lands generally, they were frequently clergymen. But in France none of those traditional callings diverted the *philosophes* from their image of themselves as freelance intellectuals of the entire society.'[2]

Fifthly, though untied to any institutions and unbound by any divisive loyalties, the *philosophes* were more than a collection of individuals. They constituted a closely knit group bound together by a dense network of communication: *la république des lettres, les sociétés de pensée*, clubs, voluminous correspondence, mutual reviewing, mutual visitings, their own papal court at Voltaire's home at Ferney, their own judicial and punitive system with opinion sitting on the jury bench. They were a group, an autonomous group, and a group which introduced opinion, writing, speech and language in general as a social bond to do away with all social bonds.

Sixthly, the establishment of *la république des lettres* could not have occurred at a more opportune time. This was a century of adminis-tration, organization, management; a century when habits became the object of legislation, and a way of life was problematized as culture; a century which radically redrew the old boundaries between private and public and magnified the size of the latter to unheard-of proportion; a century which needed know-how, skills, expertise to do what had previously been done naturally and matter-of-factly; a century in which power needed, and sought, knowledge.

I do not propose that this list of conditions is complete. One can surely add a few more; any historian of early modern France (of whom I am not one) will have no difficulty in locating other, perhaps quite dramatic, respects in which that country differed at that time from other times and other countries. And yet the list seems suf-ficient for our purpose, as even in its present form it conveys the sense of a historical situation full of tension generated by the bringing together, condensing and confronting with each other of problems which other countries or times experienced in succession or not at all; and it contains enough 'pull' and 'push' factors to account for this formidable historical process of which the power/knowledge compound is a lasting residue.

The phenomenon described in historical literature as the rise of absolutism was — sociologically speaking — a process of redeploy-ment of political power in the wake of, or simultaneously with, the waning of the feudal principle of association between landowning rights and administrative duties. Power shifted away from the land estates; while retaining both property and wealth, the aristocracy lost its role as the 'political class'; at any rate, a place in the hier-archy of political power ceased to come to noblemen 'of right', as part of their inheritance of their estates. Power divorced from land-owners was reassembled at the top. The absolute monarch was the first specimen of the Weberian 'modern state' distinguished by claiming a monopoly of the means of violence; the subjection of all the inhabitants of the land to the coercive powers of the monarchy alone, employed by the rules set by the self-same monarchy, was the major mechanism for transforming those inhabitants from feudal subjects into citizens of the modern state – and thus from participants of corporate rights and duties into individuals. A direct link of dependence now tied together individual citizens and the king: citizens had duties towards the state, and the state had duties towards the citizen – all together and each one separately. Whatever administrative organ mediated between the two extremes of the absolutist system, it could do so only by royal assent or behest; all power came from the top.

The 'depoliticization' of land estates laid at the door of the royal court a task no government had confronted before – at least not on a similar scale. Alexis de Toqueville was perhaps the first to emphasize this most seminal, though unanticipated, consequence of absolutism. In France,

> having been divested of his power, the lord no longer felt bound by his traditional obligations. And no local authority, no poor relief committee or parish council had taken them over. . . [T]he central government had, somewhat venturesomely, accepted sole responsibility for this duty. Every year the Council allotted to each province a sum of money taken from the public funds for poor relief. . . Each year the Council issued orders for the setting up in various places (specified by itself) of poor houses, in which impoverished peasants were given work at a low wage.

But poor relief was only one small matter among thousands which the centralized state had to pick up, as they laid abandoned all around the country. Means of violence were not the only power factor the absolutist monarchy claimed a monopoly on.

> Ministers of state had made a point of keeping a watchful eye on everything that was happening in the country and of issuing orders from Paris on every conceivable subject. As time went on and with the increasing efficiency of administrative technique, this habit of surveillance became almost an obsession with the central government.

The inevitable outcome of this new and unprecedented preoccupation of the state was an equally unprecedented 'top-heaviness' in the emerging political system. Central offices grew fast in size and influence. As d'Argenson had already observed in 1733:

> the amount of office work imposed on our heads of departments is quite appalling. Everything passes through their hands, they alone decide what is to be done, and when their knowledge is not as wide as their authority, they have to leave things to subordinate members of their staffs, with the result that the latter have become the true rulers of the country.[3]

The enormity of the tasks facing them was the cause of both the breath-taking powers and the frightening weaknesses of absolutist rule. The powers must have seemed bewildering to the contemporary observer: a government entitled to legislate for an enormous territory, overriding local differences and setting universally binding standards; powers, moreover, reaching into areas of life never before subject to legislation and external management – and hence, seemingly, operating in a free, unoccupied space, in a sort of a political no man's land, where the will of the legislator met with no constraints. In these virgin lands of politics, at least, the king played the role of God; nothing less than the creation of human society 'from nothing' was his task. Helvetius had no doubts on the matter: Who shall frame the laws? 'Enlightened despots!'[4] While Turgot advised Louis XVI that nothing 'need prevent you from altering the laws they laid down or the institutions to which they gave their approval, once you accept that such a change is just, beneficial and feasible'.[5] Absolute power was a power which saw society as an empty land to be colonized, given laws, knitted into a selected pattern.

If this image of a truly fabulous strength was one side of the absolutist coin, its weaknesses were the other. Indeed, one was inseparable from the other. Building on an empty site demanded a bold, but carefully sketched design; there was none available, as the task had never arisen before. The design was likely to be as grandiose as the task was formidable – so it called for a technique of management more potent even than that used long ago for the single-purposed co-ordination of hydraulic empires. The technique, when invented, was likely to require the gathering, storing and processing of information on a scale never needed, nor available, under the hierarchical, graduated power structure of feudalism. But no one aspect – drawing the design, developing the technique or its implementation, handling the necessary information – could rely on traditional skills or customary institutions. If anything, old habits and social skills appeared as so many obstacles standing in the way of the new order. Necessarily, they were perceived as superstitions or prejudices, defending factional and selfish forms of life against the public interest (that is, against the new order). New skills were therefore needed, and a new elite of skill; one untied to the past mechanisms of privilege and thus able to rise above the retrograde interests of estates or localities.

The category which was least likely to produce such skills and to turn into a new elite was the landed nobility, which, in the words of de Tocqueville, 'was regarded in the age of feudalism much as the government is regarded by everyone today . . . [T]hey kept order, administered justice, saw to the execution of the laws, came to the rescue of the oppressed, and watched over the interests of all.'[6] One inalienable aspect of administration by nobles was that the scale of administrative jurisdiction was reduced to that of the land estate. Aristocratic administration could only assure the reproduction of society in so far as this society remained fragmented into federated localities. The governing horizons and administrative zeal of the landed aristocracy were tightly interwoven with their property rights and circumscribed by the boundaries of the latter. They had no foundation of their own and not enough flexibility to be easily redeployed in the service of a centralized government and a centralized legal system which cut across the boundaries of noble estates.

In a recent study Ellery Schalk found out that at the start of the modern period in French history nobility 'was thought of as a profession or function – something one did – rather than something one inherited'.[7] In fact, Schalk has collected ample evidence showing unambiguously that nobility was perceived (and conceived of itself) as being both things at the same time, in close conjunction. Such a close, indivisible union between 'inheriting' and 'doing' was the most remarkable trait of its image and legitimating formula. It was the necessity to choose between the two, and the possibility of conceiving of 'inheriting' without 'doing' (and, sooner or later, vice versa) that marked the end of the era of aristocratic ascendancy and opened the road for a new elite.

Nobility entered the early modern era as the 'warrior class'. The two notions remained synonymous as long as the two sets of men they designated overlapped, thanks to the military profession practised and monopolized by members of noble families. In early modern writings the synonymy is articulated, argued and defended – already a sinister sign of the impending divorce. Throughout the sixteenth century, the discourse of aristocratic legitimation was organized around the concepts of *race* and *vertu*; the first stands for what later will become known as the 'pedigree', while the second stays close to its latin etymology (from *vis*, force, to *vir* – man, the masculine; *vertu* had the semantic overtone of prowess, fighting against odds, gaining mastery – the meaning we still put into our somewhat civilized idea of the *virtuoso*. At the start of the modern era, the valiancy encapsulated by *vertu* had only a military application; holders of *vertu* were knights; *vertu* was an attribute needed by soldiers). It is assumed that nobility is the conjunction of both *race* and *vertu*. Yet the very articulation of the union, and the insistence with which the union is restated in ever more numerous publications, allows for the possibility that there might be cases where the marriage has not been consummated. There are two, not one, criteria for nobility; if so, then logically speaking they may, or may not, meet in one and the same person. But if one of them is missing, then the 'nobility' of that person is flawed and questionable.

More and more often, *noblesse* is discussed as a *profession* or *vocation* (function). For Montaigne, for example, the military function was 'the proper, the only, and the essential form' of French nobility. The proper form is evidently a form which at least in principle is not automatically assured. And the inevitable happens: first timidly, then more vigorously, the divorce is warned against, diagnosed, bewailed. As early as 1539–40 Guillaume de la Perriére published *Le mirroir politique*, a book which set the agenda of the legitimation debate for the rest of the century and beyond, in which he complains that 'One of the greatest errors we observe at present is that some nobles of our times confine themselves to their heredity [*race*], hoping to be nobles without virtue.' That was the diagnosis, and here comes the prescription for the cure: 'if from their youth [your children] are well instructed, they will show themselves nobles and of good morals and habits; and on the other hand, if they are poorly instructed and brought up, they will always be *villains*, bad and vicious.' De la Perriére's concern did not necessarily stem from moral compunction. There were other, more tangible, causes for alarm and a sense of urgency, as Francois de l'Alouëte testified in *Traité des nobles et des*

vertus dont ils sont formés a few decades later (in 1577): as the consequence of the nobility not living up to virtue 'it is no longer those
from the most noble and ancient families that are called to occupy
the highest positions of honour and it is no longer the *gentilhommes*
who hold the charges and offices of the *maison de Roi* nor those of the
judiciary, but it is very often the most infamous and *vils* peasants
and other such *roturiers.*' And in 1582 Louis Musset spells it out: one
is not noble regardless of what one does, simply because of one's
ancestors.[8]

A number of new and revolutionary ideas were formulated in the
course of the sixteenth-century legitimation debate. To start with,
the old idea of *vertu*, the central attributes invoked in all past legitimations of social superiority and the right to rule, slowly, almost
imperceptibly, shed its former military connotations. It acquired a
wider meaning, referring now to those skills demanded by public
life, and particularly to those skills needed by an administrative ser-
vant of the king. The political context, rapidly changing with the advent
of the absolute monarchy, had no use for knightly prowess, but a
great deal of use for zealous and knowledgeable officers of government and law. If the old meaning of *vertu* was cut to the measure of
the feudal hierarchy of power, the transformed meaning answered
the new demand. Yet other new formulations seem much more consequential. First, the idea that *vertu* is not a birth gift, but a quality
which has to be acquired or earned (a clear shift from the ascriptive
to the achievement-oriented argumentation). And, secondly, a still
more seminal conception: *vertu* can be only attained through instruction. It is a matter of guided education, and not just of displaying
innate propensities.

A curious semantic confusion follows. On the one hand, the term
noblesse is still used in its descriptive sense – as a summary name for a
collection of families with pedigrees and titles, constituted as an entity
by the combined force of tradition and law. Among other things, it
was inherent in the structure of the Estates General which, significantly, was not convened through the whole period of dramatic
change under discussion. Some authors praised it, some castigated
or ridiculed it – according to their political provenance or class sym-
pathies. On the other hand, however, *noblesse* is now used as a normative or evaluating concept, as the name of an ideal, coveted form
of humanity, referring to free-floating attributes, divested of a
'special relationship' with any of the legally defined sections of the

nation. *Noblesse* in the second sense is something which the *noblesse* in the first sense must work for, if it wants it, as much as anybody else. At the threshold to the seventeenth century Pierre Chanon wrote in *De la sagesse* of *noblesse personelle*, or *acquise*, as distinct from *noblesse naturelle*; loyalties did not bar insight, but dictated an opposition of terms not likely to clear the confusion. Nobility as excellence, as an entitlement to a distinguished public role and function, had shattered the anchor which used to tie it down to the nobility of pedigree. It was now, so to speak, on general offer. And the bids could be made through education alone.

During the period from the end of the sixteenth century to the middle of the seventeenth, academies for nobles were established and flourished all over France. There were numerous publications arguing the case for institutionalized education and sketching curricula and syllabi for the ideal school. The academies, in Pluvinel's neat expression, were to be *écoles de la vertu*. *Vertu* itself was discussed in its modernized sense: the declared purpose of the academies was to train noble offspring for public offices, and to add that grace and polish necessary to survive and to progress in life at court – the new site of public life for which the customary uncouth, raw conduct was singularly inopportune. Proposed curricula did contain quite considerable sections devoted to the martial arts; but the latter were treated in their symbolic rather than any practical sense, as status signs and the badges of a cherished tradition. Horse riding, hunting and duelling skills took precedence over military know-how more directly relevant to the battlefield. Their subtly transformed role becomes apparent from their new company of skills seldom associated with *noblesse* a century before. According to one of the proposed curricula, the noble alumni were to be taught 'the customs and habits of other peoples, how to conduct themselves in politics and in war, the knowledge of Antiquity, honour, gracious conduct and manners [*gentillesse*], and a thousand other important things that will ignite their curiosity to go and search out beauty and perfection'.[9]

To sum up: with the rise of absolutism, hereditary or titled nobility (diluted, let us add, beyond recognition through the massive purchase of offices associated with titles) lost its collective role as the political class. Nobility as an ideal of excellence, and a legitimation of political influence, lost little of its appeal. It has now, however, been sundered from heredity and pedigree. Instead, it has acquired a new, but equally intimate connection: with education. To acquire excellence, men must be taught. They need teachers. They need those who know. It is the experience of passing through the hands of the teachers that now becomes the decisive stage on the road to *vertu*. And there is no clear reason why teachers can only perform the transplant of *vertu* on pedigreed humans.

It is to the teachers we now need to turn.

With a sociological insight rare in historians of his time, Augustin Cochin wrote: 'The body, *la société de pensée*, explains the spirit, the shared convictions. The Church preceeds here, and creates, its Gospel; it is united for, not by, the truth. The Regeneration, the Enlightenment, was a social, not a moral or intellectual phenomenon.'[10] Cochin, killed in his prime in the trenches of the First World War, was a historian of the French Revolution. The event he wished to understand was the brief episode of the Jacobin Terror. It was this inquiry which led him back to *les philosophes*. From his posthumously published passionate pamphlets one learns his tentative findings: Jacobin politics can be comprehended only as a continuation, as a fulfilment, of the form of life of *les philosophes*; and viewing the story of *les philosophes* in the light of its Jacobin, practical, stage offers a key to their own mystery. It allows us to see the Enlightenment as a mode of life, not a collection of ideas.

Cochin's slim books waited, virtually unread, for almost 70 years to be rediscovered by François Furet.[11] In Furet's own work, they met with some equally half-forgotten observations of Alexis de Tocqueville. Together, they fed into a new, detached, self-consciously sociological conception of the early, heroic era in the history of modern intellectuals. A conception which, so it seems, could not be arrived at but from the vantage point of the post-modern age and its 'partial intellectuals'.

De Tocqueville introduces the topic of the intellectuals at the point where we left the story of the nobility:

> A powerful aristocracy does not merely shape the course of public affairs, it also guides opinion, sets the tone for writers, and lends authority to new ideas. By the eighteenth century the French nobility had wholly lost this form of ascendancy, its prestige had dwindled with its power, and since the place it had occupied in the direction of public opinion was vacant, writers could usurp it with the greatest ease and keep it without fear of being dislodged.[12]

There is no dispute with the chronology of events, but the process seems now to have been much more complex than de Tocqueville suggests. Portraying the process as a mere 'change of guard' in front of an unchanged palace misses the true revolutionary significance of those 'men of letters, men without wealth, social eminence, responsibilities, or official status', who 'became in practice the leading politicians of the age, since despite the fact that others held the reins of government, they alone spoke with authority'.[13] Those men of letters, the forerunners (and to this very day the archetype and the utopian horizon) of modern intellectuals, did not 'take over' the leadership over public opinion. They *became* a public, they *created* public opinion, they won for this creation of theirs an authority enabling them to negotiate or compete with the power of such others as 'held the reins of government'. True, they appropriated a refurbished and redesigned weapon of virtue which fell from the wearied hands of the hereditary nobility; true, the demise of the nobility prepared a fertile ground for such a refurbishing and redesigning. But here the analogy ends. It is difficult even to sustain the idea of historical succession. At no time was the old nobility a leader of public opinion in the sense that men of letters later became. It was not only (or, rather, not in the first place) political leaders who changed; politics itself did. Unlike the politics of the past, it now had a space for the authority of men of letters.

In the words of François Furet, the substance of this new politics was a whole new world of 'political sociability', grounded on *opinion* – 'this confused thing formed in cafés, salons, loges and "societies"'.[14] The sites of this complete and self-enclosed world of new politics were far removed from the seats of real administrative power and political control. People occupying them could, therefore, afford an outside view of problems which for the administrators and law-givers appeared as matters of practical action. They could afford to think of political matters in terms of principles, rather than practicalities or the art of the possible. They never had an opportunity to submit their ideas to the test of feasibility; the only test which counted was the agreement of other, similar participants in the debate. A new, truly revolutionary criterion of truth had been thereby generated: consensus.

In this, the new social setting for the production and dissemination of ideas differed sharply from everything remembered from pre-modern Europe. It stood not against the mode of life of the aristoc-racy: the latter's power was one of arms and administrative control, not of ideas. It stood against the Church, its polar opposite. The pro-duction mechanism of ideas grounded in *la république des lettres* presented a novel, and radical alternative to ecclesiastical hierarchy. The vertical structure of the Church provided thinkers and writers with an unshakeable and transcendental foundation of truth: the divine wisdom, certainty embodied in the stability and continuity of the Church. The Reformation shattered such stability; worse still, it introduced polyvalence to the heretofore unified hermeneutics of God's truth. As a result, pious certainty gave way to Pyrrhonian crisis,[15] which haunted the new, secular breed of philosophers throughout the sixteenth and seventeenth centuries. It was to this crisis that the horizontally structured *république des lettres* provided an answer: new foundations for certainty, a new court of appeal. Consensus.

Horizontality of structure gave the immigrants to the *république des lettres* a freedom from well-defined, vertical structures of power which rebounded in their consciousness as 'freedom of thought'. In-deed, however severe the constraints imposed on individual thinking by the consensus of the collectivity, they seem diffuse and soft by comparison with the 'command economy of thought' represented by the Church. The experience of freedom was further reinforced by the separation from state power. Unlike their colleagues east of the Rhine, French *philosophes* did not occupy public posts; or, rather, individual members of *la république* earned their living in so broad a variety of trades and institutions, that their respective dependencies cancelled each other out; no single external power was influential enough to outweigh the rest. Freedom of thought had, of course, another side, somewhat less prepossessing and hence less celebrated: powerlessness. The pressures of sacred and secular power were all the less obnoxious the farther they stayed from the reach of *les philosophes*.

This unique social setting found its articulation in a series of counterfactual rules of secular truth-seeking, which endowed *les philosophes* with a lasting role in the formation and history of modern intellectuals. The rules are still with us, whether spelled out and exposed, tacitly obeyed or projected as outer limits of desired pro-gress, as in the famous utopia of 'undistorted communication' of Jürgen Habermas.

In a *société de pensée*, Cochin observed, 'the participants appear free, liberated from all attachment, any obligation, every social function'.[16] 'The members must,' adds Furet, 'in order to play their role, cleanse themselves of all concreteness and particularity, of their real social existence . . . *Société de pensée* is for each of its members characterised by being related to ideas only.'[17] These are, of course, counterfactual assumptions, as the citizens of *la république des lettres* differed from each other in every conceivable respect. As in the wider society, there were rich and poor, powerful and powerless, well connected and outcasts among them. But the only power which was explicitly allowed to be invoked inside *la république* was the power of idea, of argument, of logic, measured by the yardstick of consensus. To quote Cochin again, *la république* 'is a world where one chats, where one cannot but chat, and where every intelligence seeks the agreement of all, the opinion, the same way as in the real world it seeks a product and an effect'.[18] As human opinion is the only social foundation of the new certainty, argument is the royal road to truth. Truth is man-made, human reason is the highest authority, man is self-sufficient as the ordering force of human reality, reality itself is pliable, ready to be made, unmade and remade according to human – good or ill – will. A setting integrated solely by the argument and opinion of socially undefined individuals is reflected in a vision of the world shaped and reshaped by subjective will: a world with no constraints, only with adversaries.

La république des lettres was, therefore, a mode of life, grounded socially in a widespread and closely knit network of reciprocal communication, and intellectually in a set of counterfactual conventions which made such a network operational. Both conditions of its existence became available in the very particular, and perhaps unrepeatable, political situation of one society, which carved out an area of autonomous action free from intervention of political powers. This situation lasted long enough to enable the new mode of life to institutionalize and so attain a certain immunity towards later twists of political history; but not long enough to allow this mode of life to freeze into a marginal innovation of some historical interest but no political significance.

Isolation from power (experienced as autonomy) did not last too long for reasons briefly discussed above. The absolute monarchy faced administrative tasks of an unprecedented magnitude, which could not be handled by traditional means. Dislocations in social structure devalued the customary mechanisms of social control and integration and put on the agenda problems new not just in their size but in quality. The seemingly unlimited power was now concentrated in the hands of the absolute monarch tempted to embark on experiments to reshape the social body, as the latter now seemed tractable and malleable by comparison with the enormity of the tools of power. But this called for a grand design for a better society; experts, specialists, advisers – those who 'know better' – were needed.

When consulted on such matters, the citizens of *la république des lettres* could only respond by projecting onto the huge screen of 'good society' what they knew best and were most satisfied with: their own mode of life. Many years later, in 1931, Ludwig Wittgenstein wrote in his notebook:

> If I say that my book is meant for only a small circle of people (if it can be called a circle), I do not mean that I believe this circle to be the élite of mankind; but it does comprise those to whom I turn (not because they are better or worse than others) but because they form my *Kulturkreis*, they are people of my Homeland, in opposition to the rest who are *foreign* to me.[19]

This is, of course, a profound insight into the psychological condition of the intellectual hierarchy of values, one which became possible only towards the end of the era that *les philosophes* set in motion; the cosy familiarity of a well-understood and easily practised style appears here in its true shape, as the particularity of a social circle, rather than a universally valid form of life. Psychological conditions of the projection we mentioned above could, however, be very similar to those spelled out by Wittengenstein, even if group peculiarity disguised itself then as the attributes of the human species, and the counterfactual mask of group members presented itself still as the purified nature of 'man as such'.

The questions asked were not of *les philosophes*' making. The answers were. And they could not be moulded of anything else but the collective experience of *la république des lettres*.

3

Sociogenesis of the power/knowledge syndrome

Les philosophes saw the world in a way different from their predecessors. They saw the world as composed of individuals left to their own resources, needing the light of knowledge to cope with their life tasks, waiting for the wisdom of the state to supply them with the proper conditions and the proper guidance. True, this was a new way of looking at the world. But the world *les philosophes* looked at was a new world; a world different from that of their predecessors.

'Fear at all times, fear at all places', thus Lucien Febvre described human world as it stood at the threshold of the modern era.[1] It was a frightening world, perhaps too horrifying for the feeble human psyche, as its dangers were too formidable for their frail human defences. There was, of course, the perpetual human fear of death – still exacerbated by the fresh memory of recurrent wars and plague. There was the fear of capricious and untamed nature; fear of personal misfortune, of losing health or face – and a long list of ordinary, timeless human fears. But perhaps the strongest fear of all was the horror of a new and ever growing uncertainty. This one was anchored in the margins of the familiar and the habitual, but these margins were beginning to press hard at the boundaries of the world of daily life. These margins were populated with beggars, vagabonds, bohemians; through the glasses of popular fear they appeared as lepers, disease carriers, robbers. They were a threat aimed at the very foundations of human existence, a threat all the more dreadful for the absence of social, customary skills fit to absorb, neutralize or chase it away.

The only weapon the denizens of the pre-modern era learned to use to defend their security, however feeble, and to combat danger, was their own 'dense sociability' (Phillippe Ariés), the 'complex game of human relations' (Robert Muchembled).

> Peasants and town dwellers alike had to rely on themselves to guard their security – physical as much as psychological. Security was sought through a set of social solidarities. In the same way as they put clothes on their bodies to protect themselves from frost, they surrounded themselves with successive layers of human relations which they called the family, kin, and rural or town community . . .
>
> Town community gave the ultimate form to the effective and real relations of solidarity, in all its dimensions of the family, friendship, neighbourhood, diverse corporations. Like the walls, those symbols of the city, they drew the horizon which separated the dangerous 'outside' and the 'inside', where various bonds of sociability tied together . . .
>
> This means that the sociability of the era needed a relatively restricted space, close and frequent contacts, sites for encounters neither too numerous nor too distant, to express itself in full.[2]

What strikes us most in the picture of the communal world is that the available means of production of security (and indeed, the fundamental conditions of human cohabitation), however effective they might have been in the traditional setting, reacted badly to an extension of their social space. By their very nature, they could only be operated in a relatively small group, on a relatively confined territory. They were also geared to a relatively stable setting, where points of reference, the other partners in the solid network of solidary relations, stay fixed over a protracted stretch of time – a period long enough to learn their mutual rights and duties, develop obligations, be put to the effectivity and reliability tests.

Security grounded in 'dense sociability' could not be transplanted on an expanded, or fluid social setting – as the essential skill employed in its production was the ability to make 'the other' familiar, to transform him or her into a fully defined person with a fixed station inside the familiar world. This skill could be applied to all 'others' as long as they remained firmly 'within sight'. Villagers and town dwellers alike knew most of the others they were ever likely to meet, because they had ample opportunity to watch them – to watch continuously, in all their functions and on most diverse occasions. Theirs were communities perpetuated and reproduced by mutual watching. This 'transparency', of which modern utopia writers would dream as a sign of ideal society, was daily reality; a natural product of the permanent and total openness of the life of each and every member of the community to the gaze of all others. If so, however, then the limits of that gaze defined the size of the world in which secure social life could be produced and maintained.

The small and stable, and hence tightly controlled, world of the pre-modern man came under heavy stress in the sixteenth century, to be irretrievably shattered in the next. For England, the beginning of stress has been located in the half-century starting in 1590; it was then that the 'impact of dearth and plague together with the poverty and vagrancy which was accentuated by a rising population' began to be felt.[3] There was a sudden increase in the global size of the population. But apart from the demographic boom, the rearrangement of land property and a connected rise in the efficiency of agricultural technology prevented traditional rural communities from absorbing new hands and filling new stomachs. A rising number of men and women become economically redundant, and consequently socially homeless. It is interesting to note that exactly at the same time as the old world of communities and corporations went through its terminal disease, the European guild theory, lauding brotherhood, friendship and mutual help as the principles of human organization, reached its most impressive peak in the works of Bodin and Althusius.[4]

The change had two related consequences, both highly visible and experienced by contemporaries as the collapse of social order. The first was the sudden appearance, and continuous numerical expansion, of 'masterless men' – dangerous by all measures suggested by traditional bases of social order, as they stayed (or, rather, moved) beyond the reach of any of the extant methods of social control or regulation. 'Masterless men' did not belong anywhere, they had no superior to bear social responsibility for their behaviour, and no concrete community – village, town or parish – to demand obedience in exchange for subsistence. The second result was the sudden influx of 'vagabonds' (the same 'masterless men', but seen and defined in their other capacity as a homeless, nomadic population) into the small and inflexible world of local communities. 'Vagabonds' were people too listless and too numerous to be tamed and domesticated by the customary method of familiarization or incorporation. They appeared and disappeared from sight without warning, they stubbornly remained strangers and vanished before the community could absorb them by subjecting them to its all-penetrating gaze. 'The medieval system of frankpledge, whereby every resident of a jurisdiction was legally responsible for every other, was useless when it came to dealing with itinerant strangers.'[5]

Separating the masterless–vagabond population into a category of its own, and endowing it with sinister and dangerous powers, was a reflection of the inadequacy of the extant means of social control. Sociologically speaking, the masterless vagabonds exposed the obsoleteness of the traditional mechanisms of social reproduction; as a result, they focused upon themselves the anger and anxiety born of a new uncertainty. Fear was self-corroborating; it was also unabating, as the ongoing processes of enclosure and engrossing threw more and more people onto the roads, and as the mobile habits of the masterless multiplied their real numbers in the public consciousness; each masterless man visited, and frightened, many localities in a short stretch of time.

Reaction to the symptoms of the bankruptcy of customary social control was swift and radical.

To start with, the traditional concept of the poor as the blessed of God and favourite object of Christian charity, was given a thorough overhaul.

[T]he stereotype of the sturdy beggar developed, which diverged sharply from the Franciscan idealisation of poverty in the High Middle Ages. The stereotyping was the work of a wide range of learned authorities and was ultimately enshrined in law . . . Destitute, rootless and masterless, he seemed part of a conspiracy to destroy society.[6]

[T]he erstwhile children of Jesus had by the middle of the eighteenth century assumed a less beatific countenance and were generally depicted as violent, drunken, and menacing.[7]

In England John Gore depicted vagrants as rootless and dangerous because they lived without God, magistrate and master; in France, Guillaume le Trosne wrote of them as a race both undisciplined and dangerous, engaged in '*une rébellion sourde et continuelle*'. The new socially accepted definition of the poor was focused on the moral opprobrium attached to an inability to earn one's living. It was not so much the ennobling impact of work which counted, as the fact that working always implied having a master, belonging to a community, and otherwise remaining in sight and hence under control.

Being out of work, on the other hand, escaping social control – staying 'socially invisible'. It was the elusiveness of the masterless men's social identity that was most frightening, and from which there was only a short step towards a suspicion of conspiracy, a malevolent collusion against established society and its order. The poor were denounced as staying deliberately out of work, in Robert Crowley's words as being 'caterpillars in the Commonwealth' who 'licked the sweat from the true labourer's brow' or, in Thomas Adams' view, preferring to be sick than work.[8] The main danger, however lay not so much in the immanent moral abomination of poverty, as in the resulting danger emanating from the state of rootlessness.

Perhaps the most seminal impact of this massive redundancy which exploded communities as the essential units of social order, was the triggering off of a series of legal initiatives which, in the long run, totally transformed the role of the state in the reproduction of society. Communities could not cope with new problems. They did not have enough economic resources. Above all the 'I watch you, you watch me' system of communal control, working so smoothly (and hence unnoticed) before, cracked once the mutuality grounded in joint membership was undermined. The resulting crisis called for a redeployment of social power.

Michel Foucault turned the attention of social historians to the emergence of 'surveillance' or 'disciplinary power', to the development of the 'gaze technique of social control' which occurred at the beginnings of the modern era and rendered the latter a period of bodily drill and pernickety regimentation of each and every aspect of human behaviour.[9] We have seen, however, that such power was not new; it was not born with the advent of modern times. It remained a paramount method of social control throughout the pre-modern period. What indeed happened in the early modern era was the bankruptcy of the traditional agents of surveillance power. Disciplinary control could not, therefore, be exercised matter-of-factly, as in the past. It had now become visible, a problem to be taken care of, something to be designed for, organized, managed and consciously attended to. A new, more powerful agent was needed to perform the task. The new agent was the state.

In England, as in France, the sixteenth and seventeenth centuries were a time of feverish legislative activity. New legal notions were defined, new areas of legitimate state interests and responsibility charted, new punitive and corrective measures invented. Behind all this flurry of activity stood the sinister spectre of the new social danger: rootless and masterless men, 'dangerous classes' as they would later be called, the vivid and ubiquitous symptom of the crisis of power and social order. At first the legislative acts of the state tried to define the new phenomenon in terms of absences: what do the dangerous people lack, what is missing in their attributes or in their environment among the 'normal' factors as defined by customary existence? This was a reaction fully to be expected in the light of what one knows about the power of historical memory, and the common tendency to 'domesticate' and neutralize the new through couching it in habitual terms and subjecting it to tested remedies. In the process, however, the 'normal' factors of social order were brought into relief, problematized and theorized; as Heidegger used to say, you do not know what the hammer is until it has broken. And so the act of 1531 defined the vagabond as 'any man or woman being whole and mighty in body and able to labour, having no land, master, nor using any lawful merchandise, craft or mystery whereby he might get his living'. This definition pin-pointed the possession of a master or a property as the conditions of normal, non-punishable conduct. By the same token it identified the way in which the infamous state of vagabondage could be rectified: by restoring such conditions. What the act of 1531 and all following acts were silent about, through ignorance rather than ill will, was that masters, land or craft workshops seemed potent remedies because throughout the remembered past they were the straps fastening people to the well-controlled setting where they could remain under the constant observation and corrective pressure of the community. The writers of the early legislation against vagabondage knew of no other means of achieving the same effect – and that was the true object of their worry.

The old means had to be exposed as inadequate and ineffective, before the issue of control-through-surveillance could emerge as a problem in its own right; as a purpose for which new, better tools were to be found or invented. It became slowly evident that returning vagabonds by force to the places to which they originally belonged would not bring desired results. They were, as far as the network of villages and towns were concerned, redundant people. Local authorities had neither the means nor the skills to deal with the growing numbers of unemployed. Turned away from their native villages, the poor fled in droves to the towns, attracted by the slender chance of anonymity and escaping eviction. Throughout Europe towns turned into 'places of refuge for the extreme poor, sometimes the hopeless and helpless; towns as monuments to rural poverty . . . The urbanisation of poverty, a poverty born in the countryside but which manifested itself in the town, created problems of public order, menaced public health and placed a strain on traditional patterns of provisioning'.[10] Above all, it placed unbearable strain on the traditional patterns whereby social order was reproduced.

The clock could not be turned back; the monotonous cycle of the communal reproduction of order could not be restored simply by forcing the rootless back to their roots. The legislators soon realized that the heart of the matter was the terrifying capacity of the vagabonds for slipping through the local nets of control-through-surveillance. Perpetually mobile and strangers everywhere, they remained, so to speak, socially invisible. The legislators shifted their attention, therefore, to the means of restoring the 'visibility' of the masterless men, and thus rendering them amenable to surveillance.

The simplest method was suggested by the practice known to every cattle-breeder: branding. Under James I the practice was extended from stray sheep to stray humans. The act of 1604 instructed that the mark be 'so thoroughly burned and set on upon the skin and flesh, that the letter 'R' be seen and remain for a perpetual mark upon such rogue during his or her life'.[11] It was hoped that the mark would distinguish the particularly dangerous people for particularly close attention and hence at least partly undo the consequences of their mobility.

But the most seminal of all reactions to the bankruptcy of communally based control was the invention of enforced confinement. Surveillance, that tested (though heretofore unnoticed) tool of communal control, could be employed deliberately, and under artificially created and maintained conditions. Vagrants had no neighbours who could watch and streamline their conduct. None of the natural 'collective supervisors' had them long enough within their sight to exert more than passing influence on their behaviour; vagrants knew how to avoid all 'supervised spaces', and how to evade staying too long in any one space. This could be counteracted, however, by forcing them into a confined territory, where they could be seen, seen all the time and watched in everything they did; where supervisors would be attached to them permanently, in sufficient quantity to assure continuous surveillance; where, consequently, their behaviour – indeed, their whole life process – could be strictly regimented, subject to an externally designated rhythm, and no longer a source of uncertainty and a threat to social order. Once so confined, the 'dangerous classes' could become again 'transparent'. And this meant harmless.

Prisons, workhouses, poorhouses, hospitals, mental asylums, were all by-products of the same powerful thrust to render the obscure transparent, to design conditions for redeploying the method of control-through-surveillance once the conditions of its traditional deployment proved increasingly ineffective. That each of these innovations of the early modern era was more than a chance invention arising out of a specific problem, is suggested by the astounding simultaneity of their appearance in spheres ostensibly distant from each other and functionally unconnected. What was at stake was not only the solution of concrete 'social problems', but a truly fundamental reshuffle of the sites of social power and a re-adjustment of the mechanism of social control to the radically changed social conditions. This universality hiding behind the apparent specificity of prisons or hospitals was later to be made apparent in the famous 'Panopticon' of Jeremy Bentham:

> the very word 'Panopticon' seems crucial here, as designating the principle of a system. Thus Bentham didn't merely imagine an architectural design calculated to solve a specific problem, such as that of prison, a school or a hospital. He proclaimed it as a veritable discovery, saying of it himself that it was 'Christopher Columbus's egg'. And indeed what Bentham proposed to the doctors, penologists, industrialists and educators was just what they had been looking for. He invented a technology of power designed to solve the problem of surveillance. One important point should be noted: Bentham thought and said that his optical system was *the* great innovation needed for the easy and effective exercise of power. It has in fact been widely employed since the end of the eighteenth century.[12]

We have seen already that there was nothing new in defining the problem of control and reproduction of order as one of surveillance. And yet the way in which the ancient method was employed in the modern era was revolutionary in a number of crucial respects. Together, they brought into being a totally novel social figuration.

Perhaps the most important change was an end to the reciprocity of surveillance. Another way of putting it is that the new institutions were grounded in an asymmetry of control. The activity of surveillance now split the affected group into two sharply and permanently separated subsections: the watchers and the watched. Asymmetry of power as such was not a new invention; it had been a constant factor in all known types of society. In pre-modern societies, however, it related to the possession of objects rather than to their owners; to things rather than people (with a few notorious exceptions such as standing armies or monasteries). Asymmetry of power operated mostly in the area of redistribution of social surplus, when producers were pressed or forced against their will to part with a section of their produce on behalf of their superiors. On the whole, the power holders were satisfied with achieving this result. They appeared on the scene, so to speak, as an active factor in the producer's life at the very moment when the surplus was ready for redistribution. How the surplus had been produced did not concern them; the regularity of production was attained by other means than the power they held – means of which they had little idea and which they did not control. The power of the prince or feudal lord was remote from the daily life of their subjects. Irregularly applied (often only in annual cycles) and focused solely on reallocation of things, it could limit itself to violence as the only relationship between the power holders and their subjects. It was necessary to convince the producers that resisting expropriation was senseless and doomed to failure and such a conviction normally took the form of a belief in superhuman guarantees of that duty. This effect could be achieved by periodic exercise of the power of coercion, supported more or less by regular, often ritualized, displays of the possession of such power. The might and splendour of the princely retinue was a public spectacle, in which the powerless were the intended watchers, while the power holders expected to be watched. The daily life of the subjects of princely power was, to be sure, subject to continuous surveillance. By and large, however, this was a diffuse surveillance, an activity in which all members of the community took part in succession or simultaneously. Surveillance was based on what the anthropologists call 'generalized reciprocity', where the right to exercise control was legitimized by the right of the controlled to reciprocate on the same or another occasion.

The institutions which the grand design of Bentham's 'Panopticon' symbolically represented were the first to apply on a massive scale, as a 'normal' technology of power in society, an asymmetry of surveillance. It put the majority, the objects of power, permanently in the position of 'the watched', without a right, or a realistic hope, ever to reciprocate or to change places with their surveillors. This change brought the division of power inside the institutions and carried in its wake two highly consequential innovations. First, the sheer continuity of uni-directional surveillance created conditions for control of a totally new quality. Not only behaviour of the subjects could be shaped in accordance with a chosen design on certain selected, critical occasions; their total way of life could now be regimented, cast into a desirable mould, regularized. A repetitive rhythm could be imposed on the movement of their bodies. Their conduct could be made independent of their motives, so that their will could be disregarded: once externally sustained habits became settled, individual motives ceased to be factors of the situation to be reckoned with seriously. Continuity of uni-directional surveillance made coercion ostensibly unnecessary, and at any rate less obtrusive; manifest at the initial stage of drill, it was bound to be called into action less and less until it could assume a latent or merely symbolic presence. Secondly, the uni-directionality of the continuous surveillance made uniform the social definition of the watched; as defined by the power relations, they were all specimens of the same category. The totality of their social status was determined by their being subjected to the same operation of surveillance, which was aimed at achieving the same, universal, behavioural routine in the case of every individual under surveillance. The tendency of uni-directional surveillance is to erase individual differences between its objects, and to substitute a quantifiable uniformity for qualitative variety. This tendency may later be reflected in the scientific 'objectivization' of human objects into categories amenable to statistical processing, in which references to individuality, personal meanings, motives, etc., is not a necessary factor. What separates the categories from each other is also a product of the power operation; in this case, of dividing practices, which sort out certain quantities of objects into positions requiring a somewhat different routine, and indeed subject them to a different routine (like dangerous or non-dangerous criminals, mentally ill, bright and retarded pupils, etc.).

Another far-reaching consequence of the asymmetry of surveillance is the demand for a specialist in a position of supervision. The act of surveillance now sets the surveillor apart from the rest of the group; it is a full-time labour requiring a total concentration of mental and physical powers, and thus bound to become an 'occupation' – a constant source of the means of existence. By its very continuity and the permanence of its direction it can, and does, set for itself ends far more ambitious than the 'diffuse' surveillance of princely power could ever have dreamt of. The task generated by asymmetrical surveillance is nothing less than a total reshaping of human behavioural patterns; an imposition of a uniform bodily rhythm upon the variegated inclinations of many individuals; a transformation of a collection of motivated subjects into a category of uniform objects. This is no mean task, needing much more than a mere application of brute force. It needs an actor armed with specialized know-how and skills, an engineer of human behaviour. Asymmetrical surveillance tends to generate the role of the 'educator', rather than one of a mere expert in coercion (though the two roles are not necessarily in opposition).

The role of an expert or of a specialist may only arise under conditions where a permanent asymmetry of power aims at shaping or modifying human conduct. And such a role was indeed another consequence of the momentous redeployment of social power associated with the birth of the modern era. Its spectacular rise was a result of the new realization that human conduct geared to the maintenance of the desired social order cannot be left to individual discretion or to those 'natural forces' which seemed to take care of it so well in the past. Institutionalization of asymmetrical surveillance provided an archetypical structure in which this realization of the 'insufficiency', 'incompleteness' or 'intrinsic immaturity' of human beings could be reforged into practical action, and thereby proved and reinforced. This practice, however, which on the one side reproduced and 'objectified' the imperfections of the human individual, set at the other end of the power spectrum the role of the educator – the specialist in bringing human beings up to the level of perfection required by social order, fittingly renamed 'the common good'. Education had now become an irremoveable constituent of power. Power holders must know what the common good (of mankind, of the whole society, or of the section entrusted to their rule) is and what pattern of human conduct best fits it. They must know how to elicit such conduct and how to secure its permanence. To acquire both these skills, they must appropriate certain knowledge which other people do not possess. Power needs knowledge; knowledge lends power legitimacy and efficiency (not necessarily unconnected). Possession of knowledge is power.

The new kind of power that arose out of this figuration had two remarkable qualities: it was a pastoral power; and it was a proselytizing power.

Again, we have to admit that neither of the two qualities was new. At least not entirely new. Both were invented, developed and tested in the centuries of pre-modern history, and the Christian Church, in the times of its spiritual rule, could be portrayed as their unsurpassable model. In Foucault's description, pastoral power was one exercised not for its own, but for its subjects' good; it had no selfish ends – only the improvement of its subjects. It dealt with its subjects singly, not collectively – in the sense that it aimed at the reform of every individual, and thereby construed the individual as the autonomous unit of the collectivity. And it assumed that the key to the individual's improvements lay hidden inside the subject's person, and hence so arranged the network of rewards and punishments that it shaped the individual as the bearer of rights and responsibilities, the site of conscience, the decision maker and the autonomous agent. Proselytizing power was distinguished by being bent on converting its subjects from one form of life to another; it saw itself as the knower and the practitioner of a superior form, and its subjects as beings incapable of lifting themselves to such a superior level. (It has to be stressed that like varieties of power described under the names of 'therapeutic power' (Kittrie) or 'tutelage complex' (Donzelot), proselytizing power does not necessarily aim at remoulding the subjects after its own image, and thus dissolving the difference between the two modes of life. What it does seek, remorselessly and uncompromisingly, is the recognition by its subjects of the superiority of the form of life it represents and derives its authority from. Such acceptance is the ultimate act of their salvation; having agreed that the ways preached by the power holders are indeed superior, they assign superiority to the knowledge that their rulers possess. Such an agreement may well solidify and eternalize the gap between the power holders and their subjects instead of bridging it, contrary to the declared purpose of proselytizing zeal.) Again, essential precepts of proselytizing power were practised and tested by the Christian Church long before the dawn of the modern era.

What was truly new in the modern power figuration was the secularization of the pastoral and proselytizing techniques; the techniques themselves were not new, but their emancipation from the hierarchical body of the Church and their redeployment in the service of the state was. This meant, however, that the aims pursued by the two techniques became much more ambitious and comprehensive than ever before. The pastoral and proselytizing power of the Church had aimed at the production and reproduction of the superiority of one faith (together with its institutionalized spokesmen) over another, or over individuals too feeble to embrace it firmly and whole-heartedly. The pastoral and proselytizing power of the state would not stop at spiritual conquest; as a matter of fact, faith was not the issue at stake. The state embarked on a war against all forms of life that could be seen as potential pools of resistance against its own rule. Nothing less was required than the acceptance of state expertise in the art of living; it had to be admitted that the state and the specialists it appointed and legitimized knew better what was good for the subjects, and how they should live their lives and beware of acting in a fashion harmful to themselves. The subjects were not only denied the ability to find their way to God; they were denied the capacity of living human life without the surveillance, assistance and corrective intervention of those in the know.

4

Gamekeepers turned gardeners

'Wild cultures', says Ernest Gellner, 'reproduce themselves from generation to generation without conscious design, supervision, surveillance or special nutrition.' 'Cultivated' or 'garden' cultures, on the contrary, can only be sustained by literary and specialized personnel.[1] To reproduce, they need design and supervision; without them, garden cultures would be overwhelmed by wilderness. There is a sense of precarious artificiality in every garden; it needs the constant attention of the gardener, as a moment of neglect or mere absent-mindedness would return it to the state from which it had emerged (and which it had to destroy, evict or put under control to emerge). However well established, the garden design can never be relied upon to reproduce itself, and never can it be relied upon to reproduce itself by its own resources. The weeds – the uninvited, unplanned, self-controlled plants – are there to underline the fragility of the imposed order; they alert the gardener to the never-ending demand for supervision and surveillance.

The emergence of modernity was such a process of transformation of wild cultures into garden cultures. Or, rather, a process in the course of which the construction of garden cultures re-evaluated the past, and those areas that stretched behind the newly erected fences, and the obstacles encountered by the gardener inside his own culti-vated plot, became the 'wilderness'. The seventeenth century was the time when the process acquired momentum; by the beginning of the nineteenth century it had by and large been completed in the Western tip of the European peninsula. Thanks to its success there, it also became the pattern to be coveted by, or to be forced upon, the rest of the world.

The passage from a wild to a garden culture is not only an operation performed on a plot of land; it is also, and perhaps more seminally, an appearance of a new role, oriented to previously unknown ends and calling for previously non-existing skills: the role of the gardener. The gardener now takes over the place of the gamekeeper. Gamekeepers do not feed the vegetation and the animals which inhabit the territory entrusted to their care; neither do they have any intention to transform the state of the territory to bring it closer to that of a contrived 'ideal state'. Rather, they try to assure that the plants and the animals self-reproduce undisturbed – the gamekeepers have confidence in their trustees' resourcefulness. They lack, on the other hand, the sort of self-confidence needed to interfere with the trustees' timeless habits; it does not occur to them, therefore, that a state of affairs different from the one sustained by such habits could be contemplated as a realistic alternative. What the gamekeepers are after, is something much simpler: to secure a share in the wealth of goods these timeless habits produce, to make sure that the share is collected, and to bar impostor gamekeepers (poachers, as the illegal gamekeepers are branded) from taking their cut.

The power presiding over modernity (the pastoral power of the state) is modelled on the role of the gardener. The pre-modern ruling class was, in a sense, a collective gamekeeper. The passage to modernity was the process in the course of which the first emerged and the second declined and was in the end displaced. This process was not a result of the invention of gardening; it had been set off by the growing incapacity of the wild culture to sustain its own balance and the annual reproductive cycle, by the disturbing disequilibrium between the volume of gamekeepers' demands and the productive capability of their trustees as long as the latter were guided by their own 'timeless habits', and finally by the inability of the gamekeepers to secure the yield they wanted while confining themselves to traditional gamekeeper pastimes.

Gamekeepers are not great believers in the human (or their own) capacity to administer their own life. They are naturally, so to speak, religious people. Having practised no 'patterning', 'moulding' or 'shaping' of the wild culture they supervise, they lack the experience from which one can fashion the idea of the human origin of the human world, the self-sufficiency of man, the malleability of the human condition, etc. Their own lack of interference with the spontaneous working of the wild culture, which has constituted the virtual 'untouchability' of the latter, is reflected in their philosophy (if they need one) of the superhuman character of the world order. The wild culture itself cannot be perceived as a *culture*, to wit, an order imposed by humans – whether by design or by default. If it is at all reflected upon, it appears as something much stronger than a human – overt or tacit – agreement may call into being and sustain. It is seen as Nature, God's creation, as a design supported by super-human sanctions and perpetuated by superhuman guardianship. Intellectually, the redefinition of social order as a product of human convention, as something not 'absolute' and beyond human control, was by far the most important milestone on the road to modernity. But for such a redefinition to happen, a revolution in the way social order was reproduced must have taken place. The gamekeeper stance of the ruling class must have revealed its ineffectiveness and yielded worries it was not prepared to cope with.

Hobbes's curt dismissal of the 'natural state' of mankind as a condition under which human life is 'nasty, brutish and short' is arguably the most quoted and best known of all ideas bequeathed to posterity by the seventeenth-century thinkers. It has received a great deal of attention and been widely accepted as the starting-point of modern social philosophy, political science and sociology. Talcott Parsons thought it possible to see the whole history of social science as the long and still inconclusive struggle with the problem that the Hobbesian metaphor put on the agenda: this problem provided the 'puzzle' around which the paradigm of modern social science could be organized. There is no denying the importance of Hobbes's prop-osition for the last three centuries of European intellectual history. What the profuse comments on Hobbes's idea have on the whole been silent about, is another puzzle: from where did Hobbes take his image of the 'natural state'? Did he simply conjure it up by the sheer strength of his imagination? Was it wholly an intellectual creation *ab nihilo*? Or, like most ideas, was it rather a response, perhaps exag-gerated and unusually powerful, but still a response to some new experience which prodded Hobbes's imagination in the direction that his mind had taken?

Unless the contrary is proven, a plausible supposition is that the latter was the case. If so, then the question is: What was there, in the world of Hobbes's contemporaries, which could inspire the frighten-ing image of the 'state of nature'?

It seems that Hobbes was the victim of an optical illusion of sorts: what he mistook for the living relics of the state of nature, were the artefacts of the advanced decomposition of a tight man-made system of social control. If anything, the worrying, alien bodies infesting his life-world were pointers to the future, an avant-garde of the society to come, the few scattered samples of what was to become the 'normal state' – a society composed of freely moving, gain-oriented individuals unbound by the now bankrupt community supervision. In a true wild culture such individuals were safely kept within the few supervised niches meant to cope with the inevitable failures of social control and their consequences; their numbers were steady, their status unambiguous, their conduct safely stereotyped and hence perceived as predictable and manageable. Now, for reasons discussed in the previous chapter, all these neutralizing factors were fast disappearing. In the cracks of the wild culture system of self-reproduction Hobbes could have thought he glimpsed the state of nature in its pristine purity.

The most significant of the eye-opening effects of the communal retreat was, however, the revelation of the essential brittleness of the principles on which human daily intercourse was based. To be sure, the very existence of such principles (not to mention their indispensability), was in itself a formidable discovery. Such principles could be hardly guessed, or construed, in relation to a society which reproduced itself 'without conscious design' and – let us add – without unpredictable side-effects of a scale too big for the policing system to tackle. Now, when the principles came to be broken too often to work properly, they became visible. Or, rather, once a society 'without design' started producing on a massive scale phenomena it did not anticipate and could not control, it was possible to ask about the real or ideal principles which had been breached, and any remedy proposed for the regrettable effects of such a break had to be in the nature of a *conscious* design. A 'social contract', a legislator or design-drawing despot were the only frames within which the problem of social order could be envisaged, once it became a problem rather than a manifestation of the nature of things.

The new perception of the relationship between (man-made) social order and nature – including the nature of man – found its expression in the notorious opposition between reason and passions. The latter was seen increasingly as the 'natural equipment' of men, something men acquire with their birth, with no effort on their part and no assistance from other men. The former, reason, comes with knowledge, must be 'passed over' by other people, who know the difference between good and evil, truth and falsity. Thus the difference between reason and passion was from the very start more than a moral opposition; it contained, implicitly but intrinsically, a theory of society, articulating the opposition between the 'natural', and also individual, roots of anti-social phenomena, and the social, organized, hierarchized mechanism of social order. It spelled out the indispensability of the supra-individual power (of the state) in securing and perpetuating an orderly relationship between men; and the morbid and disastrous effects of any loosening of the power grip, or of any reliance on the 'natural predispositions' of fellow men.

For the philosophers who thought in such terms the obvious contradiction contained in the juxtaposition of passion-ridden individuals and the state promotion of reason must have been disturbing, as Albert O. Hirschman noted.[2] Indeed, how could the precepts of reason possibly influence the conduct of men guided only by passions? As the concept of 'passions' stood for everything 'natural' in man, for everything 'wild' and not having its (artificial, designed) origin in man-made law, how could reason address itself to the 'man of passions' and find him listening and, more importantly, obeying? What Hirschman failed to note in his otherwise highly informative study, was the practical, not merely logical, character of this question. The answer was to be sought in political practice, not moral theory; the thinkers Hirschman quotes were busy developing a theory and pragmatics of social (state) power, not just debating the 'nature of man'.

The apprehensions widely shared by the participants of the debate were succinctly summarized by Spinoza: 'No affect can be restrained by the true knowledge of good and evil insofar as it is true, but only insofar as it is considered as an affect.'[3] The message, if read out in terms of the pragmatics of social order, the main preoccupation of the time, is relatively clear: emotions, the anti-social drive which knows no distinction between right and wrong, cannot be dealt with by the *voice* of reason, by knowledge as the argument and dissemination of truth; or, rather, it can be dealt with in such a way only in cases where knowledge itself becomes an 'affect'. One would conclude that the latter case may have only limited application. It would only apply to those few men for whom knowledge itself is a passion – to philosophers, and perhaps also to those chosen few in whom the philosophers stir a similar devotion. As to the others, the problem is not so much how to channel their affects in the true direction, but how to restrain or neutralize their lusts. In Spinoza's view, devotion to God, the desire to be blessed and faith in the effectivity of the road to salvation as suggested by religion, could lead to the needed result.

Hirschman found *interest* one passion which the learned debate of the era treated with rising sympathy and hope. It is easy to explain away this choice as a 'prodromal symptom' of the capitalist future, thereby casting the philosophers of the seventeenth century in the role of prophets or at least heralds of a system which took a further century and a half to materialize. This would mean, however, imputing to the philosophers a conduct they seldom practised before or after. It makes more sense to assume that while promoting interest as one good passion to stifle all other, morbid, passions, they thought through the realities of their own time and proposed to deal with contemporary problems using contemporary means (including this 'contemporaneity' which had been construed with the help of historical memory). Indeed, only with some effort can the present reader squeeze the idea of interest as explicated in the seventeenth century, into the now familiar notion of profit-orientation. The kind of interests invoked by the seventeenth-century thinkers as a remedy against anti-social passions covered a much wider area. According to La Rochefoucault's *Maxims* (1666), the most frequent were interests in honour and glory; interest in welfare or wealth was just one of many, and in no way synonymous with interest as such. One would say rather that the idea of interest was meant to capture social motives rather than natural drives; it was something artificially added to the natural predispositions, something socially induced rather than deriving from human nature. The true opposition between interests and passions was, again, the difference between a socially designed order and the unprocessed, wild, natural state of man. The substance of interest mattered less than its artificiality, synonymous with its social orientation.

There was also another dimension to the opposition between interests and passions (again unnoticed by Hirschman): this was the class dimension, that between two types of men, rather than two sides of an individual's nature, or two types of conduct in which one and the same individual may indulge. *Un homme intéressé* could be the name given to a particular phase in an individual's life; but it could also stand, and it did, for a particular class of individuals, the motivated people, people who pursue socially oriented ends, instead of being pushed and pulled by their natural instincts. Using a later distinction, one can say that what set this class of 'interested men' apart from the rest was the dominant role played in their behaviour by 'in order to' motives – this epitomy of an instrumental–rational behaviour. The interest debate was just one of the many conceptual guises in which, at the age of disintegration of the old order, the theorizing of the new class bases of social order was conducted.

The more the interested behaviour was praised as socially beneficial, the more damaging and condemnable the passion-prodded, self-oriented conduct of the raw and crude people seemed. By setting their own goal-oriented action as a standard of socially useful and laudable life, the participants of the debate defined the contours of the new class divisions and the 'terms of reference' for the new mechanism of societal reproduction. However different the conceptual garb and semantic context of the debate, its social function did not depart significantly from the one perceptively described by Nietzsche in reference to the essential categories of the moral discourse:

> it was the 'good' themselves, that is to say the noble, mighty, highly placed, and high-minded who decreed themselves and their actions to be good, i.e. belonging to the highest rank, in contradistinction to all that was base, low-minded and plebeian. It was only this *pathos of distance* that authorised them to create values and name them . . .
>
> The basic concept is always *noble* in the hierarchical, class sense, and from this has developed, by historical necessity, the concept *good* embracing nobility of mind, spiritual distinction. This development is strictly parallel to that other which eventually converted the notions *common, plebian, base* into the notion *bad*.[4]

This account of the origins of morality is of course mythological, much in the style of the *naturgeschichtliche* speculations fashionable in his time – but the power of sociological insight, with which the mechanism attaching positive signs to behavioural characteristics associated with social domination has been disclosed by Nietzsche, is remarkable. The enthronement of interest was no exception from the general rule; neither was the downgrading of the passions – which gradually came to mean, first and foremost, the base opposite of the praiseworthy 'interested' conduct of the 'better men', the style of life that became fundamental to the orderly society.

The most important perlocutionary (in Austin's terms) effect of the reason vs. passions discourse was the recasting of the poor and lowly as the dangerous classes, which had to be guided and instructed to prevent them from destroying social order; and the recasting of the way of life of the poor and lowly as a product of human animal nature, inferior to, and at war with, the life of reason. Both effects amounted to the delegitimation of wild culture and rendering the carriers of the latter legitimate (and passive) objects for cultural gardeners. According to the poignant summary of Jacques Revel, now

> the people were seen as carriers of this fossilised trace of a social and cultural archaism; it was both an indication of their subservient status and its justification. Popular practices, therefore, represented a bygone age, nothing more than a repository of the erroneous beliefs of humanity and the infancy of mankind . . . What had been denounced in the name of accepted reason or of scientific knowledge was now invalidated by being labelled the product of an inferior social group . . . The domain of the popular was now the negative world of illicit practices, odd erratic conduct, unrestrained expressiveness and nature versus culture.[5]

Revel demonstrates the solidarity which united the guardians of reason and rational interests, all their notorious disagreements notwithstanding. However hotly they defended their own particular versions of reason's superiority over natural passions, they forgot their differences whenever the condemnation of those who 'reasoned poorly or not at all' was at stake. Every incantation of the universality of the faculty of reason was invariably accompanied by a reminder that the ability to use it is a sparsely distributed privilege. The whole discourse can be best understood as an aspect of a 'closure–exclusion' operation; to quote Revel again, 'it was perpetuated anonymously by a collective voice whose identity was derived from the use of the discourse, independent of any technical capacity for expertise. The group used the discourse to define itself.'[6] Solidarity spread wide and brought together otherwise utterly unlikely bedfellows; David Hall wrote recently of a coalition of 'clergy, freethinkers, philosophers and scientists' closing their ranks by the end of the seventeenth century to deliver mankind from the awesome power of passion and superstition.

Such a unanimity between schools of thought, which history of ideas textbooks have taught us to see as engaged in a war of attrition with each other, would be a puzzle – were we, following those textbooks' habit, considering their relations separately from the socio-political figuration of the time. Otherwise, it does not look surprising at all. Clergymen, secularizers, philosophers, budding scientists –all confronted the problems of the time, the whole set of 'social demands' spawned by the imminent passage from the wild to a garden culture. And they vied with each other in offering their services as the proponents of the best recipes and the most expert practitioners of social control. The set of social demands was rapidly growing in size and urgency. In no way was it a creation of philosophical discoveries or even of a changing intellectual mood. The process was firmly rooted in the practice of the state of moving swiftly into the gaps left by failing community control. '[T]he early modern state,' writes Günther Lotte, 'took great pains to order the everyday life of its subjects. In fact, a great deal of what we know about early modern popular culture comes either from numerous ordinances, mandates and edicts issued to this end or from the records that were kept when rules were infringed.' The scope of state interference was widening so rapidly, and its regulatory zeal was so all-embracing, that 'a whole way of life seemed to be coming under attack'.[8]

The scale and intensity of the political repression which swept seventeenth-century Europe, while masquerading as a cultural crusade, was truly unprecedented. For the popular masses, the reigns of Louis XIII and Louis XIV were – in Robert Muchembled's characterization – 'un siècle de fer'. 'Shackled bodies and subjected souls' had become the new mechanisms of power. Not that long ago, a century or two before, ordinary people 'were relatively free to use their bodies at their convenience; they did not have to refrain all the time from expressing their sexual and emotional impulses'. But it was all changed now. Under the rule of absolute monarchy, social conformity suffered a complete transformation.

> It was not now the question of respecting the norms of the group to which one belonged, but of submitting oneself to a general model, valid everywhere and for everyone. This implied cultural repression. The courtier society, men of letters, nobility, rich urbanites, in other words privileged minorities elaborated between themselves a new cultural model: one of *l'honnête homme* of the seventeenth century, or of *l'homme éclaire* of the eighteenth century. A model obviously in-accessible to the popular masses; but one they were called to imitate.[9]

It is sensible to suppose an intimate link between the growing attachment felt by rulers for the uniform and universally binding cultural model, and the new, statistical–demographic, tenor of politics related to the techniques of absolutist power. Subjects, citizens, legal persons – all were essentially identical units of the state; their exemption from the local constraints (and thus their subjection to the supra-local power of the state) required their particularistic hues to be rubbed off and covered with the universal paint of citizenship. This political intention was well reflected in the idea of a universality of behavioural pattern that knew no limits for emulation. This pattern could tolerate alternatives, which claimed legitimacy by invoking localized traditions, no more than the absolute monarchy could tolerate local customs invoking ancient laws, written or unwritten, for their support. But this meant bulldozing the whole intricate structure of local cultures with the same determination and no less ferocity than that used in levelling down the solitary towers of communal autonomies and privileges. The political unification of the country had a cultural crusade as its accompaniment and the postulated universality of cultural values as its intellectual reflection-cum-legitimation. Let us borrow again from Muchembled, for the summary of the outcome:

> Popular culture, the rural as much as the urban, suffered an almost total collapse under the rule of the Sun King. Its internal coherence vanished definitely. It could not serve any more as a system of survival, or philosophy of existence. France of the Reason, and later France of *les lumières*, had room for only one conception of the world and of life: this of the court and of the urban elites, the carriers of the intellectual culture. The immense effort to reduce the diversity to a unity constituted the very base of the 'civilizing conquest' in France, as witnessed by the drive to subordinate spirits and the bodies, and by the merciless repression of the popular revolts, of deviant behaviour, heterodox beliefs and witchcraft . . . Toward the middle of the seventeenth century, the conditions had been put together for the birth of the 'mass' culture.[10]

Were we to judge the causes of the cultural crusade according to the accusations articulated by the learned critics of the time, we would in all probability assume that the old ways, now redubbed superstitions and prejudices, offended the educated elite's sense of the reasonable and the properly human. We would also have to accept that whatever the sacred and secular powers, aided and abetted by the theologians and the philosophers, did to the rural and urban populus, it was for the latter's own benefit; that the critics had only the popular interest in mind. Above all, we would be told that ancient popular habits came under criticism and had been selected as objects of prosecution and legal prohibitions because of the false, or morally wrong, ideas they promoted, ideas contrary to scientific or moral truths as proclaimed and testified by the men of knowledge.

It is easy to realize how misleading such an interpretation was, once the substance of accusations launched against popular custom is analysed; particularly, once the various criticisms are brought together and compared. According to Revel's findings, while there was continuous and active opposition to the popular way of life throughout the seventeenth and eighteenth centuries, the arguments advanced against ancient customs and reasons supplied for their suppression changed visibly over time. At the beginning of the crusade, the old customs were castigated as 'untrue', as celebrating non-existent or misinterpreted facts of history and hence promoting popular ignorance. Later, the argument shifted to the defence of 'rationality', and rural and urban festivals, processions, games and plays were declared guilty of unleashing passions and stifling the voice of reason. Finally, towards the second half of the eighteenth century, the new, centrally located sites of authoritative pronouncements were probably established firmly enough for the persecution of local traditions and their carriers to be justified in terms of their conflict with 'socially agreed' conventions and behavioural codes.[11] This succession of leading themes seems to have had no impact on the practice of the persecution. Continuity of practice underlay the ostensible discontinuity of the debate; for a sociologist, it provides the key to the true causes and mechanisms of the crusade.

Yves-Marie Bercé, in his excellent study of the fate of popular festivals in the early modern age,[12] collected striking evidence of incoherence and mutual contradictions between contemporary (and not only successive) arguments against traditional customs. For example, mysteries traditionally performed in Flanders on the streets of towns were attacked by the writers of catholic persuasion for the implicit anti-papist undertones allegedly contained in their rendering of biblical anecdotes; the protestants, on the other hand, loathed the mysteries for the naïvety and crudity of their religious representations. Yet the writers of both camps were unanimous in their condemnation of mysteries, and the hapless perpetrators of traditional festivals could expect no reprieve from either of the two rival religious powers.

From the Reformation and the Catholic Counter-Reformation, to the revolutionary zeal of the Jacobins, there runs an uninterrupted line of persecutions, which brought in the end a total dispossession and cultural disarmament of the rural and urban *classes populaires*. Total and unqualified resentment for popular habits, contempt for the irrational and grotesque, now identified with the peasant and generally 'uneducated' culture, was perhaps the only point of agreement between the spokesmen of established Churches, puritans, Jansenists, libertines, learned *philosophes* and practitioners of revolution. In his *Dictionnaire philosophique* (1766) Voltaire summed up two centuries of discourse (*and* repressive practices) when he defined *fêtes* as an occasion for the peasants and the artisans to get drunk on the days of their favourite saints, to indulge in sloth and debauchery and commit crimes.[13] The notorious debate between the 'moderns' and the 'ancients' (often mistaken by historians of ideas for the leading intellectual theme of the era, one which encapsulated the tortuous emancipation of Reason from its slavish subservience to tradition) is best understood as an aspect of this general restructuring of power in which the cultural crusade was an important manifestation as well as an indispensable condition. The radical transformation of time imagery closely corresponded to the revaluation of tradition, now embodied in the popular mode of life. 'In the eyes of the writing men who ruled the taste and the state, presentation of the past and its heritage changed completely. One did not speak any more of the times of good habits, of the Golden Age, but of the "ignorance and the barbarism of the former ages" (Fontenelle, 1688). Repeating the humanist cliches, one opposed the "gothic" vulgarity to the reason of the modern age . . .' In this re-evaluated time framework popular culture 'was considered as a relic of the past', its customs contemptible or laughable, and above all marginal, shrinking and doomed.[14]

Bercé locates the rupture between the 'educated elite culture' (the first way of life truly deserving the name of 'culture', as it organized itself around consciously accepted ideals and in equally explicit opposition to alternative modes of life) and what, by juxtaposition, was cast as the culture of the popular masses, as early as the sixteenth century. At least at that time the Church unilaterally renounced its long and happy cohabitation with local traditions and cults. A stiff, universal Church calendar had been opposed to local calendars of traditional festivities. The sophisticated, highly intellectualized and abstract religion of the theologians had been given preference over the unrefined, but exuberant and passionate beliefs of the illiterate; the very sophistication of the canon now enthroned as the only acceptable version of religious faith served as an unsurmountable hurdle for the masses and the foolproof means of keeping them permanently in a subordinate position as the objects of the pastoral action of the Church. Parish priests and parish churches withdrew from communities and set themselves apart, as supervisors and judges of the parishioners' life, rather than as its willing and friendly, *primus inter pares*, participants. Symbolically, the change was conveyed by the erection of fences around churchyards and cemeteries, and the refusal to lend church premises for peasant or urban folk fairs, dances and other festivities. Again, the behaviour of the Church was just one symptom of a much wider process of separation between 'high' and 'low' culture, the 'objectification' of the latter, and the assumption of the gardener role and a proselytizing function by the powers focused on the state.

In every area, the powerful and the wealthy were now withdrawing their participation and refusing support for the activities once common and shared, that were now redefined as one-sidedly plebian and hence unsavoury and contrary both to the precepts of Reason and the interests of society. As later developments will prove, what angered the dominant classes and prompted them to turn their backs on events in which they had taken an enthusiastic part in the past was – contrary to their own explanations – not the nature of the events and certainly not their form, but the fact that people now firmly divided into the agents and the objects of social initiatives mixed in them indiscriminately. Worse still, the popular classes took an equal part in planning and running such events, more often than not claiming leadership sanctified by tradition. The withdrawal of the powerful signalled the start of hostilities in what was to be a long struggle for authority, meaning first and foremost the right to take social initiative, the right to be the subject of social action (Touraine's struggle for historicity), rights that the dominant classes wanted now for themselves and for themselves alone. The strategic end of the struggle, never clearly spelled out, was to reduce 'the people' to the status of a passive recipient of the action, as one of the spectators of public events, which now turned into spectacular displays of the might of the mighty and the wealth of the wealthy. By the eighteenth century, the splendour and the scale of public festivities had risen rather than diminished. However 'their composition was fully aristocratic; they were the work of professionals. Popular audiences were not absent, but their participation in the spectacles, partaking of the play, were undesirable. Their enthusiasm was welcomed, but their intervention would be condemned as a manifestation of stupidity or uncouthness.'[15]

Thanks to the work of Eileen and Stephen Yeo, an impressive body of information has been collected on numerous aspects of this struggle for authority in early nineteenth-century England; the last vestiges of what once used to be a fully fledged and autonomous popular culture were attacked with formidable ferocity. The clergy of the established and nonconformist churches as well as the preachers of secular progress vied with each other in composing ever more juicy, lurid and blood-curdling pictures of the crudity and bestiality of popular customs – particularly those which had been maintained and administered by the popular classes themselves. The concentric assault on 'blood sports' such as bull-baiting and cock-fighting has been widely documented by the enthusiastic recorders of moral progress; what they failed to note, however, was the fact that the most prominent among the attackers were the very classes who made sport synonymous with hunting and collective, ritual killing of animals. R. Malcolmson, in his thorough research on popular recreations in early modern England, pointed out and resolved the paradox involved:

> Just as the Game Laws discriminated in favour of the sport of gentlemen, and did so with the approval, or at least general acquiescence, of 'public opinion' – 'Rural diversions certainly constitute a very pleasing and proper amusement for all ranks above the lowest', remarked one essayist – so the attacks on traditional recreation accommodated themselves to the circumstances of social and political power, concentrated their attention on the culture of the multitude, and fashioned their moral protest in a manner which was consistent with the requirements of social discipline.[16]

Three episodes of the many-fronted battle are particularly worth mentioning, as they demonstrate clearly the stakes of the cultural crusade.

The first is the famous case of the traditional football matches played at Whitsun on the streets of Derby. The occasion, much like the notorious horse racing of Sienna, involved the whole Derby population and supplied the purpose for leisure time activities long before the match and the topic for public discussions long after. For a long period of time the annual event enjoyed the support and benevolent patronage of the local nobility and clergy. But at the beginning of the nineteenth century the mood changed. The players came to be accused of brutal behaviour, the whole idea of a match in which everyone was a participant and in which there were only participants was compared with a pagan rite unworthy of a Christian community, and the whole event was declared dangerous to public health and order. The Mayor of Derby was flooded with depositions. The two quotations selected by Anthony Delves convey the flavour of this 'public opinion':

> [T]he assembling of a lawless rabble, suspending business to the loss of the industrous, creating terror and alarm to the timid and peaceable, committing violence on the persons and damage to the properties of the defenceless and poor, and producing in those who play moral degradation and in many extreme poverty, injury to health, fractured limbs and (not infrequently) loss of life; rendering their homes desolate, their wives widows and their children fatherless . . .
>
> [A] disgraceful and inhuman exhibition . . . a scene worthier of pagan Rome than Christian Britain . . . an annual exhibition of rude and brutal barbarism . . . of so low and degrading a nature that it should be swept away from our land as bull-baiting, cockfighting and other brutal sports had been of late years.[17]

Moral indignation mixed for good measure with crocodile tears shed over the threatened physical and moral welfare of the poor (which, whenever threatened, becomes a burden on the 'taxpayer'), only occasionally descends from the high pitch of disinterested righteousness to reveal the concerns underlying the sudden spate of protests against the ancient festivity: the struggle for public space, now increasingly understood as the policed space, an orderly space, a secure system of moats and ramparts guarding the fortresses of new social power. When in 1835 a police force was set up in Derby, it was given an unambiguous instruction: 'Persons standing or loitering on the footway without sufficient cause, so as to prevent the free passage of such a footway . . . may be apprehended and taken before a magistrate.'[18]

The eviction of popular orchestras from churches and their replacement with hired organists was another episode in the same cultural crusade and bore all the typical marks of a battle for public leadership. Vic Gammon's research leaves little doubt as to the true meaning of the campaign. The Church-sponsored press did not mince words in alerting enlightened parishioners to the necessity for quick and decisive action. '[N]othing can be more certainly fatal to the good cause', wrote the author of *The Parish Choir, 1846–51*, 'than placing the management of the music in crude and vulgar hands.' The appeals did not remain unanswered for long; already in 1857 *The Church of England Quarterly Review* noted with satisfaction that '[t]he days are happily numbered in which a fiddle and a bassoon were looked upon as the appropriate accompaniments to a church choir . . . Few churches are now without an organ.' Gammon concludes that '[i]n order to elevate the culture of the elite it was important that the culture of the poor be devolved, and be devalued in the eyes of the poor themselves; paternal tolerance gave way to middle-class condemnation . . . Thus all art should be judged by elite standards.'[19] True. But the stake of the game was not just the right aesthetic judgement, and not even the denigration of popular taste. Much more was involved – control over the sites from where judgements may be pronounced with authority. This was the true difference between the voluntary, self-appointed and self-managed 'fiddle and bassoon' players, and the professional organist, a paid employee hired and fired by the parish priest.

Eileen and Stephen Yeo unmistakeably capture the sense of events investigated in the studies collected in their book: 'As well as being about their separate subject matter, the struggles mapped in the book were also about control over time and territory. They were about social initiative, and who was to have it.' The Yeos' own contribution is the study of the beginnings of modern amateur competitive sport in Britain. They quote the *Sporting Gazette* of 1872: 'Sports nominally open to gentlemen amateurs must be confined to those who have a real right to that title, and men of a class considerable lower must be given to understand that the facts of their being well conducted and civil and never having run for money are not sufficient to make a man a gentleman as well as an amateur.' And *The Times* of 1880: 'The outsiders, artisans, mechanics, and such like troublesome persons can have no place found for them. To keep them out is a thing desirable on every account.' The redeployment of power signalled by these quotations sowed the seeds of the pattern to come: 'administrators, teachers, and "social" scientists giving the people what they needed, as much as entrepreneurs like club entertainment secretaries . . . giving the people what they wanted'.[20]

This was indeed the most crucial of the consequences of the passage from the wild culture of pre-modern times to the garden culture of modernity; of the protracted, always ferocious, often vicious cultural crusade; of the redeployment of social power in the sense of the right to initiative and control over time and space; of the gradual establishment of a new structure of domination – the rule of the knowledgeable and knowledge as the ruling force. Traditional, self-managing and self-reproducing culture was laid in ruins. Deprived of authority, dispossessed of its territorial and institutional assets, lacking its own, now evicted or degraded, experts and managers, it rendered the poor and lowly incapable of self-preservation and dependent on the administrative initiatives of trained professionals. The destruction of pre-modern popular culture was the main factor responsible for the new demand for expert 'administrators, teachers, and "social" scientists' specializing in converting and cultivating human souls and bodies. The conditions had been created for culture to become conscious of itself and an object of its own practice.

5

Educating people

Having been stripped of the shoddy vestments of tradition, people will have been reduced to the pure, pristine state of the 'man as such', exemplars of the human species. They will then share just one attribute: the infinite capacity to be acted upon, shaped, perfected. Having been bared of old and shabby clothes, they will be ready to be clothed again. This time the dress will be carefully selected, meticulously designed, and cut to the measure of common interest, as prescribed by Reason. The will of the designers is to be restrained by Reason only. Those who will have to wear the dress in the end are neither capable of, nor likely to be willing, to make the right choice. The human species knows of no limits to its power of perfection. The feature of the species does not translate, however, into the traits of its individual members. They – the individuals – lack, on the contrary, the resources necessary to transform them into true members of the proud species. Such a transformation must be guided by those who converse with Reason and hence know what the common interest demands. The tremendous potential of humanity cannot be realized without the help of the mediators, who interpret the precepts of Reason and act on them, setting conditions which will make the individuals willing, or obliged, to follow their human vocation.

This was the view shared by the elites of the early modern era. This was also, and more importantly, the logic of the new situation created by the destruction of the popular culture. In the wake of the cultural crusade, the people found themselves indeed naked and helpless, lacking the skills and communal support to meet the challenge of life and reproduce the conditions of their own survival. This artificially created void needed to be filled; the helpless needed a leader, the blind needed guides. Education was not an invention of the Age of Reason; neither was it an artefact of the intellectual revolution of which we so often read as the mother, or at least the midwife, of the modern, civilized age. Education was, rather, an afterthought, a response of the 'crisis-management' type, a desperate attempt to regulate the deregulated, to introduce order into social reality which had been first dispossessed of its own self-ordering devices. With popular culture and its power bases in ruins, education was a necessity.

The idea of education has been so closely associated in its later history with schooling, that it is difficult to realize the full scope of the original ambitions it stood for. If the idea of the school was inextricably woven into the idea of education from the very beginning of the Age of Reason, it was only in the sense of the whole society, the total human environment, being moulded in a way which makes human individuals learn, appropriate and practise the art of rational social life. In no way was education seen as a separate area in the social division of labour; it was, on the contrary, a function of all social institutions, an aspect of daily life, a total effect of designing society according to the voice of Reason. If the need for specialized schools and professional educators was admitted at all, it was only as an interim measure: to make a specific generation, poisoned in the past by wrong, irrational laws and the superstitions they bred, able to receive the blessings of Reason; to make it receptive to the new social order – and to participate in the construction of such an order that will render schools redundant. Such temporary measures, to be better distinguished from the much wider strategy of public education, *les philosophes* preferred to call *l'instruction publique*. Of that, Condorcet said with utmost clarity: 'While working on the formation of such new institutions, we ought to be preoccupied with bringing closer this happy moment when the need for them disappears.'[1] Instead, 'education' stood for a project to make the formation of the human being the full and sole responsibility of society as a whole, and especially of its lawgivers. The idea of education stood for the right and the duty of the state to form (best conveyed in the German concept of *Bildung*) its citizens and guide their conduct. It stood for the concept, and the practice, of a managed society.

To rediscover the place occupied by the concepts and practices of education in the emerging – modern – constellation of power, we

can avail ourselves of the rich crop of information contained in the
'hundreds of texts', 'innumerable discussions in the successive
Assemblies, blueprints of laws and decrees, articles scattered in the
press, civic catechisms etc.' of the revolutionary period. This will not
necessarily mean committing an error of asynchrony; the postulate
of a managed society, a society consciously designed, planned and
supervised by the centralized power, which the French Revolution
vigorously promoted, was, after all, nothing else but the end-
product of the discourse originated by the Age of Reason and con-
tinued by the Age of Enlightenment. Indeed, the discourse of the
Enlightenment reached its full maturity in the practice of the Revolution; before, it was lacking the levers powerful enough to lift its
theoretical prescriptions to the level of political practice. In the intoxi-
cating atmosphere of the Revolution the two levels seemed to merge,
and the practical measures, rather than acting as constraints on the
imagination, came to be plied freely to match the requirements of
theory. Bronislaw Baczko, a most profound analyst of the educational accomplishments and hopes of the French Revolution, concludes that the educational policy of the time was shaped by the
legacy of the Enlightenment; not in the sense of an impact exerted by
a concrete work or ideas traceable to a specific author, but in the
much more significant sense of *l'élan pedagogique*.[2] It was shaped by
the feeling that *l'éducation peut tout* (Helvetius), that one can actually
produce a totally new kind of human being, fully emancipated from
'prejudices', that the only limits to the educational potential of *la
République* are set by the ingenuity of the legislators. One can add
another indubitable mark of the Enlightenment legacy: the conviction, so clearly demonstrated in endless Assembly debates, that
every failure of enlightened pedagogical initiatives, any retardation
in the arrival of the New Man, may and should be accounted for in
terms of a conspiracy of the forces of darkness. The ideas shaped in
the context of social management, proselytism and interference with
the bodily rhythm and spirits of individuals coloured the retrospective wisdom of *les philosophes* and their political followers; the difference
between reason and prejudice, knowledge and ignorance could be
thought of only as an opposition between good and bad education,
rather than between the presence and absence of educational activity.
All forms of human conduct came to be seen from this perspective as
a product of education of sorts; the task did not consist in introducing
educational processes to an educationally virgin society, but in

replacing the old, damaging education, administered by wrong, unenlightened or ill-intentioned teachers, by a socially useful and individually beneficial education administered in the name of reason. The task consisted, in other words, in a change of educating elites. The obstacles to the speedy success of educational innovations could only be perceived as the outcome of the resistance put up by the old, not-yet-fully-eliminated, educational forces. Priests, *vieilles femmes* and ancient proverbs were selected as respresentations of the forces of darkness. Priests, of course, stood for the spiritual hierarchy of the Church – a direct rival in the struggle for intellectual domination, an alternative intellectual elite to be disempowered and displaced. More interestingly, the old wives stood for localized, communally based authority, which had to be ploughed over if the field of society was to be cultivated according to the universal design. And ancient proverbs represented the forces of tradition, re popular culture, re superstition, re the stubbornness of crude, unrefined, irrational forms of life – all the things which the cultural crusade of the last two centuries had set out to annihilate.

The enthusiastic legislative bustle of the revolutionary period can be seen, therefore, as the Enlightenment in action. It was the long practice of the rising absolutist state, the now almost complete redeployment of social power and the protracted maturation of the pastoral power of the state, that enabled the legislators of the Revolution to speak with authority. And it was in their speech that the practice found in the end its full theoretical articulation.

Let us remember that the participants of the debate on *l'instruction publique* saw education as a metaphor for society as such; after all, the schools they proposed to establish were just 'interim measures'; schools to prepare a society which itself will be a school, a society understood above all as a huge 'teach-in' institution. It seemed reasonable, therefore, to consider the task of designing the schools as the thinking through of the indispensable features of the society to come; to make them as much the condensed, miniaturized versions of the future society as possible. Thus the reading of the documents of the educational debate offers more than information on educational theory in the present, narrowly specialized, sense. They contain an entire theory of, or rather a complete design for, the kind of society and the type of preoccupations of state powers which the political descendants of *les philosophes* would wish to assure in order to bring about the kingdom of Reason.

In view of these remarks, it is indeed striking how relatively little attention the debate paid to the content of the postulated education, to the actual knowledge the schools will need to pass over to their trainees. Remember the detailed curricula scheduled for the 'academies for the noble', which drew on a well-institutionalized model of noble virtues, thus confining their own inventiveness to the introduction of a professional teacher as a mediator in the intergenerational transmission of the latter. It seems instead that – in designing future institutions of public education – media was indeed the message, and the school environment and the strictness of its regulation was the very content of intended instruction. By far the most frequent and most carefully elaborated theme of the debate was that proposing rules for the daily behaviour of the pupils; more symptomatically still, the methods by which the observation of the rules on all and every occasion ought to be assured. The method most widely considered was, not at all unexpectedly, surveillance. The future figures of pedagogical authority – the heads and teachers of the schools – were seen, first and foremost, as experts in supervision and the enforcement of discipline. This was, perhaps, one respect in which the blueprints for educational institutions came closest to their status as 'condensed miniatures' of society at large, and as training grounds for social life in general. Complete visibility of individual conduct, relations best described by the visual metaphor of 'transparency', were the paramount kinship factor uniting the structure proposed for the schools and the proposers' views of the ideal society.

To illustrate the point, let us look again into the documents researched and collected by Baczko.

The most comprehensive and the most notorious (though, as most other legislative initiatives, abortive) project of national education, prepared by Lepeletier and introduced to the Convention by Robespierre himself, characterized the model school as one in which everything would be visible, everybody would be under observation, and no detail would escape the rules. Austere discipline was to be the main feature of the model school and it would consist of a total absence of situations for which no rules existed, a complete exclusion of norm-neutral conduct.

Constantly under the eyes and in the hands of an active surveillance, every hour will be marked as one of sleep, eating, work, exercise, rest; the whole order of life will be invariably regulated . . . A salutary and uniform regulation will prescribe every detail, and its constant and easy enforcement will guarantee good effects . . . A new, strong, industrious, orderly and disciplined race [will be created] separated by an impenetrable wall from all impure contact with the prejudices of our ancient species.[3]

Another project, presented a little later by Barère, was still more exact and imaginative in expounding the same essential idea of national education. The world of total and ubiquitous regulation was portrayed as one in which all peculiarities of individuals had been erased, and the impersonal order of numbers had effaced the qualitative variety impeding the enforcement of uniform rules. Lepeletier's point about the need for confinement and isolation from the 'prejudiced species' was also given a more practical interpretation.

> A republican education will be attained above all by the experience of a transparent order of supervised equality and of pure and lasting mores: the division of pupils conforming to the principles of the republican system of measures: into thousands, hundreds, and dozens; the functions of decurions, centurions and millenions, assigned by drawing a lot; not a penny of personal money . . . Prohibition to approach the fence by less than ten steps, even to speak with one's parents.[4]

The global message was perhaps implicit and even unintended, but unambiguous: the purpose of education is to teach obedience. Instinct and willingness to conform, to follow command, to do what the public interest, as defined by the superiors, demands to be done, was the skill most needed by the citizens of a planned, designed, thoroughly and completely rationalized society. Not the knowledge passed to the pupils, but the atmosphere of drill, routine and total predictability under which the passage of knowledge would be conducted, was the condition which mattered most. The heralds of the garden culture did not expect individuals to guide their own behaviour in accordance with social interest, making their own decisions in the light of the knowledge they would have acquired. The kind of conduct that agreed with public interest would be decided by society in advance of any individual action, and the one ability individuals would need for the interest of society to be satisfied, was that of discipline.

This conclusion may come as a surprise. After all, the Enlightenment has entrenched itself in our collective memory as a powerful
drive to bring knowledge to the people, to restore clear sight to those
blinded by superstition, to give wisdom to the ignorant, to pave the
way for the progress defined as the passage from darkness to light,
ignorance to knowledge. This was what *les philosophes* preached. This
was the legitimation they offered in advance to the administrative
zeal of the Revolution. And yet, under closer scutiny, the substance
of enlightened radicalism is revealed as the drive to legislate,
organize and regulate, rather than disseminate knowledge. What
was at stake more than anything else was the need to compensate for
the intrinsic weakness of individuals through the unlimited 'educating'
potential of society at large as represented by its executive power.
Rousseau's much-quoted and still more maligned adage that 'men
must be forced to be free' did not signal an aberration from the
mainstream of a loftily intellectual philosophy. On the contrary, it
captured and articulated with shocking self-awareness the idea
which, as a response to the structural turbulence of the era underpinned the whole project of the Enlightenment: the idea that
Reason, understood as the ideal order of the social world, does not
have its site in the mind of the individual, that the two are not com-
mensurable, that each of the two is subject to a distinct and separate
set of causes and operating factors, and that when the two meet, the
first must be accorded (and has the legitimate claim to be accorded)
priority over the second. From the very start, *les philosophes* designed
a social order grounded in the pastoral power of the enlightened
despot, or the legislators, over the individuals; an order which was
much later aptly described as one of 'therapeutic state' (Kittrie),
saturated with a 'tutelage complex' (Donzelot).

The coincidence between the rule of ideas (ostensibly the mainstay
of the Enlightenment project) and the surveillance-based discipline
may seem contradictory and paradoxical only if the social roots of
the Age of Reason are forgotten. Let us recall that, in the beginning,
there was 'the crisis of the seventeenth century'. That the crisis was,
in essence, the bankruptcy, or at least the increasingly apparent
inadequacy, of the extant (and thus far untheorized) means of social
control. That this feeling of inadequacy of control, of social order
under threat, arose among the powerful and the wealthy of the time
out of the new experience of the presence of 'masterless people' – a
shifting, homeless, vagabond population, the rabble, riff-raff, *mobile*

vulgus, les classes dangereuses. That the effort to neutralize the perceived threat and to dispel the fears it emanated took the form of political practices, best summarized as the passage from wild cultures to a garden one. That now emerging garden culture involved the new responsibility of the centralized power of the state for the maintenance and reproduction of social order. And that the qualitatively novel location of controlling and order-reproducing powers created demand for a novel kind of expertise, and a novel function of paramount, systemic importance: a function of teacher/supervisor, of a professional specializing in modifying human behaviour, in 'bringing conduct into line' and staving off, or containing the consequences of, disorderly or erratic action. The project of the Enlightenment was a response to those perceptions, practical problematizations and demands. When this is remembered, the paradox evaporates. It becomes clear instead that the project was, from the start and by necessity, a two-edged one: aimed at the 'enlightening' of the state, its policies and its methods of action on the one hand, and at the containing, taming or otherwise regulating of their subjects on the other. *Les philosophes* spoke to the power holders; what they spoke to them about, were 'the people'. The act of speaking meant the dissemination of rational ideas. The subject-matter of that speech was the methodology of rationalizing the reproduction of social order.

In the light of the same consideration, another frequently noted paradox will also vanish: one of the admittedly ambiguous treatments proferred by *les philosophes* to 'the people'. As if to make the apparent paradox even more striking, the ambiguity was twofold. On the one hand, the people were seen as would-be citizens, the Shilsian 'periphery' to be eventually brought within the orbit of the 'centre' and saturated with the latter's values and norms; but, simultaneously, they were conceived of as a multitude to be kept in check, held with or without their consent, by force if necessary, under control of the 'centre' and rendered harmless from the point of view of the 'centre'. On the other hand, there was the bewildering discrepancy between the mixture of horror, contempt and derision *les philosophes* felt for the ignorant, superstitious, fickle and unpredictable *mobile vulgus* and the benevolent compassion they manifested each time they thought of *le peuple* as the prospective objects of their pastoral care and tutelage.

However psychologically puzzling ('cognitively dissonant') the listed contradictions, they lose much of their edge once considered

against the two-pronged task in relation to which the project of the
Enlightenment was conceived and developed. What made the image
of the people intrinsically contradictory was the duality of systemic
tasks as perceived from the vantage point of the state, the ruling
classes and their enlightened advisers. One task was to make the
state policy rational, that is, effective and efficient; the other was to
render the conduct of *les classes dangereuses* manageable, predictable
and thus harmless. The first task needed, clearly, the formulation
and dissemination of right, rational and adequate ideas. What the
other task needed, was not immediately obvious. The natural, instinc-
tive reaction of those who lived by ideas and deeply believed in their
creative power was to hope that the second task could be met by the
same means as the first. But, virtually at the same time, doubts sapped the initial enthusiasm: is everybody equally receptive to
Reason? Do not the true ideas require, in order to be grasped and
assimilated, a special kind of effort, of which only selected people are
capable? And, above all, would the spreading of lights prove beneficial to everybody, regardless of his or her (particularly her) place
in the total order of society?

This last question explains most of the apparent inconsistencies
one finds in the philosophers' writings about 'the people'. Whatever
their concrete proposals for the form that the education of the people
should take, *les philosophes* never lost from their sight the ultimate
purpose that the rational ideas and their distribution should serve:
the achievement, and reinforcement, of an orderly society. Order
meant diversification of social roles, uneven distribution of wealth
and other benefits society may offer; it meant the perpetuation of
hierarchy and class divisions. Rational organization of society should
assure satisfaction of everybody whatever his or her position within
this hierarchy. The same principle of rational organization militates,
however, against the idea of identical education for everybody; on
the contrary, synchronization of the scope and the content of education with the fate allotted to people by their class location is a
necessary condition of the universal acceptance of social order. This
assumption found perhaps its most outspoken expression in *La politique naturelle* of Holbach:

> Enlightened policies insure that every citizen will be happy in the
> rank where birth placed him. There exists a happiness for all classes;
> where the state is properly constituted, there emerges a chain of felicity

extending from the monarch to the farmer. The happy man rarely considers leaving his sphere; he likes the profession of his ancestors to which education has accustomed him since childhood. The people is satisfied as long as it does not suffer; limited to its simple, natural needs, its view rarely extends beyond.[5]

All the essential ideas are here: satisfaction with social order ('happiness', 'felicity') is the matter of the enlightened policy of the state, not of the enlightenment of the state's subjects; the purpose of enlightening the state is to assist its rulers in keeping the subjects where they are and preventing them from rebelling against their lot. And finally, particularly in the last sentence, we sense that condescension for the less fortunate which served as the excuse for holding them in conditions other classes would find repulsive (often misinterpreted as the wistful idealization of primitive, unsophisticated life).

On the whole, the philosophers inherited the image of 'the people' as it had been construed by the political action of the absolutist state. It had been constructed as a problem for, simultaneously, repressive measures and social policy. As an agent, 'the people' had been problematized as an unruly force and seed of rebellion. By the same token, it had been construed as an object for any action aimed at the defence and promotion of social order. Apart from such action, when left to their own resources and allowed to be guided by their own passions, 'the people' had been problematized as the carrier of the most odious, repulsive and socially damaging tendencies – exactly those which the enlightened, rationally organized state set out to extirpate. Even an incomplete list of the propositions made by *les philosophes* to this effect makes awesome reading.

Of the Enlightenment thinkers, de Toqueville's opinion was unequivocal: 'They despised the public almost as heartily as they despised the Deity.'[6] Opinion agrees with the facts, though a proviso is in order. The 'Deity' stood for the clergy and the 'hierarchical intellectuals' of the Church, and the derision *les philosophes* lavished on it was an expression of 'sibling rivalry'. The two *républiques des lettres* were fighting each other for mastery over the same contentious territory, and denigrating each other's entitlements in the course of the struggle. The contempt *les philosophes* felt for the public ('the people', to be more exact) was of an entirely different order: here an opinion was expressed of the very territory in the name of which the war was conducted. It did not augur well for the native population once the conquest would have been completed.

'The people', wrote Diderot, 'are the most foolish and the most wicked of all men.' He did not discriminate. In a way, the very essence of 'the people' was the lack of discrimination. An undifferentiated, grey mass of men and women already detached from all quality-endowing social and territorial locations, the product of two centuries of the evictions, enclosures and punitive action of the state. 'The people' was, for Diderot, simply a 'multitude'. For an article he wrote on the latter, a special vocabulary was needed: *méchanceté, sottise, déraison, hébétée.* D'Alembert added his own lurid brush-marks: the multitude, he wrote, is 'ignorant and stupefied . . . incapable of strong and generous action'. For Voltaire, 'the people' were 'les bêtes féroces, furieux, imbéciles, fous, aveugles'. They 'will always be composed of brutes'. They are, as a matter of fact, 'between man and beast'. For Holbach, the lower classes were 'scatterbrained, inconstant, impudent, impetuous, subject to fits of enthusiasm, instruments of troublemakers'.[7]

If there is one strong, persevering motif to be heard in this chorus of scorn and disdain, it is the fear of the *mobile vulgus* (in short, the mob) – the masterless men on the move, roaming the streets and the roads, congesting at will into crowds, given to explosions of anger and fury, erratic and unpredictable. This fear *les philosophes* shared with the dominant classes, with the 'party of order'. For all of them alike, 'the people' stood first and foremost for an unfulfilled and urgent political task – the imposition of discipline over behaviour, order over chaos.

The fear was true enough, as a vivid experience and as a powerful influence on the social philosophy of the Enlightenment; it was not, however, the whole truth. In addition to the need for containment – or, rather, because of it – 'the people' presented itself to the eyes of *les philosophes* as objects of tutelage and care. And all wards tend to evoke compassion, sympathy and understanding. Particularly if – as noted above – an efficient wardenship is the crucial stake in the struggle for political leadership. Not unexpectedly, there are numerous expressions of a frequently naïve, but as a rule genuine, compassion for the plight of the *classes laborieuses* scattered over the writings of *les philosophes.* It was stressed, over and over again, that 'the people' lived in penury and misery, that they had been cast in inhuman conditions, that poverty and hunger were the reward for the toil of the 'nourishers of nations' (Holbach). There was moral indignation; but there was also alarm, that leaving 'the people' for long in their present condition was pregnant with trouble – indeed it turned *les classes laborieuses* into *les classes dangereuses*, into facile 'instruments of troublemakers'.

For the thinkers with a proselytizing mission to perform, and with firm views of what the ideal form of *l'homme de lumières* would be like, the crucial question was, however, whether 'the people', given their odious characteristics and their abominable conditions, are capable of embracing enlightenment and instruction, and whether they need either of them (for their own good, or for the benefit of the social order as a whole). Answers to this question differed. Rousseau, who drew sharp boundaries for educational ambitions, leaving the peasants and the artisans on the other side ('Do not teach the child of a villager, as it does not fit them to be taught', *La nouvelle Héloize*;[8] 'The poor does not need education; one attached to his state is forced, and he would not have any other', *Émile*),[9] perhaps occupied one extreme, and Condorcet ('it is possible to instruct the whole mass of the people', *Escuisse d'un tableau historique*) the other. Any attempt to construct a coherent, non-contradictory account of the Enlightenment attitude to popular education would be admittedly contentious, as the attitudes themselves, for reasons indicated above, were far from consistent and only too often fell into overt, or implicit, conflict with each other. Of all summaries of the controversy I have found, Harvey Chisick's thoroughly researched opinion seems relatively the most cogent and reliable:

> The authors on whose works I have drawn did not discuss directly the possibility of rising the people to their own level. One can, however, form quite a clear idea of their opinions on this question by examining their reaction to the proposal that the people be given a broad, liberal education which would put them, intellectually at least, on a par with their social superiors. Members of the enlightened community were remarkably consistent in describing the effects that such an education would have on the labouring poor: they regarded it as 'dangerous'. [A long list of statements to this effect follows.] To the question 'Should the people be enlightened?' virtually all spokesmen of the Enlightenment answered with an emphatic 'No'. To the question 'Should the people be educated?' they responded with a reserved 'Yes'. The education the members of the enlightened community proposed for the lower classes were intended to improve their health,

teach skills suited to their *état*, and to enlist their minds and hearts for
religion and for the *patrie*.[10]

Let us comment that the question 'Should the people be
educated?' could not be answered in a simple negative. We have
seen already that the vision of a social world ruled by ideas barred *les
philosophes* from conceiving the possibility of an 'education-less'
state. Like Nature itself (according to the image accepted at the
time), education 'did not suffer void'. An alternative to good
teachers was bad teachers, not an absence of teaching; the enlightened state could not, therefore, resign its task of training its subjects in the skills they needed and of instilling the willingness to
behave in a socially useful, or acceptable, manner. Education – in
the sense of instruction and drill – should be in this case made to the
measure of *l'état* 'the people' occupy and will go on occupying, and
under no circumstances should it be identical with that addressed to
'the small number of sensible men' (Diderot). It has to be a carefully
planned and conducted education all the same.

'Enlightenment' was an entirely different matter. '[N]ot even
during the High Enlightenment', according to Chisick, 'were the
people deemed capable of independent thought or political choice.'[11]
The intrinsic flaws of the 'multitude' set unencroachable limits to
enlightenment, understood as the development of a capacity for
clear, rational thinking and informed decision-making. Enlightenment was something the rulers needed; their subjects were in need of
training, oriented toward discipline.

The social-intellectual movement recorded in history as 'the age
of Enlightenment' was not (contrary to the Whig version of history)
a huge propaganda exercise on behalf of truth, Reason, science,
rationality; neither was it a noble dream of bringing the light of
wisdom to the confused and the oppressed. Enlightenment was,
instead, an exercise in two distinct, though intimately related parts.
First, in extending the powers and the ambitions of the state, in
transferring to the state the pastoral function exercised previously
(in a way incipient and modest by comparison) by the Church, in
reorganizing the state around the function of planning, designing
and managing the reproduction of social order. Secondly, in the creation of an entirely new, and consciously designed, social mechanism of
disciplining action, aimed at regulating and regularizing the socially
relevant life of the subjects of the teaching and managing state.

6

Discovery of culture

The concept of 'culture' was not coined until the eighteenth century. There was nothing before in the learned language, not to mention everyday language, which even remotely resembled the complex world-view which the word 'culture' attempts to capture. This fact is shocking; it is also puzzling and intriguing to a contemporary reader, to whom the 'fashioning' of humans by their societies is one of the trivialities of existence. Today's triviality, nevertheless, was once a discovery, and one which truly revolutionized the way human life was perceived. It is worth our while to try to solve the puzzle. The solution may prove relevant to our efforts to comprehend the mystery of modernity – that great adventure of the north-western tip of the European peninsula.

People have travelled to foreign countries and looked at foreign peoples since the beginning of human time. Since the beginning of writing, they have sometimes recorded their experiences. Some were curious and noted strange, odd, occasionally bewildering or repulsive, ways of life. Most were not curious at all, and, as the fascinating and now classic study of Margaret Hogden amply testified,[1] hardly saw anything unusual in the things they were looking at. The numerous pilgrims to the Holy Land, the most ardent contributors to the 'travelogue' genre, scrupulously recorded their own progress with descriptions of the meals, shelters, robbers and impassable marshes it involved, but, except for the incomprehensibility of local dialects, they would not have noticed anything strange in the people they met. Naturally and matter-of-factly they imputed to such people's behaviour the meanings they expected to find, much like Christopher Columbus, that most enlightened and versatile sailor, would record the dolphins observed from his captain's deck as the sirens dancing on the ocean waves.

This was a peculiar, selective kind of collective blindness. It did not prevent people – learned and illiterate alike – from seeing and knowing that residents of various countries are different from each other. The difference, however, did not seem to present a challenge and did not call for explanation. It was what it was, like all other differences between things; the way God ordained things to be in the days of Creation; the way 'Nature' – the created world – has been since then. For centuries, the most learned among men lived without the distinction, so dear to our hearts and political passions, between the 'natural', genetic, and 'nurtured', man-made, differences between people. There was no room for as much as a supposition of the latter in the writings of the foremost scholarly authority of the Middle Ages, Isidorus of Seville: 'In accordance with diversity of climate, the appearance of men and their colour and bodily size vary and diversities of mind appear. Thence we see that the Romans are dignified, the Greeks unstable, the Africans crafty, the Gauls fierce by nature and somewhat headlong in their disposition which the character of the climates bring about.'[2] Skin colour, height of the body, temperament, customs, political institutions – all remained, if at all noticed and recorded, at the same level: they were perceived as the manifestation of a natural and perpetual diversity of the human race, meaningful only as an aspect of the pre-determined, pre-ordained 'chain of being'. There was no trace of suspicion that some of the traits could be less long lasting than others; that they may change with time; or that (God forbid) they could be changed deliberately, by human action and according to human designs. Such a perception outlived its time. Even deep in the eighteenth century, sounding somewhat outdated by the standards of that age, the great taxonomist Linnaeus would find, among the species of *homo sapiens, Homo Europeus* 'with eyes blue, governed by law', *Homo Asiaticus* 'with black hair, ruled by opinions', and *Homo Afer* 'with frizzled hair and silky skin, women without shame'. It was not only the noted differences between races, nations and countries that were seen as natural and hence eternal and pre-ordained. The same perception applied to differences between social stations within the same society (the ideal of perfection was distinct for every estate and every trade – transgression was sinful, as all human tampering with the divine order of things) or between sexes. One of the most learned men of his time,

Dante Alighieri, had no doubt as to the latter: '[T]hough we find it written that the woman spoke first, it is, however, reasonable for us to suppose that the man spoke first; and it is unseemly to think that so excellent an act of the human race proceeded even earlier from woman than from man.' In writing these words, Dante followed in spirit, if not in letter, a long tradition going back at least as far as St Paul of Tarsus: 'Does not even nature itself teach you, that, if a man have long hair, it is a shame unto him? But if a woman have long hair, it is a glory to her: for her hair is given her for covering.'

What was, therefore, well nigh totally absent from the pre-modern perception of the world was an idea of the temporaneity and mutability of human characteristics; and the idea of differentiation between the characteristics themselves, with some remaining by and large resistant to human choices and purposeful actions, others being relatively pliable, given to manipulation and change. The universe in all its complexity and inner diversity, complete with hundreds of recorded, true or imaginary, human races and ways of life, and the daily observed sharp distinctions between rural and urban dwellers, estates, trades and sexes, presented itself to contemporary eyes as a stable, harmonious construction. An object of respectful contemplation, perhaps even diligent study, but otherwise remaining steadfastly and forever beyond the reach of human practice.

Such a world-view is exactly the one to be expected in an *oikoumene* composed of wild cultures – ways of life with in-built mechanisms of self-balancing and self-reproduction, modes of coexistence which never presented themselves even to their own political rulers as 'managerial problems', as objects needing purposeful intervention simply to remain what they were. It was ultimately the lack of experience of such intervention that prevented the thought of a man-made nature of the human world, of its conventional and historical character, from being born. What we are now apt to dismiss as cultural blindness fitted well with a life-world in which the only human control efforts were aimed at things rather than human bodies; in which power specialized in supervising the circulation of products while remaining indifferent to their producers; in which the mode of life of the powerful stayed sharply distinct from the customs and habits of their subjects, but was never made into an ideal to be emulated by the latter; in which the powerful never embarked consciously on a campaign aimed at changing the ways of life of their subjects, and hence could never conceive of those ways of life as an 'object', a matter to

be 'handled' and 'acted upon'. Not until the 'natural' differences
between people are meddled with do these differences stop being
'natural' and appear as 'historical', to wit, actual or potential
objects for purposeful human action.

Throughout most of the Middle Ages, the belief in the
'naturalness', in the pre-ordained character of human forms,
remained undisturbed in Europe thanks to the firmness of control in
which the continent was held by the hierarchy of the Church.
Hierarchical unification of thought could only be reflected in certainty
about truth, guaranteed by divine origins and the grounds of all
existence. It was only at the threshold of the modern era that that
certainty was shattered; it was undermined by the internal schism
within the Church, which, for the first time in centuries, was powerful enough to produce centres of resistance too formidable to be
marginalized into heresies. A parallel departure of great consequence was the formation of absolute monarchies – again the creation of centres of power great enough to cast the differences between
countries and nations on obviously human, earthly and temporal
foundations. Finally, one factor of arguably the greatest impact on
the 'discovery of culture' was the gradual fading out of 'wild
cultures' and the parallel realization of the necessity of 'gardening'.
The first reaction to the crisis of the old powers was, as one would
expect, the dissipation of certainty and the advent of scepticism.

Scepticism (or, as it is dubbed today, relativism) is a frame of
mind reflecting a world in which no version of the truth or the
supreme values of goodness or beauty enjoys the support of a power
so evidently superior to any rival powers that it may credibly claim
its own superiority over alternative versions. We live in such a world
today. Our ancestors entered such a world in the final centuries of
the Middle Ages; in the sixteenth century, they were already well
aware that they lived in such a world, and their philosophy showed
beyond reasonable doubt that they did.

The sixteenth century was the era of Pyrrhonian crisis – the void
between the collapse of the old, Church hierarchical grounds of certainty and the painstaking construction of new, secular grounds of
universal truth. Long forgotten arguments of the ancient sceptics
were resuscitated and quickly moved into the very centre of scholarly
debate. If we remember that a sceptic is a person who doubts that
necessary and sufficient grounds or reasons can be given for our
knowledge or beliefs, we will realize how well fitted were the resur-

rected arguments in the experience of scholars who suddenly found themselves facing a clash of irreconcilable values and visions of reality, which showed no signs of impending resolution because of the fine balance of supporting forces. 'Obviousness' may be only a function of the monopoly of power. In the absence of such a monopoly, the resistance of rival versions of equally 'self-evident' truths becomes too obstinate and immune an argument to offer hope for an unambiguous resolution of controversy. All truths, including one's own, appear to be tied to 'the time and place'; all truths, including one's own, seem to make sense only inside the boundary of a country, the realm of a reign, the tradition of a nation, according to the principle *cuius regio, eius religio*.

In the sixteenth century, the tightly knit, harmonious chain of being suddenly disintegrated into a disorderly collection of qualitatively distinct and autonomous forms, already devoid of the intrinsic unity guaranteed by divine design, but still lacking the *ex post facto* unity imposed, or aimed at, by a new secular power formidable enough to consider seriously the possibility of moulding the diversity into a unity of design of its own. The first reaction to the collapse of old certainties was dismayed shock – wittily portrayed in a thoughtful study by Richard H. Popkin.[3] The earth tremors sent by the crumbling Gothic edifice, the cacophony of battle cries made by the armies unlikely either to win, surrender or compromise, found their sublimated philosophical equivalent in growing doubts in the validity of knowledge as such, the possibility of 'proving' its soundness, the likelihood of finding apodictically binding arguments in favour of acceptance (or rejection, for that matter) of any proposition engaged in battle with an alternative one. For the descendants of generations of schoolmen acting under the cosy shelter of divinely guaranteed certainty, this enforced lack of self-confidence was a sufficient cause for philosophical despair. Some tried to hope against hope that the old certainties could be somehow salvaged from the débâcle by sticking to the tried weapon of *petitio principii* – tacitly assuming in the debate what the debate was meant to demonstrate. This way the debate could go in circles forever, the spokesmen for despair and the equally desperate exhumers of certainty speaking past each other rather than to each other (a contemporary reader would not fail to be struck by the similarity to the philosophical discourse of our own Pyrrhonian crisis). Others – more realistically – sought a way out from the increasingly barren, circular argument, by adopting a middle-of-the-way, cautious attitude, characterized above all by trimming the excessive ambitions of the seekers of universal truth. Such an attitude involved granting validity to the sceptical attack against all potential grounds of certainty, and seeking comfort in justifying whatever 'uncertain' knowledge was left after surrender in terms of its modest, yet indispensable and not at all negligible uses.

If Borges was right when he said (of Kafka) that every great writer creates his own predecessors, and if this rule extends to great schools of thought, then modern pragmatism, particularly in its most recent version proposed by Rorty, may well render Mercenne and Gassendi its spiritual ancestors. Without ever using the term, they did articulate a 'crisis management' strategy which implied all the assumptions and tactical suggestions of modern pragmatism. They agreed with the Pyrrhonists that our knowledge does not have, and is unlikely ever to acquire, indubitable and dogmatic grounds for self-certainty; they stoutly refused the temptation to seek new justification of such certainty in the wake of the bankruptcy of the old one; and yet they sought consolation in convincing themselves and their audience that the business of scientific study is worth pursuing even if seen, humbly, as the construction of tentative, working hypotheses on the grounds of tentative, limited experience. It is worth pursuing not so much because it leads to a foolproof, unshakable truth about reality, but because it offers practical guides to our actions. (To go even further back in history, to another period of crumbling certainties, let us recall that a similar compromise with scepticism was offered almost two millenia earlier by Cerneades.)

As we can assess retrospectively, Mercenne's and Gassendi's solution, however attractive (and however sensible it may seem to readers at the end of the twentieth century), proved to enjoy only temporary popularity. A new age of certainty was advancing, which would consider proto-pragmatist modesty undignified and evidently at odds with its own infinite potential. A person with a much more important role to play in the three centuries which followed the proto-pragmatist compromise was Descartes, with his insistence on the necessity and the possibility of certainty, with his resolute refusal to settle for anything less, and his astonishing insights into the essence of all possible grounds for certainty. His *malin génie*, the evil spook capable of tinkering with our perception and hence of sowing seeds of doubt in the truthfulness of what we know, could ultimately be exorcised only by a power too powerful and overwhelming to be ever suspected of anything reproachable, particularly a willingness to deceive. As it were, 'the desire to deceive without doubt testifies to malice and feebleness'; it is a mark of 'subtlety of power'. If we were only confronted with a power which is not feeble or subtle, which is, on the contrary, strong and firm, we would be pretty certain of our certainty. For Descartes, such a power was God; but this was to be the less relevant and transitory aspect of his insight.

In the meantime, however, there was Montaigne – justly forgotten by the age of certainty which succeeded the age of Pyrrhonian doubts and equally justly rediscovered and celebrated once the new certainty started to fade. Our century sees Montaigne as a father of modern anthropology, a giant who from the height of his vantage point saw above and beyond *les philosophes* whom he dwarfed, a messenger of future wisdom, and a stranger in his own time. Whatever else can be said of Montaigne, a stranger in his own time he was not. Everything he said about the fragility and inconclusiveness of human mores fitted perfectly the mood of a century which had lost its self-confidence. Indeed, one cannot imagine an anthropology better geared to the time of Pyrrhonian crisis. What else could it be, but a resolute statement of the lack of resolution? A staunch refusal to accept that one way of life can prove its superiority over another, one set of opinions can demonstrate its advantage over another? An emphatic rejection of all criteria of righteousness except human usage and convenience? And an insistence, in Mercenne–Gassendi style, that human usages do not need a superhuman sanction, as they serve well the business of daily life?

> I am ashamed when I see my countrymen steeped in that silly prejudice which makes them fight shy of any customs that differ from their own; when they are out of their village, they seem to be out of their element . . . Not only every country, but every city and every profession has its own particular form of civility . . . Every nation has many habits and customs which to any other nation are not only strange but amazing and barbarous . . . We all call barbarism that which does not fit in with our usages. And indeed we have no other lever of truth and reason but the example and model of the opinions and usages of the country we live in . . . He who would rid himself of this violent prejudice of custom will find that many things are accepted with undoubting resolve, which have no support but in the hoary beard and wrinkles of the usage which attends them . . .

The principal effect of the force of custom is to seize and grip us so firmly, that we are scarcely able to escape from its grasp, and to regain possession of ourselves sufficiently to discuss and reason out its commands. In truth, since we imbibe them with our mother's milk, and the world shows the same face to our infant eyes, we seem to be born to follow the same path; and the common ideas that we find current around us, and infused into our souls with the seed of our fathers, appear to be general and natural. When it comes that what is off the hinges of custom we believe to be off the hinges of reason: God knows how unreasonably for the most part.[4]

Less than a century later Descartes will still confront a world dissipated into a myriad of more or less known customs and more or less bizarre ways of life, a world in which no single mode of life could show anything but its own familiarity to itself as its passport to acceptance. To Descartes, however, such a world would present a problem; it would be both frightening and infuriating, and hence a stimulus to act, promptly and urgently. Descartes would bewail the lesson such a world offered: that one could not believe anything with certainty, of which one had been convinced *merely* by example and custom. Relativity of human ways and opinions was not something with which Descartes would reconcile himself – complacently, resentfully or enthusiastically. It was a trouble, a worry, a challenge to be met and fought away by finding grounds, more solid than *mere* example and custom, for accepting some opinions with certainty and, with the same certainty, rejecting all others. Descartes would be first, at the dawn of a new era of certainty, to denigrate and dismiss 'the way people do things' as 'mere' customs, deprived of authority in the magnificent discourse of truth. Husserl would be the last, at the dusk of the same era, to rule 'the way people do things' out of court. The first verdict was a declaration of a youthful power which believed it could reach where no other powers tried or could, the second a desperate attempt to hold on to something that other powers, holding each to its own, lost all interest in.

To Montaigne, relativity of human ways was neither a problem, nor a solution. It was just the way the world was. Montaigne had no problem to solve; there seemed to be no power around (as yet) either sufficiently self-confident or strong to demand that its usages be recognized as truth, the whole truth and nothing but the truth (and, by the same token, all others to be declared 'mere' prejudice and given an outright, or suspended death sentence). There seemed to be no power around likely to be an interested customer for the criteria of absolute truth. On the contrary, the idea that all human ways, however different from each other, are equally well (to wit, equally feebly) grounded, and that, consequently, there is no need to make much fuss about the difference, suited rather well the world hanging on an uneasy truce and compromise between precariously balanced powers, preoccupied rather more whole-heartedly with the defence of their own respective realms, than with making a case for the conquest of neighbouring ones. However, this state of affairs was shortly to change. And then the self-same springs of human ways and thoughts, which Montaigne joyously admired as good reasons for mutual understanding and tolerance, would be redeployed: as the *casus belli*, the excuse for a cultural crusade, the war-cry of forces bent on absolute domination and needing an absolute truth to match their ambition.

Already in 1930 (in his invaluable historical study, 'Civilisation, évolution d'un mot et d'une groupe d'idées')[5] Lucien Febvre drew attention to an amazing fact: though there is hardly anything easier than to coin a noun with an *isation* ending once a verb with an *iser* suffix is in general use, for many decades, indeed for the better part of the eighteenth century, a procedural verb, *civiliser* (to civilize) was widely used by men of letters on both sides of the Channel, while the noun *civilisation* had yet to be introduced. The fact sheds some of its mystery, however, once we learn that the entry of the idea of civilization and culture in their verb-procedural form was in no way an isolated case. On the contrary, as M. Frey (*Transformations du vocabulaire français a l'époque de la Révolution*) had demonstrated, the language of eighteenth-century France seemed to develop a particular liking for procedural verbs ending with *iser*. Learned writers and politicians alike spoke and wrote of nothing with greater enthusiasm than of *centraliser, fédéraliser, municipaliser, naturaliser, utiliser* and similar actions undertaken, or at least contemplated, by powers strong and ambitious enough to treat the surrounding reality as pliable, amenable to transformations, soft and malleable and able to receive a form designed by those in the lead – and at the same time imperfect, wanting and in need of a better form. This vocabulary shows the eighteenth century as an age of action; a determined action, as it were, an action simultaneously self-confident and one that valued certainty highly. Before it could become a description of the human world (or a well-defined part of this world), *civilisation* must have entered power rhetoric as a project, a declaration of intention and a design for action.

Etymologically, the origins of the word *civilisation* look complex. Its form suggests close kinship with the relatively ancient idea of *civilité*, which use had been documented for at least a century preceding the introduction of the verb *civiliser*. *Civilité* meant courtesy, good manners, mutual reverence demonstrated by carefully followed and meticulously applied rules of demeanour; as Furetière noted in 1690, it stood for 'manière honnête, douce et poli d'agir, de converser et ensemble'. As such, it was by and large an internal affair of nobility, of a class of once powerful feudal warlords, now reduced by the absolute monarchy to a bevy of courtiers, trying desperately to survive in a world where to fall was as easy as to rise meteorically, as both depended on making the right friends and influencing the right people (among whom the king, of course, was the rightest). It was, in Febvre's evaluation, nothing more than a 'veneer', a language designed specifically to hide emotions and conceal intentions, to declare one's agreement to prevent one's own emotions and intentions from interfering with peaceful interaction, seen by one and all as a condition of collective survival. In 1780, however, when the other, ostensibly related, concept of *civilisation* had already acquired an entirely different connotation, a certain abbé Girard found it possible to sustain this traditional interpretation of *civilité*: 'civility is to men what public cult is in relation to God: an external evidence of internal sentiments'. It was this meaning of *civilité*, coupled with the apparent etymological link between *civilité* and *civilisation*, which allowed Norbert Elias to locate the roots of his 'civilizing process' in the court of Versailles, and to depict the process itself as an emulation of manners associated with social distinction and privilege by classes motivated first and foremost by collective envy and the struggle for promotion.

The similarity of terms, however, conceals more than it reveals. We have seen in earlier chapters that the republic of letters had close links with the circles of nobility and the court itself. No wonder they used the same vocabulary; no wonder either that men of letters couched their ideas, however radically novel, in a language likely to strike a chord of familiarity and sympathy among the audience, and among the most important part of that audience – the enlightened despots or monarchs earmarked for such a role. This circumstance, however, does not by itself determine a continuity of meaning behind a similarity of form. After all, the concerns of *la république des lettres* extended well beyond the small snakepit in which the courtiers fought for their survival. There was nothing in the mode of existence of the courtly nobility which could possibly inspire the elaboration of the idea of *civilité* into that of *civilisation*. Everything in the mode of life, and in the social location, of *la république des lettres*, pointed on the other hand towards a set of ideas in search of a concept – the very same ideas which would subsequently find their home in the term *civilisation*.

To follow Febvre's argument once again: seen from the point of view of its content rather than its form, the verb *civiliser* reveals remarkable similarity with a quite different, but also longer established, verb: that of *policer*. The latter was from the start oriented towards the society, or the political domain, as a whole. It connoted the idea of preservation of order, elimination of violence from human intercourse (or, rather, the monopolization of violence in the service of state-supported law), safety of public space, a public sphere closely supervised and kept within well-defined, easy to decipher rules.

With some oversimplification, one can say that what united the verb *civiliser* with the verb *policer* and, at the same time, distinguished it from the old idea of *civilité* was that it denoted an operation to be performed on the network of inter-human relations, rather than on human individuals taken apart; what, on the other hand, united the verb *civiliser* with the idea of *civilité*, and at the same time distinguished it from the verb *policer* (which it soon replaced and almost totally eliminated from public discourse), was that it referred to the attainment of the desirable pattern of inter-human relations through reforming the individuals involved. 'To civilize' was a mediated activity; a peaceful and orderly society (the ideal already grasped in the notion of *société policé*) was to be reached through an educational effort aimed at society's members.

There was, however, a crucial difference hidden even in this admittedly limited similarity between the programme of civilizing and the ideal of *civilité*. The latter was, as we have seen, 'a veneer': a behavioural mask forced upon a tamed, but essentially unreformed, still passion-ridden, body. Civility was an etiquette: a code of demeanour to be learned and followed faithfully, a set of rules anyone admitted to the society of the chosen was asked to accept and obey, while others were expected to settle for obedience to the rules as a

sufficient proof of loyalty to the group and eligibility for membership. Civility was concerned with the masks, not the faces. It neither
attempted, nor wished to reach beneath the mask; the face, the
'private' side of the individual, it considered irrelevant and hence
exempt from regulation. Not so the ideal of civilizing; here the
motives of the individual, the suppression of passions inside the
individual, the victory of reason over emotions on every individual
battleground, were at stake. To civilize was to engage in a strenuous
and continuous effort to transform the human being through education and instruction. As Diderot spelled out with his usual clarity,
'to instruct a nation, is to civilize it: to extinguish knowledge, is to
reduce it to the primitive state of barbarism'.

The project of civilizing linked inseparably the achievement of the
desirable pattern of human conduct with the dissemination of *les
lumières*; the latter was an activity which constituted the specialized
domain of *les philosophes*; the project of civilizing, therefore, postulated in addition to a specific form of society an unambiguous choice
for its operators and guardians. In this sense, *civilisation* was the collective bid of men of science and letters to a strategically crucial position in the mechanism of reproduction of social order.

An enormous distance separated the ambitions of the civilizers
from the sceptical modesty of Montaigne. No longer was there any
tolerance for localized, nation-bound ways of life. The new order
was not to be safeguarded by collective experience grounded in
historically developed customs. Those, on the contrary, had to be
broken. Tradition had to be denied authority; after all (as we have
seen in chapter 4) it had already lost its grip on human relations and
thereby demonstrated its ineffectiveness. To the absolute state, about
to take the guardianship of social order in its own hands, whatever
remained of the localized traditions must have appeared as so many
obstacles on the road to the orderly society. All power needs truth;
absolute power needs absolute truth. In so far as it was coupled with
the entrenchment of the state monopoly of power, the civilizing
project had to invoke values and norms which demonstratively set
themselves above all and any local tradition. In the same way as the
modern absolute state made all locally based powers parochial,
retarded and reactionary, the civilizing project which supplied such
states with legitimation and strategy had to make locally grounded
ways of life backward, superstitious and barbaric.

The eighteenth century, according to Febvre, knew of no 'ethnic'
or 'historical' civilizations. Those would be contradictions in terms;

indeed, a plural form of the noun *civilisation* would be an oxymoron. The civilizing project was in its innermost essence an effort to stamp out all relativity, hence all plurality of ways of life. What emerged was an absolute notion of 'human civilization', a coherent and unitary notion which brooked no opposition and contemplated no compromise and no self-limitation. It was an explicitly (though in most cases unreflectively) hierarchical ideal,[6] whether seen against the background of a national society, or the human species as a whole. It took for granted that the civilizing action would eventually draw the whole of mankind under its influence; the form of life it preached and hoped to install seemed so unproblematically superior to any other, known or imaginable, that *les philosophes* hoped that its triumphant march would be guaranteed by its self-evident attractions. As a typical statement of the time, Febvre quotes from Mohean: 'One should not be surprised that a brute and savage man would be driven to adore a man civilised and perfected.'

To sum up: the concept of *civilisation* entered learned discourse in the West as the name of a conscious proselytizing crusade waged by men of knowledge and aimed at extirpating the vestiges of wild cultures – local, tradition-bound ways of life and patterns of cohabitation. It denoted above all else a novel, active stance taken towards social processes previously left to their own resources, and a presence of concentrated social powers sufficient to translate such a stance into effective practical measures. In its specific form, the concept of *civilisation* also conveyed a choice of strategy for the centralized management of social processes: it was to be a knowledge-led management, and management aimed above all at the administration of individual minds and bodies. As such, the concept may be viewed as an interpretation, from the vantage point of the mode of life of *la république des lettres*, of the structural transformations analysed above in chapter 4.

The same power activism presided over the 'discovery' of culture. The late twentieth-century reader would naturally expect this discovery to be related to the widening of the mental horizons of the enlightened West, or to the dawning recognition of the plurality of human ways. The truth was exactly the opposite.

At the beginning of this chapter we noted, as an apparent curiosity, certain cultural blindnesses which remained the characteristics of the West through most of its history right up to the period of the decline of medieval society. What we would call today 'plurality of cultures' was right in front of European eyes all this time; it was looked at, but not seen – not, at any rate, in a way noticeably different from the fashion in which the diversity of God's creation in general was contemplated. What happened in the early centuries of the modern era was not a sudden revelation of long and unjustly neglected truth, or a sudden arousal of previously dormant curiosity. The processes which were to be captured in the idea of 'culture' were confined inside West European society. In the beginning, 'culture' stood (in this case etymological links are, indeed, illuminating) for the intention and the practice of 'gardening' as a method of ruling society. Both the intention and practice were reactions to structural dislocation of which the rapidly falling efficiency of the localized mechanisms of societal reproduction was the most striking and alarming result.

Culture, a concept long associated with farming work, was exquisitely well fitted to serve as the master metaphor for the new mechanisms of social reproduction – both designed and centrally operated. In the vocabulary of land-farming and husbandry, culture meant activity, effort, purposeful action (in this vocabulary, an expression such as 'wild culture' would, in the sixteenth century, be a contradiction in terms). To culture (cultivate) land, meant to select good seed, to sow, to till, to plough, to fight weeds and undertake all the other actions deemed necessary to secure an ample and healthy crop. This was exactly the shape of the task in relation to human society, as it appeared in the wake of the bankruptcy of self-reproducing mechanisms. The forms human life and conduct assumed did not seem any more part of the 'nature of things' or part of a divine order which would neither need nor stand human intervention. Instead, human life and conduct appeared now as something which needed to be formed, lest it should take shapes unacceptable and damaging to social order, much like an unattended field is swamped with weeds and has little to offer its owner.

Philippe Bénéton, the author of the most recent comprehensive study of the early history of the idea of culture,[7] locates the beginnings of the metaphorical use of the culture concept in the second half of the seventeenth century. By 1691, it started to shed and to forget its metaphorical past, and to be used on its own, without help of qualifying terms, to denote the 'formation of spirit'. Again, as in the case of the concept of *civilisation*, it took half a century more for culture to be used (by Vauvenergues, in 1746) as a description of the product of educating activity, rather than the activity itself. 'Always used in the singular, it reflected the unitary ideal of the eighteenth century and its universalist perspective; it applied to Man – with a capital "M" – beyond all national or social distinctions.' In Bénéton's words, this concept of culture was marked by three traits: optimism (belief in the unlimited malleability of human characteristics), universalism (belief in one ideal applicable to all nations, places and times) and ethnocentrism (belief that the ideal shaped in eighteenth-century Europe represented the pinnacle of human perfection which other parts of the world would have to, and wish to, emulate). 'Culture and civilization', Bénéton concludes his survey, 'are *mots de combat*, which assume a political function.'[8]

The appearance of the concept of culture and civilization, first in a procedural, then in a descriptive form, signalled the advent of a 'new certainty' and a temporary end to the relativism of the sceptical age. The new certainty, which after the Pyrrhonian interlude came to replace the church-based certainty of the Middle Ages, was of a new brand. The self-sufficiency and perfectibility of man formed its declared profession of faith. What they implied, however, was sociologically infinitely more important than what they explicitly stated: the formation of human life and cohabitation was now the duty and responsibility of earthly, human powers. Certainty was something to be achieved, and kept alive, by purposeful activity. In practice, it was to be measured by the latter's ability to overwhelm, and to reduce to insignificance, all alternative claims to truth. The new certainty was to be grounded in the alliance of power and knowledge. As long as the alliance remained intact, there were no reasons for scepticism.

7

Ideology, or building the world of ideas

We must now return to the constitution of the intellectual life-world, as institutionalized in the republic of letters, in *les sociétés de pensée*, described briefly in chapter 2; after all, it was in this constitution that the 'new certainty' was to be grounded, and it was the resulting solidity – real or counterfactually assumed – of the intellectual life-world, which was to be represented as the validity of the output. The way in which the intellectual life-world had been constituted by the late eighteenth century set also the outer parameters for the possible capital which knowledge could bring to its marriage contract with power.

We saw that the community of *les philosophes* was brought about, sustained and reproduced solely by the activity of discussion. As Habermas would restate two centuries later, with retrospective wisdom of the time when eighteenth-century hopes turned into twentieth-century frustrations, discussions cannot be conducted without the participants assuming the possibility of mutual understanding and, eventually, reaching a consensus. One element in the Habermasian vision of such an 'undistorted communication' which came under particularly severe criticism was, however, another condition allegedly implicit in any act of discussion: that no powers, divine or secular, no difference in social statuses between the participants, no economic or political resources must be allowed to bear on the outcome of the discussion; the only power which may be employed, and counted, on the road to a valid consensus, must be the power of argument. To the critics of Habermas this seemed a nebulous idea, so jarringly at odds with twentieth-century experience of public debate as to put the image of undistorted communication on the shelf where other beautiful dreams of good-willing sages gather dust. (This was the conclusion reached by critics who took Habermas's vision as a practical proposition for attaining consensus in our own world, rather than as an 'ideal type', a baseline from which the practically attained consensus can be criticized and proved invalid.) Spelled out in the late twentieth century, the idea of undistorted communication appeared as much out of touch with actual public discourse as Weber's idea of bureaucracy as the fortress and source of rationality appeared, when compared with actual administrative systems that are plagued with trained incapacity, goal-displacement, the clash between skills and offices and other incurable diseases. One notes easily that the criticisms of 'undistorted communication' and 'ideal bureaucracy' have been aimed at an assumption strikingly similar to both: that, when entering communication or bureaucratic systems, participants may shed and leave outside their social roles, or at least all those ingredients of their social statuses which are declared irrelevant, and thus impermissible, in the light of the idealized goal of communication (valid consensus) or bureaucracy (rational action). It was this assumption that seemed particularly fantastic – to the extent of totally invalidating the respective ideal types as viable propositions for practice.

This twentieth-century wisdom reflected the experience of twentieth-century intellectuals as much as its absence reflected the experience of *les sociétés de pensée*. In the light of the latter experience, the idea of an unqualified equality of participants before the court of Reason did not seem at all nebulous; neither had it to be explicitly phrased and written into a 'statute book' as a postulate to be pursued and enforced. On the contrary, such an equality was experienced as a natural characteristic of the discussion itself. The only resource used as a raw material, processed and forged into the end-product of this particular factory, were words. This was not, therefore, a zero-sum game; the volume of available linguistic resources, the only resources which counted for the time being (to wit, as long as *les sociétés de pensée* enjoyed their freedom, consisting in their total disengagement from all effective earthly powers), did not diminish by being 'used up' by others. To language, everyone had – in principle – an equal access. Beyond language, the members of the republic of letters had little chance to venture.

It was perhaps at this precocious period in the history of modern intellectuals that a peculiar vision of the world was forged out of the

collective experience; a vision of a world made of words, constructed
of ideas, ruled by ideas, bound to surrender to the power of ideas.
An image which explored, and played with, virtually all the thinkable versions of idealism – an image of the world which assigns to
ideas priority over material reality. Or, rather, such a description of
philosophical consciousness of the time is incorrect, drawing as it
does on a later formulation of the problem. For *les philosophes*, ideas
were *the* world. In no way was this belief an aberration, as the life-
world of their material existence, *les sociétés de pensée*, was indeed spun
by the activity of producing and processing ideas. It was this collective experience, by itself neutral in relation to philosophical
divisions, that spawned an essentially idealistic world-view once it
was brought in contact with the seats of earthly powers.

'We exist', said Destutt de Tracy, 'only through our sensations
and our ideas. No things exist except by ideas that we possess of
them' (*Mémoire de 2 floréal* (April 1796)). Mercier, at the same
meeting, was more specific still: 'Everything which is outside
thought is in nothingness . . . Ideas – they are all that exists . . .
The thought, in an infinite order, is always a key to another
thought.'[1] By the time these words were spoken, at a session of
the National Institute founded in 1795, contact with the seats of
earthly powers had already taken place. The members of the
Institute, the collective heir of the glory which the practice of the
Revolution lavished retrospectively on the theories of *les philosophes*,
had already left the self-contained world made of ideas. What they
took with them was the only capital that that world contained in
abundance: words and the skill of handling them. It was only
natural that – once called by the earthly powers to advise on the
construction of a new, better society – they offered the one product
and the one kind of production they were best at; and that the only
flesh they were able to put into the urge for a new social order was to
be drawn from the world they came from, knew best and felt at
home in. What used to be the self-awareness of the republic of letters
was now turned into a chart for society as a whole. 'The good society'
that the political state was now told to bring about was the republic
of letters writ large. In other words, the image of good society, in the
National Institute's version, had to be, and was, an extrapolation of
the collective experience, of the mode of life, of the life-world, of its
members. Deliberately or not, such an image was also a bid for
power. A world made of ideas was, by necessity, a world ruled by

people who produce and distribute ideas; a world in which discourse is the central and crucial activity; in which those engaged in discourse are equally central and crucial to the fate of society.

The image of society advanced by the National Institute was a version of Francis Bacon's 'House of Solomon' – a society ruled by sages. What, for Bacon, was a utopian dream, a genius's premonition of a society to which no practical possibilities contained in his own time could point, became a viable proposition after a century and a half of the absolutist state, particularly in the atmosphere of total mobilization engendered by the Revolution. It seemed a glimpse of a society waiting round the nearest corner of history. As Theodore Olsen observed,[2] Bacon's project 'could not develop until its proponents could command men, goods, funds, and energies on a national or continental scale. Those who could do this were the believers in the developed progressivism of the nineteenth century and, specifically, those whose sense of group will was formed on a scale large enough to encompass the necessary resources.' Intellectuals of the time of the National Institute had every reason to believe that they met such conditions. The revolutionary state developed the power potential – and the ambitions of power – even beyond the formidable achievements of absolute monarchy; as to the will to mobilize resources in the service of redesigning society – this was present in abundance. The might of the state, and the volume of things it was able, and likely, to accomplish, seemed particularly huge as it easily dwarfed all remembered predecessors.

The particular kind of knowledge to preside over the House of Solomon, to merge with political power, to be power, Destutt de Tracy called 'ideology'. He introduced the word as the name of a science concerned with the 'generation of ideas', and which was meant to replace other sorts of intellectual work which had pursued similar interests in the past, yet in an unsatisfactory manner, such as metaphysics, or psychology.[3] In Emmet Kennedy's description, ideology was understood as

> genealogically the first science, since all sciences consisted of different combinations of ideas. But it was specifically the basis of grammar or the science of communicating ideas, logic, or the science of combining them and reaching new truths, education, or the science of forming men, morality, or the regulation of desires, and finally 'the greatest of arts, for the success of which all others must cooperate, that of regulating society . . .'[4]

According to the Dictionary published by the French Academy, *Idéologie* stood for 'science des idées, système sur l'origine et la fonction des idées'. A person specializing in ideology was to be called an 'ideologist' – by association with other, established scientists such as physicists, chemists or biologists. The word *ideologue* was to be introduced later, as a derogatory and ironic name devised by the detractors of de Tracy's project (Chateaubriand and, above all, Napoleon). The most remarkable and noteworthy thing about the new science which the National Institute proposed to develop was, however, not its definition, but the fact that it was the only science proposed to explore society; in other words, not what the proposal introduced, but what it eliminated or pre-empted. Ideology was to be *the* science of society; or the *science* of society could be only ideology. By the same token, society was identified with production and the communication of ideas; to study the latter, was to know everything there was to know, everything of practical importance for anyone seeing society as an object of action. (A few decades later, Auguste Comte will propose ostensibly to rectify the partisanship of the name by replacing it with 'sociology'; but the way he will describe the new discipline will not significantly depart from the contents suggested by Destutt de Tracy's brainchild.)

There is hardly a sentence in all of Marx's writings more famous than 'Philosophers so far only explained the world; the question, however, is how to change it.' The sentence is taken, by admirers and detractors alike, as an epitomy of Marx's radicalism and Marxism's uniqueness; within the walls of twentieth-century academia Marx's adage sounded strangely out of place, as a challenge to what the established inhabitants had long before accepted as their role within a division of labour which most of them saw no reason to question and renegotiate. Both the guardians of the walls and those suspected of wishing to explode them were on the whole too busy praising or denigrating the message contained in the adage to reflect upon the correctness of the sentence itself as a description of Marx's predecessors. This oversight is a cause of regret, as a closer look at Marx's condemnation/appeal would have simply revealed Marx's project as a belated restatement of the routine Enlightenment understanding of philosophy and its tasks. The first, condemnatory, part of Marx's sentence would have been, to an extent, true, if written a century or so earlier; it was evidently incorrect, written as it was after Condorcet, Cabanis, Destutt de Tracy and the National

Institute. The second part of the sentence, on the other hand, was hardly original. What else did the philosophers of the preceding century do, if they did not debate ways of changing the world, and toy with practical applications of their blueprints? In this second part of the sentence, Marx merely reported the state of philosophy they considered too obvious and uncontroversial to be made explicit.

Indeed, whatever the philosophers gathered around the National Institute did, it was shot through by their passionate urge to remake: to remake everything – individuals, their needs and desires, their thoughts, their actions and interactions, the laws that set a frame for such interactions, those who set the laws, society itself. The principle of selecting the topics for philosophical study and reflection – the only acceptable principle, as it were – was the usefulness of the latter in promoting, inducing and attaining the change. To express the same in Schutzian language, the topical relevances of their philosophy were determined solely by one motivational relevance: that of societal transformation.

This was anything but a contemplative philosophy. Philosophy preached and practised by the National Institute was politics pure and simple, which would explode the walls of any specialized educational establishment. Roederer, appointed by Napoleon as the equivalent of a minister for education and arts, described his philosophical credentials in words which would fill any academic philosopher's heart with horror: 'Philosophy is not any more contained in the books of the sages – it burst out, as the light cast by the Sun; like this light, it has now scattered all over the Earth, it shines high above everybody's head, it is reflected in most of the social institutions, it fills the air which we all breathe.'[5] This was a vision of a philosophy in action, an active philosophy, philosophy as power, transforming everything it touches. Aeons divided this philosophical programme from Wittgenstein's resigned admission: 'Philosophy leaves everything as it was.' Destutt de Tracy would find it tough to comprehend Wittgenstein's verdict; for him, there was little doubt that, if only the study of ideology took off as expected, 'it will be easy for us to indicate to people the rules (of thought and action) they must follow'.[6]

Like physics or chemistry, ideology was to be an instrument of mastery over its object. 'To know it, in order to master it', this attitude to Nature which they saw no reason to question, the ideologists extended to society and its members, again without any urge to reflect on the peculiarity of the latter task. In his project for the *Éléments d'idéologie*, a book meant to provide the theoretical foundation for the philosophy of action, de Tracy proposed to lean entirely on the systematic observation of savages, the peasants of remote villages, children and animals – admittedly the kind of beings unlikely to be credited with the capacity for self-regulation, and thus natural objects for domestication, taming, drill or training. In the book itself, he referred to the authority of Pinel, who 'proved that the art of curing the demented is in no way different from the art of regulating the passions and directing the opinions of ordinary people; in both cases, it consists in forming their habits.'[7] Society and its members were perceived by the ideologists as, first and foremost, an object for purposeful action; as a material which ought to be studied like any other material one wishes to employ in constructing desirable designs. For the construction to be successful, the inner qualities of the material, its structure, flexibility, durability, etc., must be well understood. Condorcet dreamt of the eventual representation of human societies as 'grandiose geometrical constructions' in which everything which happens is subject to constant and fixed causes, in which no mystery is left, and no room is provided for the accidental and the unexpected.[8] Cabanis would not admit that actions aimed at the human body and those directed towards the human spirit present practical problems of different quality:

> Medicine and morality, branches of the same science – the science of man – rest on a common foundation. It is from physical sensibility, or from the organization which determines it, that ideas, sentiments, passions, virtues, vices, movements of spirit or the diseases or health of the bodies derive . . . Through the study of the constant relations between physical and moral states, one can lead man towards happiness and transform good sense into a habit, and morality into a need; one can expand human abilities . . . (and cause) their progressive, and forever unlimited perfection.

For Cabanis, medicine was a model and an inspiration for all future education – the educationalists' work on the human spirit and body following closely the pattern developed by doctors.[9]

In comparison with *les philosophes* of the pre-revolutionary period, a subtle yet seminal change took place on the road to the National Institute and its project of ideology. We have seen already that *les philosophes* selected, as the addressee of *les lumières*, the legislating powers of the state. It was the monarch, the despot, the legislator, who was to be enlightened; 'the man' as individual was to be affected indirectly, via the social conditions redesigned according to the precepts of Reason. *Les philosophes* did develop the idea of bringing the lights directly to the subjects of the state, but this idea never occupied pride of place in their designs for a good society. The activity of education, like *les lumières* themselves, was to focus on the task of enlightening the legislators and other persons in charge of the adminstration of society and human interaction. Among the ideologists, not without prodding and encouragement by the now seemingly omnipotent state in command of – by former standards – unlimited resources, the idea of education moved into the very centre of the programme. It was still to be carefully differentiated and doled out in sharply unequal measures depending on the place assigned to a given category of subjects in the total design for the good society. (De Tracy, for example, would insist that for the working classes what counted as the purpose of education was 'not fine development and subtle discussion, but sane results'.)[10] But the centrality of education as a whole in the project of ideology expressed itself most importantly in the shifting of responsibility for the production and reproduction of 'good society' from the holders of the secular political power of the state to the professional spokesmen of Reason, showing their own science, ideology and expertise, founded in this new, but indubitably 'first' science, as the legitimation for their unique position. However subtle and often imperceptible the modulations of terms and the shifts of accent, the changes in the idealized balance of power were in no way negligible. To put it bluntly, the descendants of the counsellors of the legislators now made a bid for the job of legislating itself. The project of ideology was a manifesto proclaiming more than anything else that the function of administering a civilized, orderly and happy society belongs naturally to scientifically trained professionals. With the advent of the new science of ideology, the new generation of philosophers stopped discussing Reason as an all-powerful law of nature; liberty, equality and fraternity were not any more articulated as the precepts of Reason which society must sooner or later obey due to the law of progress. All former laws and tendencies of the natural order of things now become the products of the scientifically based, expertly performed work of the specialist in the cultivation of human spirits and bodies.[11] Only a few years later, in 1822, Auguste Comte, the

most audacious of ideologists, will make the bid in terms that left
nothing to the imagination:

> Spiritual anarchy has preceded and engendered temporal anarchy. In
> the present epoch the social malady depends much more on the first
> than on the second cause . . . The nature of the works to be executed,
> of itself sufficiently indicates the class on which their execution must
> devolve. Since these works are theoretical, it is clear that those whose
> professed aim is to form theoretical combinations, in other words
> *Savants* occupied with the study of the sciences of observation, are the
> only men whose capacity and intellectual culture fulfill the necessary
> conditions. It would be evidently abnormal to entrust the work to any
> but the greatest intellectual forces we can command and to men who
> pursue a method of which the superiority is universally recognised.[12]

This claim was made on behalf of 'sociology', a new name for the
science branded 'ideology' by Destutt de Tracy. The name changed,
but the ambitions remained – and the inherent link with the discourse of power, if anything, was spelled out more clearly than ever
before, instead of remaining implicit.

It was against this power rhetoric intrinsic in the project of
ideology that Napoleon, after years of flirting and amicable relations
with the ideologists, during which he lavished upon the more outspoken members of the group prestigious, though merely cere-
monious, distinctions as senators and tribunes, finally launched
his barrages. Emmet Kennedy explains the gradual cooling of
Napoleon's enthusiasm by the emerging conflict between his author-
itarianism and the ideologists' dedication to republican ideals. The
temporary nature of the alliance seems, however, to have been
determined in advance by the power ambitions inextricably woven
into the very idea of ideology and of the social function of its experts
– an idea which had to bring its preachers and practitioners into
open conflict with state powers once it became clear enough for the
rulers of the state to comprehend. Gradually, the ideologists turned
in Napoleon's eyes into competitors for state power; at some point
they became the very epitome of rival political forces – so radically
different was their conception of the administration of society. No
wonder Napoleon blamed the ideologists for being morally responsible for the failed Malet conspiracy of December 1812:

> We must lay the blame for the ills that our fair France has suffered on
> ideology, that shadowy metaphysics which subtly searches for first

causes on which to base the legislation of peoples, rather than making use of laws known to the human heart and of the lessons of history. These errors must inevitably and did in fact lead to the rule of blood-thirsty men. Indeed, who was it that proclaimed the principle of insurrection to be a duty? Who educated the people and attributed to it a sovereignty which it was incapable of exercising? Who destroyed respect for and the sanctity of laws by describing them, not as sacred principles of justice, the nature of things and civil justice, but only as the will of an assembly, composed of men ignorant of civil, admin-istrative, political and military law?[13]

The trend-setter in so many other vital aspects of modern times, Napoleon also drew the essential parameters and terms of reference for one of the most salient and persistent conflicts of the new era: that between scientifically trained experts and practitioners of politics, between the entitlements to power referred to the knowledge of 'laws of society' and those which refer to 'civil, administrative political and military' experience; between 'first causes', the weapon of the intellectuals, and 'sacred principles', the war-cry of the poli-ticians. Once the slogans and propaganda terms have been removed, what remains of the trenchant indictment is a clear-sighted vision of the essential, insoluble conflict of two interest groups competing for the administration of society, unable to pro-mote their respective claims in terms other than a war of principles and conceptions of social order.

One other aspect of Napoleon's insight is worth mentioning at least in passing. In the subsequent history of experts vs. practitioners rivalry the argument of 'the rule of bloodthirsty men' will become recurrent. The conflict between the experts and the practical poli-ticians will be over and over again represented by the latter as a con-flict between those who think they 'know better' and hence would have no scruples in forcing their ideals down the throats of those whom they rule, and the politicians, pragmatists by nature, who beware of moving forward too fast for the 'people' to follow them, and who put the 'art of the possible' above any stiff doctrine. For at least a century following Napoleon's squabble with the ideologists this conflict was to be treated seriously by both sides of the con-troversy. The descendants of the ideologists on one side, and the rulers of the state on the other, were united in their belief that, given the precarious, untested and on the whole unreliable techniques of power, the authority of law and its underwriters, attractiveness of the political formula, and the will to obey the state which Weber (at the very moment when such a will began to lose its relevance for the reproduction of social order) was to call 'legitimation', were indispensable supports for the state. As long as both sides believed that, the otherwise abstruse and abstract problem of the 'sources of legitimacy', the kind of expertise required for the practice of ruling, and the criteria with which to measure the entitlements of rulers, remained in the very centre of the power conflict. The problem was never to be solved, either in theory or in practice. It simply lost its significance as the modern state grew in confidence as to the efficacy of the techniques of policing, surveilling, categorizing, individualizing and other methods of modern bureaucratic administration. Having lost all its relevance to the practical business of politics, the problem became, uncontestedly, the private property of philosophers.

It was in this original meaning of the term that the science conceived and cultivated by the National Institute was subjected to a scathing critique and ridiculed by Marx and Engels in their 'German Ideology'. Presenting the doctrines of Bauer and Stirner as a German version of the philosophy of the French ideologists, seemed to Marx a certain way to discredit them and deprive them of any authority they might have claimed. By 'ideology', Marx understood exactly what had been intended by the authors and preachers of the idea: an idealist theory of society, one which calls the philosophers to 'liberate people from the chimeras, the ideas, dogmas, imaginary beings under the yoke of which they are pining away', one according to which social reality is made up of ideas, which fight some ideas, fertilize other ideas and give birth to yet more ideas, while human beings suffer because of wrong ideas and get eventually saved by good ones. The assault against 'German Ideology' was aimed against philosophical idealism which, in Marx's view, obfuscated the true determinants of the human situation and the genuine springs of human action; and which removed from the philosophical agenda the truly crucial question: Why do ideas, good or bad alike, tend to be accepted and believed in the first place? Marx objected to extrapolating the philosophers' mode of life on the theory of society, and called for the study of society to be located at the level where material conditions of life are produced and reproduced.

It takes a collective myopia, inflicted by the post-Mannheimian adventures of the ideology concept, to overlook that 'German Ideology' was a critique of idealism, and as such a critique of the validity of uses to which the term ideology, redefined in its twentieth-century reincarnation, was later put. Yet this is exactly what most of the contemporary commentators did, searching the 'German Ideology' for, however inchoate or precocious, a 'theory of ideology'; a theory understood, in its present fashion, as a theory of ideas which produce human actions, to wit, something Marx bluntly refused to treat seriously. The inability (or unwillingness) to read out the correct meaning of Marx's message is in itself an excellent key to the interpretation of changes to which the concept of ideology was subjected in its second lease of life; and, indirectly, to the understanding of those shifts in the social location and collective practices of its users which hide behind the semantic convolutions of the concept.

The new, post-Mannheimian, concept of ideology implies the tacit acceptance of a theory of society which the old concept, as used by Destutt de Tracy and his contemporaries, promoted. Behind the apparent semantic discontinuity, there is a continuity of discourse; indeed, it is this continuity which has made the articulation of a new meaning possible. The attractiveness and usefulness of the new concept depends ultimately on a theory of society which depicts ideas as causes of human action; which presents beliefs as major, if not the only, factors of societal integration; which accepts that 'legitimation', that is, the intellectually articulated rights of the rulers to rule, is a major, if not the only, factor generating popular obedience to power and thus responsible for the reproduction of social order; which maintains that the power of power rests in its capacity to manipulate the production of ideas and beliefs; and which considers a similar manipulation of ideas as the royal road to the eventual delegitimation, and thus dismantling, of any given power structure. The theoretical chart of the human universe has remained, therefore, the same, just as it was sketched by the ideologists with a pen moved by their understanding of the role they did or were destined to play, and with ink drawn from the resources which their social location supplied. The true novelty engendered by Mannheim's resuscitation of the long-forgotten word was its attachment to one part of the chart only. In Mannheim's use, ideology retained the derogatory flavour associated with it since Napoleon's outburst of rage; but the table, so to speak, was turned against Napoleon's descendants.

Mannheim's ideology stood for what the original ideologists wished to use their ideology to fight and destroy: prejudices, superstitions, erroneous judgements, ignorance. Such afflictions haunting

human understanding and disarming human intellectual capacities
were now ascribed to the partiality of cognitive perspective, caused
by narrowly circumscribed, routine and repetitive group practices.
As such, they were most likely to be found among the bureaucrats,
the military, the conservative politicians – categories of actors
enslaved by their own uncontrolled patterns of behaviour produced
by collective specialized learning, actors inclined to conceive of
tasks at hand in terms of their collective memory, and so remaining
hostages to their own past. Read carefully, these features responsible
for the ideological (in Mannheim's sense) character of group consciousness reveal remarkable similarity to the selfsame attributes
which Napoleon brandished as the proofs of the professional politicians' unique ability to rule. Mannheim's *Ideology and Utopia* reads
indeed as the belated answer of the National Institute to Napoleon's
strictures.

To the partiality and deforming potential of other perspectives,
one universal cognitive perspective is now opposed; a perspective
which ties itself to no perspective, which hovers above all particularized social locations and hence sees all locations as particularized,
which is confined to no localized routine practice and so reveals all
routine practices as parochial and founded solely by their own
respective pasts. This 'perspective to put paid to all perspectives'
was, for Mannheim, a defining feature of the intellectuals (or the
'intelligentsia', the elite of the educated). This feature anointed the
intellectual with a mission, and the right, to adjudicate between
ideologies, to reveal them as ideologies, as partial and prejudiced
world-views, to disclose their lack of universal foundation and hence
their invalidity outside their own homeground, their essential
'untransferability', and inadequacy of credentials when confronted
with universal standards of truth.

In Mannheim's reformulation, there was no room left for the enlightened despot. Mannheim's ideology was not an offer of valuable
services to the legislators. It was not an application for the
counsellor's job. The unbridgeable gap between those who know
and those who rule has been placidly accepted as the way the human
world is organized, and given well nigh ontological solidity. This
does not mean, however, that Mannheim's version of ideology
renounced that bid for power which stood behind the original concept. Mannheim's intellectuals are still intent on designing social
orders and the policies best fitted to the task of their production;
indeed, they are now the only category entitled to entertain such

ambitions. Only now they do not view political leaders as the carriers of universal designs – or, indeed, as allies or partners in implementing the job. Mannheim's intellectuals stand above the politicians (at a level the latter would never be able to reach while retaining their identity as politicians), as their analysts, judges, critics. Instead of power being made knowledgeable, knowledge may try to become powerful.

Mannheim's reformulation may be plausibly interpreted as an attempt to resuscitate the old idiom of intellectuals as legislators at a time when the social conditions, which originally made such an idiom possible, all but disappeared. Mannheim's panache made the ideologists' pretensions to advise the high and mighty look meek and cowardly by comparison; but the high and mighty of Mannheim's time did not listen. Unlike Napoleon, they would not flatter Destutt de Tracy, nor his descendants, with their attention – even with their anger. Not that Mannheim was a lesser scholar than Cabanis or Volnay; but the state which Napoleon's descendants administered was far removed from one unsure of its technical efficiency and hence eager to seek its foundation in the virtues of its citizens or in the nation's patriotic zeal. It did not need ideas to generate the obedience of its subjects; what is more, it believed now – not unjustly – that ideas would not make much difference anyway. In Mannheim's time, the state administration of the reproduction of social order was firmly and securely based in panoptic, disciplinary and bureaucratic technology which left as little room for 'absolute truth' as Mannheim's concept of ideology left for the enlightened despot. Mannheim's revision of the ideologists' legacy was the last act of the old drama – not the beginning of the new one. Once again, the owl of Minerva spread its wings at dusk.

The trouble with dusk, however, is that it is quickly followed by night; the virtues of Mannheim's suggestions could not remain visible for long. A generation later the idea of ideology offered by Mannheim seemed as partial as the categories of consciousness it was meant to unmask and criticize. Mannheim's version has been proclaimed as being merely a negative concept of ideology, while what was needed was a positive concept. This, however, leads us beyond the era of the legislators, and well into the time of the interpreters. We will have, therefore, to delay the discussion of the latest stage in the convoluted history of the world made in the image of the philosophers.

8

The fall of the legislator

From at least the seventeenth century and well into the twentieth, the writing elite of Western Europe and its footholds on other continents considered its own way of life as a radical break in universal history. Virtually unchallenged faith in the superiority of its own mode over all alternative forms of life – contemporaneous or past – allowed it to take itself as the reference point for the interpretation of the *telos* of history. This was a novelty in the experience of objective time; for most of the history of Christian Europe, time-reckoning was organized around a fixed point in the slowly receding past. Now, while rendering the thus far local, Christian calendar, well nigh universal, Europe set the reference point of objective time in motion, attaching it firmly to its own thrust towards colonizing the future in the same way as it had colonized the surrounding space.

The self-confidence of the enlightened elite of Europe was projected on adjacent categories of mankind, in measures strictly proportional to the perceived closeness of kinship. Thus the group distinguished by an enlightened way of life was seen as decidedly superior in relation to their own ignorant and superstitious working classes or villagers. Together, educated and uneducated Europeans constituted a race which had already situated itself on the side of history that other races were – at best – only struggling to reach. Rather than deriving its own self-confidence from its belief in progress, the educated elite forged the idea of progress from the untarnished experience of its own superiority. Rather than drawing its missionary, proselytizing zeal from an uncritical belief in the infinite perfectibility of man, the educated elite coined the idea of the pliability of human nature, its capacity for being moulded and improved by society, out of the experience of its own role in the disciplining, training, educating, healing, punishing and reforming aimed at categories other than itself. Collective experience of a category cast in a 'gardener' role in relation to all other categories, was recast as a theory of history.

As if following Marx's methodological precept about using the anatomy of man as the key to the anatomy of ape, the educated elite used its own mode of life, or the mode of life of that part of the world over which it presided (or thought it presided) as the benchmark against which to measure and classify other forms of life – past or present – as retarded, underdeveloped, immature, incomplete or deformed, maimed, distorted and otherwise inferior stages or versions of itself. Its own form of life, ever more often called 'modernity', came to denote the restless, constantly moving pointer of history; from its vantage point, all the other known or guessed forms appeared as past stages, side-shoots or culs-de-sac. The many competing conceptualizations of modernity, invariably associated with a theory of history, agreed on one point: they all took the form of life developed in parts of the Western world as the 'given', 'unmarked' unit of the binary opposition which relativized the rest of the world and the rest of historical times as the problematic, 'marked' side, understandable only in terms of its distinction from the Western pattern of development, taken as normal. The distinction was seen first and foremost as a set of absences – as a lack of the attributes deemed indispensable for the identity of most advanced age.

We have already discussed one of such conceptualizations: the vision of history as the unstoppable march of *les lumières*; a difficult, but eventually victorious struggle of Reason against emotions or animal instincts, science against religion and magic, truth against prejudice, correct knowledge against superstition, reflection against uncritical existence, rationality against affectivity and the rule of custom. Within such a conceptualization, the modern age defined itself as, above all, the kingdom of Reason and rationality; the other forms of life were seen, accordingly, as wanting in both respects. This was the first and most basic of the conceptualizations providing modernity with its self-definition. It was also the most persistent and clearly the most favoured by those whose job it was to conceptualize. It posited, after all, the conceptualizers themselves as in charge of the levers of history and presented them, strategically, as the most important and powerful agents of change. This conceptualization, as we remember, was already implicit in the thinking of *les philosophes*; it found its full expression in the writings of Condorcet and other ideologists; it was codified by Comte and since then taken as a canon and obligatory framework of the Whig version of history; it reached its culminating point and fullest elaboration in Weber's vision of history as progressive rationalization, and of modern society as a radical break which disclosed its own past as, above all, the long dominion of irrational conduct.

To Marx, as Marshall Berman recently reminded us in his beautiful and profound analysis of modernity, ours was the age in which 'everything solid melts into air, everything sacred is profaned'; an age of the breath-taking pace of development, of the multiplication of material wealth, of the ever increasing mastery of humankind over its natural environment, of the universal emancipation from all, real or imaginary, restrictions which constrained and hampered human creative potential for an interminably long part of history. This, to Marx, was the effect of the sudden eruption of the material means of mastery over nature, together with the ability and the will to use them; that, in its turn, was the outcome of a new organization of the productive effort of humanity – one in which the productive activities of individuals had been rhythmicized, routinized, co-ordinated, subjected to a purposeful design, supervised and put to the task of operating the tools, the power of which was no longer restricted by the limited capacity (and so the horizon) of their petty owners. To Marx, the modern age would eventually discard the few remaining limits to practical mastery over nature; the means of production, he insisted, were already 'social' in their character, and the private character of ownership, however grand in scale yet short of universal, will be the last 'solidity' to melt into air. 'Human freedom' (identified with freedom from necessity, identified in its turn with Nature) would then be complete.

Not all conceptualizations, of course, sung such unqualified praise of modernity. Towards the end of the nineteenth century, in particular, the modern age appeared to many a mixed blessing. The great achievement of humanity, no doubt, but at a price; a heavy price, perhaps. It became increasingly clear to the educated elite that the anticipated kingdom of Reason had been slow to materialize. More importantly, it was somewhat less clear that it ever would.

The kingdom of Reason was always at bottom the rule of its spokesmen. Such a rule was now a remote, and receding probability. Humanities failed to humanize, that is, the designs of social order and the strategies for their implementation were produced and administered by categories other than the humanizers themselves, and the unity between the growing power of the 'civilized' part of mankind and the growing centrality of its civilizers had been broken. Conceptualization had acquired a dramatic tinge; the images of historical progress became more and more reminiscent of a Greek tragedy, where nothing is ever achieved without a sacrifice, and the sacrifice may be as painful as the achievement is enjoyable.

The Faustian man of Nietzsche and his followers was carved in the image of the modern age, proud of its power and its superiority, considering all other human forms as inferior to itself. But the Faustian man could no longer – unlike his philosophic or entrepreneurial predecessors – casually refer his own self-confidence to the inexorable and omnipotent powers of spiritual or material progress; he had to carry modernity, this greatest achievement of the human race, on his own shoulders. The Faustian man was a romantic, not a classicist or positivist. He was the maker of history, not its product; he had to make history against all odds, forcing it to submit to his will and not necessarily counting on its willingness to surrender. History remained what it was to its Whig courtiers: the triumph of the daring, the courageous, the insightful, the profound, the clear-headed over the slavish, cowardly, superstitious, muddled and ignorant. But the triumph was not now guaranteed – particularly not by forces other than the wilful effort of prospective victors. This struggle will be costly, as all struggles are. In all conquests, there are victims as well as victors. The Faustian man must reconcile himself to the need for marching over the bodies of the weak. And he is a Faustian man because he does.

Another dramatic vision of modernity has been inspired by Freud. This one depicts modernity as a time when the 'reality principle' attains domination over the 'pleasure principle', and when people, as a result, trade off part of their freedom (and happiness) for a degree of security, grounded in a hygienically safe, clean and peaceful environment. The trade-off may be profitable, but it comes about as a product of the suppression of 'natural' drives and the imposition of patterns of behaviour which ill fit human predispositions and offer only oblique outlets for instincts and passions. Suppression is painful, it leaves psychological wounds which are difficult to heal. The price of modernity is the high incidence of psychotic and neurotic ailments; civilization breeds its own discontents and sets the individual in a permanent – potential or overt – conflict with society.

Shortly after *Civilisation and its Discontents* appeared, sending waves of shock and admiration far and wide, young Norbert Elias decided to subject Freud's hypotheses, presented as they were in intuitive and ideal–typical form, to the test of historical research. Elias's decision resulted in the remarkable *Civilising Process*, which opened new horizons for socio-historical study by reaching a heretofore unexplored and neglected kind of historical source and bringing 'daily life' into the focus of historical investigation. Elias demonstrated that the 'suppression of instincts' which Freud deduced from the nature of mature modernity, was in fact a historical process which could be pinned down to specific time, place and socio-cultural figurations. One of the many brilliant observations of Elias's study was the idea that the successful culmination of the process consists of the historical episode of suppression being forgotten, pseudo-rational legitimations being supplied for newly introduced patterns and the whole historical form of life being 'naturalized'. A radical interpretation of Elias's study would see it as a direct attack upon Weber's Whiggish vision of modernity as an era of rationality. The powers which brought about modern society and preside over its reproduction have been denied the sanction of Reason. The essentially progressive character of their accomplishment has not, however, been put in question.

A complex hate–love attitude towards modernity saturates Simmel's vision of urban society, closely related to the somewhat later interpretation Benjamin gave to Baudelaire's seminal insights. The combined image is one of tragedy – of twisted dialectics of inextricable contradictions: the absolute manifesting itself only in the particularity of individuals and their encounters; the permanent hiding behind fleeting episodes, the normal behind the unique. Above all, the drama of modernity derives from the 'tragedy of culture', the human inability to assimilate cultural products, over abundant because of the unbound creativity of the human spirit. Once set in motion, cultural processes acquire their own momentum, develop their own logic, and spawn new multiple realities confronting individuals as an outside, objective world, too powerful and distant to be 'resubjectivized'. The richness of objective culture results therefore in the cultural poverty of individual human beings, who now act according to a principle *omnia habentes, nihil possidentes* (as Günther S. Stent inverted the famous principle of St Francis).[1] A frantic search for objects to be appropriated vainly seeks to replace the repossession of lost meanings. Simmel bewails the advent of 'partial intellectuals' (a term later coined by Foucault) and the passing of a time when the erudite *Principles of Political Economy* were the common property of all enlightened contemporaries and extensively reviewed by such 'non-specialists' as Dickens or Ruskin. This is a vision of modernity as seen through the eyes of a capital city intellectual, dreaming of a continuation of the role bequeathed by *les philosophes* under conditions which render it all but impossible; conditions brought about by nothing else but the tremendous success of the philosophers' legacy.

The above is a very sketchy, simplified and in no way complete list of the visions of modernity which summoned enough following and made enough impact on the public consciousness to be recognized as traditional or classic. They differ from each other; sometimes they stand in sharp opposition to each other. For many decades the differences and oppositions overshadowed any common features and dominated social scientific debate. Only quite recently, owing to a new cognitive perspective, have the differences begun to look considerably less important – as no more than family quarrels. What the new perspective made salient, on the other hand, was exactly that close kinship bond between the apparently antagonistic views, which at the present stage of the debate would tend to overshadow the differences.

The family bond seems to have been constituted by at least three shared characteristics.

First, all listed visions and most of their contemporary alternatives or variants assumed, whether explicitly or implicitly, the irreversible character of the changes modernity signified or brought in its wake. They might have been enthusiastic, caustic or downright critical regarding the balance between good and evil within the form of life associated with modern society, but they hardly ever questioned the 'superiority' of modernity in the sense of subordinating, marginalizing, evicting or annihilating its pre-modern alternatives. None of the visions entailed (at least not organically) doubts as to the eventual ascendancy of modernity; most assumed the inevitability of such ascendancy. (Although this was not necessarily in the deterministic sense; it was not in the sense that the advent of modernity was historically inescapable, but in the sense that – once it has emerged in one part of the world – its domination, or pehaps universalization, would be unstoppable.) Seeing modernity as the highest point of development encouraged the interpretation of preceding social forms as describing or measuring their distance from modernity, as manifest in the idea of developing countries.

Secondly, all the listed visions conceived of modernity in processual terms: as an essentially unfinished project. Modernity was open-ended, and inevitably so; indeed, the open-endedness was seen as the paramount, perhaps defining, attribute of modernity. Against the intrinsic mobility of modernity, the pre-modern forms appeared stagnant, organized around the mechanism of equilibration and stability, almost devoid of history. This optical effect resulted from choosing modernity as the vantage point from which to contemplate features of alternative societies; and choosing to consider modernity as the historically, or logically, later form. This choice enclosed and objectified other social forms, and prompted them to be perceived as finished, complete objects – a perception which had been articulated as their intrinsic timelessness. To return to the visions of modernity: they all tried to capture the process of ongoing transformations *in statu nascendi*; they were, in a sense, mid-career reports, conscious of describing a movement with a destination not yet fully known, one that could only be anticipated. In the vision of modernity, only the starting-point was more or less firmly fixed. The rest, precisely because of its underdetermined character, appeared as a field of design, action and struggle.

Thirdly all visions were 'inside' views of modernity. Modernity was a phenomenon with a rich pre-history but with nothing visible beyond it, nothing which could relativize or objectivize the phenomenon itself, enclose it as a finished episode of – by the same token – confined, limited significance. As such, the way this 'insider' experience of modernity had been articulated, supplied the frame of reference for the perception of non-modern forms of life. At the same time, however, no outside vantage point was available as a frame of reference for the perception of modernity itself. In a sense, modernity was – in those visions – self-referential and self-validating.

It is precisely this last circumstance which has recently changed; its change could not but affect the rest of the family resemblances which united the traditional, or classic visions of modernity. To put it correctly, the change brought to the surface the very presence of the family traits, and their limiting role, now seen as responsible for the historical relativity of the classic visions. What has happened in recent years could be articulated as the appearance of a vantage point which allows the view of modernity itself as an enclosed object, an essentially complete product, an episode of history, with an end as much as a beginning.

Such a vantage point has been supplied by the post-modernist debate. On the face of it, this debate is just another name for the discourse organized around a family of notions, of which the most popular and widely commented upon are the concepts of post-industrial or post-capitalist societies. Whatever the connections and similarities, the differences, however, are formidable. The idea of post-industrial society does not necessarily constitute a break with the way in which modernity was traditionally conceived. More often than not, this idea refers simply to internal transformations within the Western type of civilization, allegedly reconstituting its continuing superiority in a novel fashion and on a changing socio-economic basis. Far from undermining such a superiority, the transformations pointed out as symptomatic of the post-industrial or post-capitalist stage reinforce the image of the Western socio-cultural system as a pinnacle of development or a most advanced form of human society which other forms either approach or are bound to recognize as superior. The post-industrial discourse emphasizes also the continuity of development; the post-industrial is seen as a natural product of industrial development, as a next phase following the success of the preceding one – and, in a sense, fulfilling the promise and the potential contained in its own past.

It is, on the other hand, the post-modernist discourse that looks back at its immediate past as a closed episode, as a movement in a direction unlikely to be followed, as perhaps even an aberration, the pursuit of a false track, a historical error now to be rectified. In doing so, the post-modernist debate does not necessarily oppose itself to the factual propositions construed within the post-industrial discourse; the frequent confusion notwithstanding, the two debates do not share their respective subject-matters. The post-industrial discourse is about the changes in the socio-economic system of a society which recognizes itself as 'modern' in the sense spelled out above: the changes discussed do not imply that society needs to stop identifying itself in such a way. The post-modernist discourse, on the other hand, is about the credibility of 'modernity' itself as a self-designation of Western civilization, whether industrial or post-industrial, capitalist or post-capitalist. It implies that the self-ascribed attributes contained in the idea of modernity do not hold to-day, perhaps did not hold yesterday either. The post-modernist debate is about the self-consciousness of Western society, and the grounds (or the absence of grounds) for such consciousness.

The concept of post-modernism was coined first; introduced as a designation of the rebellion against functionalist, scientifically grounded, rational architecture, it was soon taken over and extended to assimilate the profound changes of direction visible all over the territory of Western art. It proclaimed the end of the exploration of the ultimate truth of the human world or human experience, the end of the political or missionary ambitions of art, the end of dominant style, of artistic canons, of interest in the aesthetic grounds of artistic self-confidence and objective boundaries of art. The absence of grounds, the futility of all attempts to draw the limits of artistic phenomena in an objective fashion, the impossibility of legislating the rules of a true art as distinct from non-art or bad art, were the ideas which gestated first within the discourse of artistic culture (much as two hundred years earlier the conquest of the cultural field preceded the expansion of *les sociétés de pensée* on to the area of political and social philosophy). Only later did the notion of post-modernism, originally confined to the history of arts, begin to expand. It had opened the eyes of intellectual observers to those features shared by the transformations in contemporary arts and the fascinating shifts of attention, anti-traditionalist rebellion, and strikingly heretical new paradigms competing for domination in philosophy and the philosophically informed social sciences. Eyes were opened to the similarity between the erosion of 'objective grounds' in art and the sudden popularity of post-Wittgensteinian and post-Gadamerian hermeneutics in social sciences, or the vitriolic attacks of the 'new pragmatists' against Carthesian–Lockean–Kantian tradition in modern philosophy. It became increasingly plausible that these apparently disparate phenomena were manifestations of the same process.

It was this process, or rather the conditions under which it was taking place, that has been called here post-modernity (as distinct from post-modernism, which refers to the collection of works of art or intellectual products created under the conditions, or within the period, of post-modernity). Unlike the notion of a post-industrial society, the concept of post-modernity refers to a distinct quality of intellectual climate, to a distinctly new meta-cultural stance, to a distinct self-awareness of the era. One of the basic, if not *the* basic, elements of this self-awareness is the realization that modernity is over; that modernity is a closed chapter of history, which can now be contemplated in its entirety, with retrospective knowledge of its practical accomplishments as much as its theoretical hopes.

Thanks to this element of the new self-awareness called post-modernity, modernity, serving thus far as the Marxian 'anatomy of man', has been for the first time relegated to the position of 'the ape', which discloses the unsuspected, or unduly neglected aspects of its anatomy when examined with the *ex post facto* wisdom of post-modernity. This wisdom rearranges our knowledge of modernity and redistributes the importance assigned to its various characteristics. It also brings into relief such aspects of modernity as went unnoticed when looked upon from the inside of the modern era simply because of their then uncontested status and consequent taken-for-grantedness; which, however, suddenly burst into vision precisely because their absence in the later, post-modern, period makes them problematic. Such aspects, first and foremost, are those which bear relation to modernity's self-confidence; its conviction of its own superiority over alternative forms of life, seen as historically or logically 'primitive'; and its belief that its pragmatic advantage over pre-modern societies and cultures, far from being a historic coincidence, can be shown to have objective, absolute foundations and universal validity.

Indeed, this is exactly the kind of belief which the consciousness of the post-modern era is most conspicuously lacking; all the more striking is the solid presence of such a belief in the self-consciousness of modernity. From the post-modern perspective the episode of modernity appears to have been, more than anything else, the era of certainty.

It is so because the most poignant of the post-modern experiences is the *lack* of self-confidence. It is perhaps debatable whether the philosophers of the modern era ever articulated to everybody's satisfaction the foundations of the objective superiority of Western rationality, logic, morality, aesthetics, cultural precepts, rules of civilized life, etc. The fact is, however, that they never stopped looking for such an articulation and hardly ever ceased to believe that the search would bring – must bring – success. The post-modern period is distinguished by abandoning the search itself, having convinced itself of its futility. Instead, it tries to reconcile itself to a life under conditions of permanent and incurable uncertainty; a life in the presence of an unlimited quantity of competing forms of life, unable to prove their claims to be grounded in anything more solid and binding than their own historically shaped conventions.

Modernity, by comparison, seems never to have entertained similar doubts as to the universal grounding of its status. The hierarchy of values imposed upon the world administered by the north-western tip of the European peninsula was so firm and supported by powers so enormously overwhelming, that for a couple of centuries it remained the baseline of the world vision, rather than an overtly debated problem. Seldom brought to the level of consciousness, it remained the all-powerful 'taken for granted' of the era. It was evident to everybody except the blind and the ignorant, that the West was superior to the East, white to black, civilized to crude, cultured to uneducated, sane to insane, healthy to sick, man to woman, normal to criminal, more to less, riches to austerity, high productivity to low productivity, high culture to low culture. All these 'evidencies' are now gone. Not a single one remains unchallenged. What is more, we can see now that they did not hold in separation from each other; they made sense together, as manifestations of the same power complex, the same power structure of the world, which retained credibility as long as the structure remained intact, but were unlikely to survive its demise.

The structure has been, moreover, increasingly sapped by the resistance and the struggle of categories cast (practically by the power structure, theoretically by the associated value hierarchy) as inferior. It is the measure of the effectiveness of such resistance that no power today feels able to claim an objective superiority for the form of life it represents; the most it can do is to demand, following Ronald Reagan's example, the right to 'defend our way of life'. All absolute superiorities met a fate similar to the one perceptively observed by Ian Miles and John Irvine regarding the West over East domination: as far as the objections of the 'underdeveloped' part of the world go, '[w]ith increasing global instability, this claim may become more than a moral plea: it may be enforceable through political or economic action.'[2] Indeed it may, if it has not been already, and in view of this possibility the philosophical pursuit of the absolute foundations of Western superiority must sound increasingly hollow: the fact which was to be explained, has disappeared.

How different this situation appears when compared with the intellectual and moral comfort of uncontested domination, which, as Richard L. Rubenstein recently observed, made the self-consciousness of the modern era, from Calvin to Darwin, so confident in professing its moral evaluations masquerading as statements of objective truth:

> Darwin's vision resembles a Biblical theology of history: the plight of those who suffer must be viewed from the larger perspective of the Great Plan. In the Bible, God is the Author of the Plan; in Darwin it is 'Nature'. In both, history derives its meaning from the fate of the fortunate few. Of greatest importance is the fact that both Calvinism and Darwinism provide a cosmic justification for the felicity of the few and the misery of the many.[3]

With the many no longer accepting obediently their misery, even the felicitous few do not seem to have much demand for cosmic justification of their felicity. Practical and effective means of defending their felicity against rising threats seem to possess more urgency and promise more benefit.

The 'shrinking' of Europe, and the humbling of the values with which it grew used to identifying itself, is not, of course, a phenomenon reducible solely to changes in the world's balance of power. The changes are real enough (and large enough at least to problematize the previously taken-for-granted European superiority), but by themselves they would not generate a crisis of confidence in the 'absolute foundations', if it were not for the dwindling confidence of those who once theorized European superiority. Those who once scanned the world as the field to be cultivated by Europe, armed as it was with Reason, tend to speak today of the 'failed' or 'yet unfulfilled' project of modernity. (Modernity, once the 'background' one does not reflect upon, has suddenly been perceived as a project now that its attributes have begun to disappear one by one.) In the same way as the intellectual climates which preceded it, the contemporary crisis of confidence is an intellectual construction; it reflects, as before, the collective experience of those who articulate the self-identities of their times and societies; the only category of people which describes and defines itself, and which cannot describe or define itself in any other fashion but through describing and defining societies of which it is a part.

The pessimistic and defensive mood of the intellectuals, which presents itself as the crisis of European civilization, becomes understandable if seen against the difficulties the intellectuals encounter whenever attempting to fulfill their traditional role; to wit, the role which, with the advent of the modern era, they were trained – and trained themselves – to perform. The contemporary world is ill fitted for intellectuals as legislators; what appears to our consciousness as the crisis of civilization, or the failure of a certain historical project, is a genuine crisis of a particular role, and the corresponding experience of the collective redundancy of the category which specialized in playing this role.

One aspect of this crisis is the absence of sites from which authoritative statements of the kind the function of intellectual legislators involves could be made. The external limitations of European (or Western) power form only a part of the story. Another part, arguably more consequential still, comes from the growing independence of societal powers, within Western societies themselves, from the services intellectuals were able, eager and hoping to supply. This process has been well captured by Michel de Certeau:

> The old powers cleverly managed their 'authority' and thus compensated for the inadequacy of their technical and administrative apparatus; they were systems of clienteles, allegiances, 'legitimacies' etc. They sought, however, to make themselves more independent of the fluctuations of these fidelities through rationalization, the control and organization of space. As the result of this labour, the powers in our developed societies have at their disposal rather subtly and closely-knit procedures for the control of all social networks; these are the administrative and 'panoptic' systems of the police, the schools, health services, security etc. But they are slowly losing all credibility. They have more power and less authority.[4]

The point is, that the state is not necessarily weaker from this demise of authority; it simply has found better, more efficient ways of reproducing and reinforcing its power; authority has become redundant, and the category specializing in servicing the reproduction of authority has become superfluous. Whoever insists on continuing to supply such services just because he or she is well qualified and efficient in producing them, must perceive the situation as critical.

The new technology of power and control also needs experts, of course; but the traditional intellectuals–legislators would hardly recognize this new demand as geared to their skills and ambitions. A witty but profound description of new power routines is contained in a recent study by Stanley Cohen:

> Orwell's terrible image of totalitarianism was the boot eternally trampling a human face. My vision of social control is much more mundane and assuring. It is the eternal case conference, diagnostic and allocation board or pre-sentence investigation unit. Serious-looking PhDs are sitting around a table. Each is studying the same computerized records, psychological profiles, case histories, neat files punched out on the word processor. The atmosphere is calm. Everyone present knows that no amount of criticism of individual treatment methods, no empirical research, no dodo-bird verdicts can slow the work down. The reverse is true. The more negative the results, the more manic and baroque the enterprise of selection becomes: more psychological tests, more investigation units, more pre-sentence reports, more post-sentence allocation centres, more contract forms, more case summaries, more referral notations, more prediction devices.[5]

There is hardly any way left leading from this self-propelling, self-perpetuating, self-divisive, autonomous and self-sufficient mechanism of expert knowledge, back to the kind of generalized expertise entailed by the traditional role of the legislators. From the vantage point of memory (or the 'unfulfilled project of modernity') realities of modern power routines may be seen, as they indeed are, as a bureaucratic displacement of the educated experts, as an act of expropriation – intellectuals having been deprived of the functions and entitlements they grew to see as their own.

There is also another factor exacerbating the intellectual lack of self-confidence. The hope that the modern, that is, the rationally administered, highly and increasingly productive, science-based world would eventually generate patterns of social organization fit to be universalized is fading, as the disenchantments accumulate: none of the patterns so far produced inside the modern world is likely ever to respond to the expectations born of intellectual practice. To put it a different way, no pattern so far produced, or likely to be produced as things go at the moment, promises to render the social world hospitable to intellectuals in their traditional role. This realization finds its outlet in the widespread feeling, admirably captured by Agnes Heller and her colleagues from the post-Lukacsian school, that the modern world faces a situation without good choices. The choice is, indeed, between the 'dictatorship over needs' in the Soviet-type system, and the consumer society of the West – one that has taken all the lids off human desires, and has left no space for the limiting role of values, breeding instead an incessantly growing volume of dissatisfaction parallel to the unstoppably swelling volume of commodities. In the system of the first type, the intellectuals have been, so to speak, liquidated as a class, that is, they have been collectively expropriated of their shared function of generating and promoting the values the state and its subjects are expected to implement and observe. Values are now articulated by the state itself, but above all they are (in practice, if not in theory) by-passed as the means of societal reproduction and all but replaced by techniques of coercion, manipulation and panoptic control. In a system of the second type, the practical effects on the position of the intellectuals are virtually the same, once all the obvious differences between the two systems are granted: values have been turned into attributes of commodities, and otherwise rendered irrelevant. It is therefore the mechanism of the market which now takes upon itself the role of the judge, the opinion-maker, the verifier of values. Intellectuals have been expropriated again. They have been displaced even in the area which for several centuries seemed to remain uncontestably their own monopolistic domain of authority – the area of culture in general, 'high culture' in particular. In David Carrier's realistic assessment, 'aesthetic judgments directly imply economic judgments. To persuade us that a work [of art] is good, and so convince the art world [i.e., the sellers and buyers of art] that it is valuable, are two descriptions of one and the same action. Truth of criticism is relative to what art-world people believe . . . theory becoming true when enough of these people believe it.'[6] The power of adjudication passing away from their hands, the intellectuals cannot but experience the world as one without values 'worthy of the name'. They would, on the whole, agree with the sombre premonition of Georg Simmel, jotted down on the eve of the First World War: 'unlike men in all these earlier epochs, we have been for some time now living without any shared ideal, even perhaps without any ideals at all.'[7] In such a mood, it takes a lot of courage to persist in presenting the values of one's choice as absolutely binding. Some would undoubtedly do just that, bracing themselves for the noble, yet not evidently effective, role of the voice crying in the wilderness. Many others would consider pragmatic modesty a more reasonable choice.

This has been a very preliminary list of hypotheses which may possibly account for the crisis of the traditional legislator's role (the crisis which seems to stand behind the current post-modernist discourse). Social reality hiding behind the notion of post-modernism, and, more importantly, the generic name of post-modernity, requires of course a much more thorough analysis. We will try to undertake such an analysis in the remaining chapters, or at least make an inventory of its necessary ingredients.

Analysis of post-modernity, however conscientious, must bear the same 'until further notice', incomplete character, as the traditional theories of modernity once did; constructed from within modernity, they perceived the latter as a yet unfinished, and hence organically open-ended, process. Analysis of post-modernity cannot be anything more than a mid-career report. Its propositions must be tentative, particularly in view of the fact that the only solid and indubitable accomplishment of the post-modernist debate has been thus far the proclamation of the end of modernism; as to the rest, it is far from clear which among the many topics of the discourse signal lasting and irreversible tendencies, and which will soon find their place among the passing fads of a century notorious for its love of fashions. This uncertainty extends to the issue most crucial to our topic: the changing social location, and hence the role, of the intellectuals. There are many signs that the traditional role (performed or aspired to), portrayed by the metaphor of 'legislators', is being gradually replaced by the role best captured by the metaphor of 'interpreters'. Is this, however, an irrevocable transformation, or a momentary loss of nerve?

In the century or so immediately preceding the advent of modernity, Europe went through a similar period of uncertainty, and the proto-pragmatism of Mercenne or Gassendi was its response. That period did not last long. Soon the philosophers joined forces in exorcizing the ghost of relativism that the proto-pragmatists tried to accommodate. The exorcism has gone on ever since, never fully successful. Descartes's *malin génie* has always been with us, in one disguise or another, his presence confirmed by ever renewed desperate attempts to annihilate the threat of relativism, as if no such attempts had ever been undertaken in the past. Modernity was lived in a haunted house. Modernity was an age of certainty, but it had its inner demons; its was the security of a besieged fortress, confidence of a commander of a so far, thank God, stronger army. Unlike the medieval certainty of the schoolmen, the certainty of modern philosophers constantly entailed the poignant awareness of the *problem* of relativism. It had to be an embattled, militant certainty. A momentary loss of vigilance could cost dearly. It did, occasionally.

Is the time we live in another such occasion? Or does it differ from the previous ones? Is the current crisis of certainty the effect of a temporary loss of vigilance? Is it a typical interim period which follows, and precedes, successive forms of societal organization? Or is it the first sighting of the shape of things to come?

None of these three possibilities can be accepted, or rejected, with confidence. At this stage, the best one can do is try to take stock of possible scenarios and their socially grounded probabilities.

9

The rise of the interpreter

Pluralism is not a recent experience. By itself, it cannot serve as a sufficient reason for the recent upsurge of the post-modernist intellectual climate in which pluralism of experience, values and criteria of truth stoutly refuses to be treated as a transitory feature of the yet incomplete reality, and a feature to be eliminated in the process of maturation. '[P]luralization of diverging universes of discourse', Jürgen Habermas remarked, 'belongs to specifically modern experience . . . We cannot now simply wish this experience away; we can only negate it.'[1] Habermas here brings together two distinct kinds of pluralism, to be sure: one, deriving from the division of labour of sorts, the mutual separation of discourses concerned with truth, judgement and taste, which Habermas considers as the crucial feature of modernity as such, something the philosopher and social scientist have been living with for at least a couple of centuries; and another, pluralization of communally and traditionally contexted discourses, which reclaim the localization of truth, judgement and taste which modernity denied and set to overcome in practice. The second kind of plurality is not a recent development either; what is (so it seems) recent, is the recognition of the second type of pluralism as no less permanent and irrevocable than the first one. It is this recognition that is hard to reconcile with the spirit and the practice of modernity. By bringing the two kinds of pluralism together, Habermas, as it were, precludes the possibility of considering the present situation of the Western intellectual as essentially novel, and calls for rather far-reaching changes in the way the intellectual services have been traditionally dispensed.

Instead, Habermas can only perceive recent shifts in the intellectual world-view as a sort of aberration; a regrettable hardening of attitudes which in their more benign form were with us for a long, long time; an event engendered by a lapse of comprehension or theoretical errors; an ailment to be cured by better comprehension and a proper theory. What has indeed happened, according to Habermas, is the sharpening up of the time-honoured controversy between historicism (an attitude which admits historical plurality of truths, yet expects science to supply both the substance and the legitimacy of consensual knowledge) and transcendentalism (which aims at distilling the characteristics of *all* rational action which *must* be presupposed), into a barren polarization between relativism (which denies the possibility of agreement between truths) and absolutism (which seeks universal reason outside, and independently of, rational practice). The last two strategies are simultaneously mistaken; what is in fact the most mistaken aspect of them is that the gap they created between alternative philosophical strategies is so wide that one cannot expect any more the polarized strategies to mitigate mutually their respective extremisms.

There is no denying that both relativism and absolutism coexist as well-pronounced tendencies in contemporary discourse, the second being forced by the strides made by the first into obliquely confirming its presuppositions (the absolute cannot any more be sought in practice – either as an empirical generalization, or as logical premises). If the two hardened versions of the old controversy are indeed interdependent, it seems that the active role in their dialectic entanglement belongs to the view that all further search for supra-communal grounds of truth, judgement or taste is futile (if it has not been futile all along). Such a view, described as relativist, has been in recent years expressed with a force unprecedented for at least two centuries.

Lonnie D. Kliever's articulation of the novelty of the contemporary view of pluralism is as poignant as any one can find in recent writings:

> The dispersion of political power and the freedom of religious assembly within non-hierarchical societies represent differences and disagreements *within* a shared commitment to one nation and one God. Pluralism by contrast assumes no such overarching unity or loyalty. Pluralism is the existence of multiple frames of reference, each with its own scheme of understanding and criteria of rationality. Pluralism is the coexistence of comparable and competing positions which are not to be reconciled. Pluralism is the recognition that

different persons and different groups quite literally dwell in irreducibly different worlds.[2]

Kliever goes on to emphasize that in a pluralistic world, there are no 'uncontested systems of reality definition'. All theoretical attempts to negotiate an agreed solution to the contest having failed in practice, we *must* admit, Kliever insists, that 'forms of life are logically and psychologically self-legitimating'. One can live with such admission nicely, Kliever thinks, providing, however, that this admission is as universal as the earlier agreement on the plausibility of the project of universal truth. What Kliever is afraid of, is the continuation, in a pluralist world, of the strategies and ensuing behaviour which derived their sense from the assumption of universal foundations of truth. What may prevent the danger is a sort of a self-inflicted modesty adopted and practised by all 'forms of life' coexisting in the pluralist world. Without such modesty, without reconciling oneself to the 'equality of limitation' between forms of life, old authoritarian habits would soon reassert themselves and the pluralist world would turn into one of 'multiple absolutism'. It is against this new threat, specific to the situation of pluralism establishing itself in the wake of the protracted rule of an authoritarian, monistic world-view, that Kliever wishes to mobilize the intellectuals. The new intellectual task, in his view, is to fight against partial, local absolutisms with the same energy with which their predecessors fought for an 'impartial', universal one. Relativism, far from being a problem, is for Kliever a solution to the pluralist world's problem; moreover, its promotion is, so to speak, a moral duty of contemporary intellectuals.

It is arguable whether the pluralism Kliever diagnoses is a turn in the structure of the world or in the intellectuals' perception of the world. There are valid arguments to support both possibilities. We have briefly scanned some of the arguments pointing to the first possibility. As to the other, the gradual abandoning of the pursuit of ultimate judgement by intellectuals overwhelmed by the incurable plurality of forms of life, the field of art supplies a most conspicuous example of the processes involved.

A pithy portrait of the state of arts at the age of post-modernity has been painted by Matei Calinescu:

Generally, the increasing pace of change tends to diminish the relevance of any particular change. The new is no longer new. If

modernity has presided over the formation of an 'aesthetics of surprise', this seems to be the moment of its total failure. Today the most
diverse artistic products (covering the whole range from the
esoterically sophisticated to sheer kitsch), wait side by side in the
'cultural supermarket' . . . for their respective consumers. Mutually
exclusive aesthetics coexist in a sort of stalemate, no one being able to
perform an actually leading role. Most of the analysts of contemporary art agree that ours is a pluralistic world in which everything is
permitted on principle. The old avant-garde, destructive as it was,
sometimes deluded itself into believing that there were actually new
paths to break open, new realities to discover, new prospects to
explore. But today, when the 'historical avant-garde' has been so successful as to become the 'chronic condition' of art, both the rhetoric of
destruction and that of novelty have lost any trace of heroic appeal.
We could say that the new, postmodernist avant-garde reflects at its
own level the increasingly 'modular' structure of our mental world,
in which the crisis of ideologies (manifesting itself by a strange,
cancerous proliferation of micro-ideologies, while the great ideologies
of modernity are losing their coherence) makes it more and more
difficult to establish convincing hierarchies of values.[3]

It is as if post-modern art has followed the advice offered in 1921
by Francis Picabia: 'if you want to have clean ideas, change them
like shirts.'[4] Or, rather, it has improved on the Dadaists' precept: if
you do not have ideas, they surely will never get dirty. Post-modern
art is conspicuous for its absence of style as a category of artwork; for
its deliberately eclectic character, a strategy which can best be
described as one of 'collage' and 'pastiche',[5] both strategies aimed at
defying the very idea of style, school, rule, purity of genre – all those
things which underpinned critical judgement in the age of modernist
art. The absence of clearly defined rules of the game renders all
innovation impossible. There is no longer any development in art,
perhaps only an undirected change, a succession of fashions, with no
one form claiming credibly its superiority over its predecessors
– which turn, by the same token, into its contemporaries. What
follows is a sort of perpetual present, restlessness reminiscent more
of a chaotic Brownian movement than of an ordered sequential
change, not to mention a progressive development. It is the state
that Meyer called 'stasis', a state in which everything is on the
move, but nothing moves anywhere in particular. In the words of
Peter Bürger:

Through the avant-garde movements, the historical succession of techniques and styles has been transferred into a simultaneity of the radically disparate. The consequence is that no movement in the arts today can legitimately claim to be historically more advanced *as art* than any other . . . The historical avant-garde movements were unable to destroy art as an institution; but they did destroy the possibility that a given school can present itself with the claim to universal validity.

This means, in fact, 'the destruction of the possibility of positing aesthetic norms as valid ones'.[6]

Post-modern art (which truly took off, according to most analysts, only in the 1970s) has gone a long way now from the iconoclastic gesture of Marcel Duchamp, who sent to an art exhibition a urinal dubbed 'Fountain' and signed 'Richard Mutt', with the explanation that '[w]hether Mr Mutt with his own hands made the fountain or not has no importance. He *chose* it. He took an ordinary article of life, placed it so that useful significance disappeared under the new title and point of view – created a new thought for the object.'[7] In retrospect, Marcel Duchamp's scandalous act, which at the time was seen as flying in the face of virtually everything that Western aesthetics stood for, seems strikingly modern rather than post-modern; what Marcel Duchamp did was to present a new *definition* of art (something chosen by the artist), a new *theory* of artwork (cutting off an object from its ordinary context and viewing it from an unusual point of view; doing in fact what the Romantics had done a century before in making the familiar extraordinary), a new *method* of artistic work (creating a new thought for an object). By today's standards, Duchamp's gesture was not that iconoclastic at all. On the other hand, it could be seen as such just because at that time definitions, theories and methods still counted and were perceived as the necessary conditions and paramount criteria of artistic judgement. There were dominant, agreed upon, universally accepted definitions, theories and methods which Duchamp could be radically opposed to and defy. In recent times, Duchamp's gestures came to be repeated and duplicated on an ever increasing scale and ostensible radicalism: Robert Rauschenberg would dispose even of the ready-made and choose instead to present as a work of art the act of erasing a drawing; Yves Klein would invite three thousand sophisticated members of the art public to a private view of an empty gallery; Walter de Maria would fill a New York gallery with 220,000 pounds of earth, and dig a deep hole in the earth near Kassel, covering it later with a tight lid so it could not be seen.[8] The problem is, however, that the overall result of the collective efforts of the new avant-garde to remove the last thinkable and unthinkable limits of artistic work is the rapidly fading radicalism of any new, present or future, gesture; and the equally rapidly growing capacity of the art world to absorb, accommodate, legalize, market and make profit on, anything, however wild or unprecedented. All possibility of using artform as a protest, either against the art establishment, or – more ambitiously – against the society which isolated artistic work from all relation to other spheres of social life, has been effectively pre-empted. To quote Bürger again: '[i]f an artist today signs a stove pipe and exhibits it, that artist certainly does not denounce the art market but adapts to it . . . Since now the protest of historical avant-garde against art as institution is accepted as *art*, the gesture of protest of the neo-avant-garde becomes inauthentic.'[9]

This is, indeed, a new situation, to which the philosophers, art historians and art critics were ill-prepared by three centuries of Western aesthetics. Post-modern art is indeed radically different from modernism. It is, from the perspective of this difference, only now, in the last decade or two, that the orderly nature of modernist art, its close kinship with an era which believed in science, in progress, in objective truth, in the ever rising control over technology and – through technology – over nature has become fully visible. Thanks to the post-modernist upheaval we can now see clearly the meaning of modernity, hidden as it was at the time under the panoply of rapidly changing schools and styles, often at open war with each other. This new perception has found cogent expression in Kim Lewin's famous essay of 1979:

> For those who stepped outside modernism, the successive styles of the modern period, which seemed so radically different from each other at the time, are beginning to merge together with shared characteristics – characteristics that now seem quaintly naive . . .
>
>   Modern art was scientific. It was based on faith in the technological future, on belief in progress and objective truth. It was experimental: the creation of new forms was its task. Ever since Impressionism ventured into optics, it shared the method and logic of science. There were the Einsteinian relativities of Cubist geometry, the technological visions of Constructivism and Futurism, de Stijl and Bauhaus, the Dadaists' diagrammatic machinery. Even Surrealist visualisations of

Freudian dreamworlds and Abstract-Expressionist enactments of psychoanalytical processes were attempts to tame the irrational with rational techniques. For the modernist period believed in scientific objectivity, scientific invention: its art had the logic of structure, the logic of dreams, the logic of gesture or material. It longed for perfection and demanded purity, clarity, order. And it denied anything else, especially the past: idealist, ideological, and optimistic, modernism was predicated on the glorious future, the new and improved.

This family resemblance between the competing schools of the modernist era has been brought into relief and made well nigh evident by the radically different practice of post-modernist art, which in sharp contrast, is '[b]ased not on scientific reason and logic and the pretence of objectivity but on presence, subjective experience, behaviour, on a weird kind of therapeutic revelation in which it is not necessary to believe or understand – it is enough if it works'. [10]

Rosalind E. Kraus saw the grid – an obsessively repeated motif of modern painting, particularly in its last phase – as a phenomenon which captured most fully the essential features of modernism in art; Kraus argued the representativeness of the grid, pointing to its virtual absence in pre-modern painting (a break with the past) and in real life (a break with society, a manifesto of the autonomy of art). [11] If there can be no objection to the first comment, the second seems to be based on a misunderstanding. Indeed, the grid in modern painting can be interpreted as the most radical and consistent attempt to capture and express, in an artistic medium, the essence of socially produced reality; it can be seen as a product of painstaking analysis of the essential features of the social world in the modern era. Levi-Strauss decoded the Nambiquara ornaments as subconscious expressions of the true shape of their authority structure, otherwise invisible behind the smoke-screen of mythology. In modern painting, arguably as the result of a fully conscious, scientific analysis, the grid decodes the work of modern authority manifesting itself in dividing, classifying, categorizing, filing, ordering and relating. Obsessive about its autonomy and concentrating self-consciously on its own media and its own techniques as the crucial (or the only) subject-matter of its work and area of its responsibility, modern art seldom broke with the *Zeitgeist* of the modern era; it shared fully and whole-heartedly in this era's search for truth, its scientific methods of analysis, its conviction that reality can be – and should be – subjected to the control of Reason. The modernist artists broadcast on the same wavelength as their intellectual analysts and critics. They confronted their analysts and critics with tasks they could handle well, and were accustomed to handle by their professional training and inherited, institutionalized, aesthetics. The analysts and the critics could find many a development in modernist art a puzzle – but they knew that this puzzle had a solution, and they had the means to find it.

The puzzle presented by post-modernist art, on the other hand, is one which truly baffles its analysts. The feeling of bewilderment and being lost in the maze of new developments results from the absence of the comfortable conviction that the new is just more of the same, an unfamiliar form of the familiar, that it is only a matter of time for it to lose its strangeness, to be intellectually tamed, that the tools sufficient for the job are available and one knows how to apply them. In other words, the uneasiness results from the inability of the analysts to perform their traditional function; the very foundation of their social role now looks threatened. What this social role has been thus far, Howard S. Becker articulates with brevity and precision: 'Aestheticians do not simply intend to classify things into useful categories . . . but rather to separate the deserving from the undeserving, and to do it definitely . . . The logic of the enterprise – the bestowing of honorific titles – requires them to rule some things out, for there is no special honour in a title every conceivable object or activity is entitled to.'[12]

This is, indeed, the hub of the matter. Throughout the modern era, including the modernist period, aestheticians remained firmly in control of the area of taste and artistic judgement (or so it seems now, in retrospect, by comparison with the situation brought into being by the post-modernist developments). Being in control meant operating, without much challenge, the mechanisms transforming uncertainty into certainty; making decisions, pronouncing authoritative statements, segregating and classifying, imposing binding definitions upon reality. In other words – it meant exercising power over the field of art. In the case of aesthetics the power of intellectuals seemed particularly unchallenged, virtually monopolistic. In the West, at least, no other sites of power attempted to interfere with the verdicts proffered by those 'in the know'.

It is true that the power of the educated, sophisticated, sublimated, refined elite to proffer binding aesthetic judgement, to segregate the deserving from the non-deserving or non-art, was always expressed in acts of militancy aimed at judgements, or practices, whose authority was questioned. It could not be otherwise; the authority of the educated (and, indirectly but most importantly, the authority-bestowing capacity of education) could not be asserted in any other way but through construction of its opposite: pretentiousness without foundation, taste without legitimacy, choice without right. The elite ruling in the kingdom of art had always had its adversary against whom the rule was exercised and whose presence supplied the necessary legitimation of the rule: the vulgar. In Gombrich's words:

> [i]n the strict hierarchic society of the sixteenth and seventeenth centuries [we would rather say: under conditions of the disintegration of the old hierarchy in these centuries – *Z.B.*] the contrast between the 'vulgar' and the 'noble' becomes one of the principal preoccupations of the critics . . . Their belief was that certain forms of modes are 'really' vulgar, because they please the low, while others are inherently noble, because only a developed taste can appreciate them.[13]

At that early time, the point at issue was the need to redefine the old hierarchy, about to lose its traditional political and economic foundations, in terms better geared to the emerging structure of authority; but the distinction between the 'noble' and the 'vulgar' could still refer to relatively obvious and undisputed divisions. The matter did become more complicated later, once the intellectually comfortable binary opposition was blurred by the appearance of an expanding middle class, ever growing in numerical strength and purchasing power. Neither coarse nor fully refined, neither ignorant nor educated to the standards boasted by the elite, neither leaving art to its betters nor able to exercise its discretion in matters artistic – the middle class immediately turned into that 'slimy' element which threatened the very existence of the hierarchy of judgement and, with it, the authority of the aesthetically trained elite. No wonder it summoned all the most poisonous arrows of the latter.

'The vulgar' remained the term of abuse, but it changed its connotation; it now referred to the petty bourgeois, the philistine, the middle class daring to make aesthetic judgements in practice, by the act of selecting between cultural offers, but without, however, recognizing the authority of the aestheticians. The middle class juxtaposed to the power of intellect the power of money; left to its own discretion, it could conceivably make the power of intellect hollow and ineffective, without even bothering to challenge it on its own territory -- the theoretical judgement of taste. It was exactly this introduction of alternative criteria for *practical* cultural choices that was perceived by the intellectual elite as the threat to its power. In Bourdieu's words:

> what makes the petit-bourgeois relation to culture and its capacity to make 'middle-brow' whatever it touches, just as the legitimate gaze 'saves' whatever it lights upon, is not its 'nature', but the very position of the petit-bourgeois in social space . . . It is, quite simply, the fact that legitimate culture is not made for him . . . so that he is not made for it; and that it ceases to be what it is as soon as he appropriates it . . .[14]

And this as long as the cultural consumer makes his own choices (it is for this reason that he has been dubbed 'vulgar', 'philistine', or, indeed, 'petty bourgeois'). It is the autonomy of artistic judgement – autonomy in regard to the judgement of the elite – that invites rage and condemnation.

Throughout most of the modern era, however, such rage and condemnation were effective; they did guard the superiority of elitist judgement in the face of real or construed inroads. They were effective because they were in the end interiorized by the victims of elitist attacks. Like Freud's conscience, the fear of 'vulgarity', of aesthetic incompetence, became 'garrisons in conquered cities' of the middle-class 'artistic selves', and the most reliable safeguards of elitist rule. This process of interiorization was admirably captured by Wylie Sypher:

> [T]he nineteenth century produced a horde of parvenus who were obliged to discount the older rituals and who were a culturally discontented class like our prosperous 'workers'. The cultural malaise attending the rise of these shopkeepers, as Macaulay frankly called them [Macaulay's term of abuse, let us add, seems bland and innocuous when compared with 'ferocious and gross presumptiousness' which 'has freed the imbecile and the ignorant from their feelings of nullity' of Hippolite Taine, or 'the commonplace mind', who 'knowing itself to be commonplace, has the assurance to proclaim the rights of the commonplace and to impose them wherever it will' of Ortega y Gasset – *Z.B.*], is disclosed in the whole uneasy notion of vulgarity, which becomes a category in upper-middle-class values. The

Victorian fear of being vulgar . . . is a penalty for being successful. The successful men must be 'refined'.[15]

The elite's disdain and contempt for the vulgar parvenu remained unabated, the standards to measure 'refinement' were set at ever higher levels, so that yesterday's parvenu would find it ever more difficult to sigh with relief 'I have arrived'. But the general structure of modern society, with its in-built cult of education, truth, science and reason (and respect for the authority of those who embodied such values) guaranteed a mechanism through which the potential threats to elitist judgement could be absorbed and thus neutralized. For all practical intents and purposes, superiority of sophisticated aesthetic judgement was never truly put in question, however often it was resented or disregarded. When insisting that '[e]verything that is beautiful and noble is the result of reason and thought' and that 'good is always the product of an art', Baudelaire, justly proclaimed a most profound thinker of modernity, was reflecting upon the firmly established authority of the aesthetic and its intellectual priests.[16]

It is exactly this authority that is now in question; it has been brought into the focus of theory, as a problem instead of an assumption, precisely because it has been rendered ineffective in practice. It has suddenly become clear, that the validity of an aesthetic judgement depends on the 'site' from which it has been made and the authority ascribed to that site; that the authority in question is not an inalienable, 'natural' property of the site, but something fluctuating with the changing location of the site within a wider structure; and that the authority of the site traditionally reserved for the aestheticians – intellectual experts on art – is not any more to be taken for granted.

In the perception of artistic experts, the evident incapacity of aesthetic judgements articulated in the traditional way (that is, in reference to the established body of knowledge and established procedures, both embodied in the self-reproducing discourse and its privileged members) to function as self-authenticating descriptions rebounds as a state of chaos. Chaos is, after all, a state of affairs we cannot predict, change and control. In Hassan's words, while modernism 'created its own form of Authority' (that is, professional aestheticians were firmly in charge), post-modernism 'has tended towards Anarchy, with deeper complicity with things falling apart'.[17] It could be that the current uses of the term post-modernity

retained some kinship ties with the original use of the concept, by
Toynbee, as a synonym for irrationality, anarchy and threatening
indeterminacy.

What appears to the philosophers of art as a state of anarchy, is
above all the inherent 'impurity' of factors participating in the
making of an *X* or a *Y* a 'work of art'; and the ensuing impossibility
of separating art from non-art, or good art from bad art, by making
statements referring only to phenomena fully and indivisibly under
the control of the philosophers themselves. Impurity results, above
all, from the rapidly expanding 'cultural consumption' that is met
by philosophers with deep suspicion, as the creation of 'mass
culture' – a debased, inferior culture, one where the vulgar and the
philistine have got the upper hand – and its inevitable accompaniment, the art market, imposing its own criteria of practical judgement and bringing forth its own sites of authority. Philosophers
naturally crave for a valid 'theory of reputation', that is, one that is
obeyed and tends towards self-authentication, which, according to
Howard S. Becker, should run along the following lines: '(1) specially
gifted people (2) create works of exceptional beauty and depth which
(3) express profound human emotions and cultural values. (4) The
work's special qualities testify to its maker's special gifts, and the
already known gifts of the maker testify to the special qualities of
the work.' This scheme rotates, of course, around the concepts of
'beauty', 'depth', 'values', etc., all of which assume the
monopolistic competence of the theorists; this kind of theory of
reputation reaffirms and reproduces the authority of the latter. The
trouble is that no theory of reputation built along these lines would
hold today in practice. In fact, Becker comments, 'the reputation of
artist, works, and the rest results from the collective activity of art
worlds'. It has been like that all along, one could object. But even if
this were the case, the role of the 'activity of art worlds' could
remain invisible to the theorists as long as the art world which
assigned reputations was confined, more or less strictly, to the
theorists themselves. The role cannot remain invisible once the loss
of control 'objectified', 'alienated' the products of the theorists'
activity and made them into a *Vorhanden*, an object for scrutiny and
reflection.

Becker's response to the newly revealed reality of reputation-
bestowing procedures is an institutional theory of art, which gives
their due to the other, impure, non-philosophical, non-aesthetic sites

of authority: art galleries, art collectors, the opinion-making media, the consumers themselves. This theory, he hopes, will solve the haunting mystery by which an X or a Y is made into a work of art, and its author into an artist. But, he adds, 'the philosophical desire to be able to decide definitely between art and nonart cannot be satisfied by the institutional theory'. Indeed it cannot. What this theory renders evident, after all, is that 'not everything can be made into a work of art just by definition or the creation of consensus, for not everything will pass muster under currently accepted art world standards. But this does not mean that there is any more to making something art than christening it.'[18]

Well, to put it bluntly, the institutional theory of art (as an institutional theory of any other value domain) sounds the death knell to the philosophers' dream of control. What has been put in the place of the absolute principles that only they had access to and only they were able to operate, is this evasive, unwieldy, unpredictable entity of 'consensus'. Philosophers, to be sure, were always in favour of it; the search for consensus was, after all, the unwritten and unspoken, but ubiquitous assumption of their own discourse. Philosophers acted after all on the assumption that the discussion (that is, their own form of being active) does not admit of any other causes of victory or defeat but the power of argument, and hence consensus must be the only measure of success. What is new is not the authority of consensus, but the fact that the kind of consensus which now seems to possess the reputation-bestowing authority is not the consensus of the philosophers. Agreement from other, non-philosophical, quarters, must also be forthcoming, and this one can in no way be sure of obtaining by the force of the argument alone. Marcia Muelder Eaton provides an excellent example of the valiant efforts made by the theorists of art to accommodate this new, confusing and worrying, shape of authoritative consensus. She comes to the conclusion that 'being seen as a work (of art) entails that we discuss it in certain ways'; she accepts that the 'we' who do the 'discussing', are – apart from the traditional discussion experts – also the 'members of social, cultural, political and economic institutions'; she struggles to discover (not to legislate!) the rules which stand behind the agreements possible between such variegated 'members' – any point, for that matter, which would enable a knowledgeable person to make an artistic judgement with at least a minimal degree of certainty; and she ends her struggle, and her book, with the following sentence: 'If Roberta Peters utters a moose call in her concert tonight, has she sung a song? Perhaps we'll have to wait for tomorrow's reviews to find out.'[19]

I have dwelled for so long on the situation in the arts not only because it is to the 'aesthetic' branch of the intellectuals that we owe above all our sense of entering the post-modern era. Another reason for the lengthy digression is the fact that (not for the first time) it is in the domain of art and art criticism that a much wider redeployment of the intellectual world and its work seems to start. Let us repeat that in no other sphere of social life has the non-interference of the non-intellectual authorities been so traditionally low, and in consequence, the authority of the intellectuals so complete and indubitable. Rather than being the soft under-belly of the intellectual domain, the world of high culture was its inner and least vulnerable line of fortification – indeed, a shining though inimitable example to us all, engaged as we are with areas of social practice which come under the control of other earthly powers. The shock of the post-modern condition was therefore felt most profoundly where it brought about the most drastic change and exploded the most solidly entrenched myths. It therefore allows us to see more clearly the mechanisms rebounding throughout the intellectual world in a widespread feeling of unease and the urge to renegotiate the traditional strategy of intellectual work, captured (or, rather, concealed) by the idea of post-modern crisis.

If the judgement of taste (described already by Kant as 'disinterested', meaning subject to reason only) occupied the very centre of the intellectual world once organized around the metaphor of the legislator, one would expect that the closer to this centre other intellectual domains were located, the more poignantly they would experience the post-modern shock. This indeed seems to be the case. Apart from aesthetics, the areas most affected by the post-modern challenge are those philosophical discourses which are concerned with the issues of truth, certainty and relativism, and those which deal with the principles of societal organization. More often than not, these discourses generated legitimations for realities already structured by extant hierarchies of power; as long as such structures remained intact and unthreatened, however, there was little to distinguish between the articulation of legitimacy and legislating. Today, hierarchies are neither intact nor unthreatened. The tasks of legitimizing and legislating suddenly appear wide apart, once the reasons to assume the legislating power of legitimation have been progressively eroded. How can one argue the case for or against a form of life, for or against a version of truth, when one feels that one's argument cannot any more legislate, that there are powers behind the *plural* forms of life and plural versions of truth which would not be *made* inferior, and hence would not surrender to the argument of their inferiority? Suddenly, the two-centuries-old philosophical voyage to certainty and universal criteria of perfection and 'good life' seems to be a wasted effort. This does not necessarily mean that we do not like the terrains to which it has brought us; on the contrary, it is the refusal of others to admire them and to follow us there which makes us worry and prompts us to look for a new, stronger tune for the praise we still wish to sing. If we wish to defend the direction our journey took us, we need to redefine, retrospectively, its sense.

Ernest Gellner is arguably the staunchest and the most profound defender of the peculiar form of life born in the north-western tip of the European peninsula four centuries ago which has subordinated all other forms of life for the last two hundred years. His is perhaps the most convincing plea on its behalf:

> On balance, one option – a society with cognitive growth based on a roughly atomistic strategy – seems to us superior, for various reasons, which are assembled without elegance; this kind of society alone can keep alive the large numbers to which humanity has grown, and thereby avoid a really ferocious struggle for survival among us; it alone can keep us at the standard to which we are becoming accustomed; it, more than its predecessors, *probably* favours a liberal and tolerant social organization . . . This type of society also has many unattractive traits, and its virtues are open to doubt. On balance, and with misgivings, we opt for it; but there is no question of an elegant, clear-cut choice. We are half pressurised by necessity (fear of famine, etc.), half-persuaded by a promise of liberal affluence (which we do not fully trust). There it is: lacking better reasons we will have to make do with these.[20]

This statement is modest – and, in a sense, apologetic. It is self-conscious of its inadequacy in terms of the extant criteria of the elegance of philosophical proof. It justifies the *raison d'être* of the philosophical tradition, which devoted its life and energy to exorcizing the ghost of pragmatic relativism, in pragmatic terms – an ultimate irony, as it were. And the argument it employs (again self-consciously,

I am sure) is circular: this system is better because it caters for the things which it taught us to like better – like that 'standard to which we are becoming accustomed'. There is nothing intrinsically wrong with such an argument. On the contrary, it seems much more human and realistic than the philosophical elegance it proposes to replace. That is, if we first agree to abandon philosophical pretentions to universality.

Gellner's reasoning has a decisive advantage over many other arguments, similar in their self-inflicted modesty, pragmatism and circularity. It is honest about its own purpose, which is the defence of the world which we, the intellectuals of the West, shaped by the two centuries of recent Western history we collectively helped to shape, find to approximate closer than any other world we know to the standards we set for a good society. To phrase it differently, Gellner's argument makes explicit a case for the kind of world which may provide (and has been providing, with qualifications, for some time) a suitable setting for the Western intellectual mode of life; and may also create a demand for the traditional (legislating) role that Western intellectuals have learned to perform best. This makes Gellner's argument particularly interesting; it demonstrates how difficult, if not downright impossible, it is to argue the superiority of the Western type of society in objective, absolute or universal terms. At its best, the argument must be self-constrained, pragmatic and, indeed, unashamedly circular.

Other reactions to the post-modern condition tend to be rather more confused. What they are outraged or horrified by, and what they wish to save against all odds, is more often than not hidden behind new universal philosophies of history or universal strategies for philosophy and/or social science. Some, perhaps the least interesting ones, refuse to admit realities which supply relativist arguments with somewhat different, and arguably stronger, grounds than before, treat diagnoses of irreducible pluralism of the world as a collective aberration, and continue to produce 'footnotes to Plato'. Other reactions, perhaps more numerous, probably more exciting and certainly more vociferous, face the pluralism point blank, accept its irreversibility and propose to reconsider the role a philosopher, or an intellectual in general, may learn to perform in such a hopelessly plural world with the same measure of respectability and profit that the legislator's role once brought. Such propositions, however, are normally stated in a fashion which prevents rather than helps us to understand their purpose; unlike in Gellner's case, the proposals to abandon the dream of the absolute are argued in absolutist terms. They are presented as new and improved versions of the old-style all-embracing theories of 'human nature', or the 'nature of social life', or both.

Whatever the structure of the argument, the reactions of the second category all point – overtly or implicitly – to a new role that intellectuals may usefully play, given their historically accumulated wisdom and skill: the role of interpreters. With pluralism irreversible, a world-scale consensus on world-views and values unlikely, and all extant *Weltanschauungen* firmly grounded in their respective cultural traditions (more correctly: their respective autonomous institutionalizations of power), communication across traditions becomes the major problem of our time. This problem does not seem temporary any more; one cannot hope that it will be solved 'in passing' by a sort of massive conversion guaranteed by the unstoppable march of Reason. Rather, the problem is likely to stay with us for a long, long time (unless, that is, its life expectation is drastically cut by the absence of an appropriate tonic). The problem, therefore, calls urgently for specialists in translation between cultural traditions. The problem casts such specialists in a most central place among the experts contemporary life may require.

In a nutshell, the proposed specialism boils down to the art of civilized conversation. This is, naturally, a kind of reaction to the permanent conflict of values for which the intellectuals, thanks to their discursive skills, are best prepared. To talk to people rather than fight them; to understand them rather than dismiss or annihilate them as mutants; to enhance one's own tradition by drawing freely on experience from other pools, rather than shutting it off from the traffic of ideas; that is what the intellectuals' own tradition, constituted by ongoing discussions, prepares people to do well. And the art of civilized conversation is something the pluralist world needs badly. It may neglect such art only at its peril. Converse or perish.

A majority of the most influential recent developments in philosophy and social science point in the direction of such a specialism. To name only a few: the passage from the 'negative' to a 'positive' notion of ideology, which accepts that all knowledge is ultimately grounded in essentially irrational, arbitrarily chosen assumptions, related deterministically or randomly to partly enclosed traditions and historic experiences, and which replaces the old division between 'ideological' (wrong) knowledge and 'non-ideological' (true) knowledge with one between a knowledge system unaware of its localized character and one which employs such awareness in the service of rationalizing (that is, making communicatively effective) the exchange between knowledge systems; the rediscovery of hermeneutics and the enthusiasm with which philosophers and social scientists greeted Gadamer's *Truth and Method*, a sophisticated manifesto against methodical truth and true method, which attempts to redefine the task of philosophy or social science as one of interpretation, a search for meaning, making 'the other' comprehensible, making oneself understandable – and thus facilitating an exchange between forms of life – and opening up for communication worlds of meaning which otherwise would remain closed to each other; neo-pragmatism of Rorty's variety, which denigrates the ascendancy during the past three centuries of the Carthesian–Lockean–Kantian tradition as an effect of unfortunate historical accidents, wrong options and confusions, which declares a philosophical search for universal and unshakable foundations of truth as misdirected from the start, and which suggests that philosophers, instead, should focus their attention on continuing the civilized conversation of the West without the comforting, but misleading conviction of its universal validity.

None of these recent developments signals disenchantment with the kind of setting the West provided for the execution of the intellectual vocation (at least not in their mainstream manifestations). Appearances and shock effects notwithstanding, they are all in the end forms of defence of the Western intellectual mode of life under the condition of distress caused by the progressive dissolution of certainty once grounded in the 'evident' superiority of Western society. Gadamer hopes that the hermeneutically conscious philosophy and social science will help to clarify, expand and enrich our tradition, our home, the starting-point and horizon of our understanding and wisdom, the site of our dialogical, civilized co-existence with others – and so will help to preserve our tradition by opening it to other traditions. Rorty is quite outspoken about the purpose of this willingness to talk, to listen to people, to weigh the consequences of our action upon other people, and suggests that it is the proper subject-matter for philosophy: its purpose is to continue the conversation which is unmistakeably our project, the European intellectual's way of life. New philosophy and social science abounds with appeals for a shared vocabulary, a common world, a community of meanings. It is cut to human size, homely, cosy, comfortable like a family home. Like Marx's moths, we are attracted by the light of the candle on the family table once the universal sun fades.

'Community' is indeed the central concept of the self-consciously post-modern philosophy and social science. It has come to replace reason and universal truth, and the one method leading to both. It is in community, rather than in the universal progress of mankind, that the intellectuals of the West tend to seek the secure foundation of their professional role. What is this role to be?

For an answer let us turn to Richard J. Bernstein, a most perceptive analyst of the post-modern philosophical scene.[21] A careful reading of his *Philosophical Profiles* reveals a twofold destination: between communities (traditions, forms of life) intellectuals are called upon to perform the function of interpreters; inside their own community, they are still to play the role of legislators of sorts – their role now consisting of adjudicating or arbitrating in cases of controversy (obviously, controversies *between* and *inside* communities are ascribed different philosophical statutes). Inside the community, philosophers have the right, and the duty, to spell out the rules which decide who are the rational discussants and who are not; their role is to assess the justification and objectivity of views, and to supply the criteria for criticism which will be binding because of those criteria. Inside the community, philosophers may and should assure the survival of certainty, the dominion of reason – though this time by the strength of their own work alone.

At first sight the distinction seems convincing. It revokes the experience of, say, a university seminar, when everybody present is hoped by everybody else to 'share vocabulary', be a member of a 'common world', participate in the 'community of meanings'; to such tacit hopes we refer in our seminar contributions, indeed the latter would not be possible without such hopes. It is because we believe that a consensus about the essential assumptions of the discussion (that is, the conditions of communication) has been once and for all reached or remains in force at least for the duration of the debate, that we can seek agreement on the validity of different, even contradictory, statements made in the debate. There are rules which make such an agreement possible in principle; for example, the authority of 'facts' or 'empirical evidence'; the authority of logical

consistency. Such rules allow us to decide 'who are the rational participants and who are not'. We can decide 'on the truth of the
matter', or at least on what is to be done for the truth of the matter to
be established. This experience differs sharply from, say, a
negotiating session, between spokesmen of admittedly inimical
camps, regarding which contradiction of interests, purposes, points
of view, selection of relevant facts, etc., are assumed; there would be
little hope for the authority-bestowing capacity of truth, or the ability
of logical consistency to outweigh an asymmetry of power resources.
The two experiences give plausibility to the distinction between,
respectively, the intrinsic (intra-communal) and extrinsic (inter-
communal) role of the intellectuals, between the roles of legislators
and interpreters. The problem is, however, how to draw the distinction between the situations which call for one or other of the two
roles?

The erosion of the universal ascendancy of the setting within which
the Western intellectual tradition developed and took shape exposed
the previously invisible link between the pragmatic validity of such
tradition and the commonality of the 'form of life' or the 'community
of meanings'. The question is, however, how large is the community?
Whom does it entail? Where should its boundaries be drawn?

In his search for an effective definition of a nation, Ernest Gellner
found out that

> [n]ations as a natural, God-given way of classifying men, as an
> inherent though long-delayed political destiny, are a myth; national-
> ism, which sometimes takes pre-existing cultures and turns them into
> nations, sometimes invents them, and often obliterates pre-existing
> cultures; that is a reality, for better or worse, and in general an ines-
> capable one . . . Nations can be defined only in terms of the age of
> nationalism, rather than, as you might expect, the other way round.[22]

Nations are a peculiar kind of community, but Gellner's insight has
evidently more general applications. It has a direct bearing on our
problem. It reveals the community – this philosophical name for a
territory inside which the intellectuals may still deploy their legislative skills – as, first and foremost, a postulate, a project, a strategy,
a declaration of intention and the action which follows it. The problem is not 'which particular collection of men can be described as a
true community', but to which particular collection we address the
type of behaviour seen as valid, effective, and so 'rational', inside a

'community'. Communities are not units of 'natural, God-given classification', but products of a differentiating and separating action. Communities are, and must be, constituted by such actions.

Using Gellner's reasoning on the relation between nations and nationalism we have implied that the projecting origin of an ostensible unit of classification is not exactly a novelty. Transformation of variety into unity, substitution of '*the* culture' for a diversity of forms of life, has been a most prominent feature of Western intellectual history. What seems to be new, and presenting problems without tried solution, is that the present-day 'communalism', unlike the 'nationalism' described by Gellner, is essentially a philosophical enterprise only, deprived of the backing which nationalism enjoyed from the emerging powers of the absolutist state. The proselytism of the early intellectuals rode to its success, so to speak, on the wave of history; it was geared to the power aspiring to spiritual ascendancy, to societal integration and control grounded in legitimation and patriotic loyalty. Communalism does not seem to share in the historical luck of nationalism.

For the better part of their history, Western intellectuals drew the blueprints of a better, civilized or rational society by extrapolating their collective experience in general, and the counterfactual assumptions of their mode of life in particular. A 'good society', all specific differences between numerous blueprints notwithstanding, invariably possessed one feature: it was a society well geared to the performance of the intellectual role and the flourishing of the intellectual mode of life. The world of the intellectuals was politically divided. They threw in their lot with one or other of the class opponents engaged in a bitter conflict for the power resources of the state. Each choice, however, was argued and legitimized in terms of the hope that the selected class would desire, and be able, to create or sustain a society comfortable for intellectual pursuits; a society which admits in practice the centrality of specifically intellectual domains (like culture and education) and the crucial role of ideas in the reproduction of communal life.

No historical agent seems today to answer this description. There is no historical focus for the hope that the world might be made safe and comfortable for intellectual work. It has perhaps been the awareness of this aspect of the new age which has found its somewhat sublimated expression in Touraine's 'disappearance of historical agent' or Habermas's 'legitimation crisis'. What both expressions convey is the deep-down realization that the ambitions which grounded the validity of the intellectual mode of life have failed. There is no would-be enlightened despot seeking the counsel of philosophers. There are only philosophers desperately trying to create communities, and sustain them with the power of their arguments alone. The only communities so far which were created in such a fashion and effectively sustained were their own.

10

Two nations, mark two: the seduced

For many years now, the 'Puritan' has occupied a disproportionally large place among intellectual preoccupations. Not the Puritan of the regicidal, iconoclastic and witch-hunting Roundheads; not the Puritan of the pious, God-fearing and superstitious New England exiles; nor any particular historical Puritan, for that matter. The object of intense intellectual attention has been a Puritan laboriously patched together, from the skilfully selected writings of sages and saints, around the design supplied by the model of modernity as the site of reason and rationality. Weber's moral tale armed the intellectuals with a most powerful aetiological myth of modernity. (The tale must have been flattering for the tycoons of capitalist industry: it presented their fortunes as an un-aimed for, unanticipated, side product of a saintly life, asceticism and the search for noble ends. But then it is not at all clear whether the tycoons cared about this sort of flattery and whether they counted among the avid readers of fairy tales.) The intellectuals, more than anyone else, liked Weber's tale immensely. In the myth of the Puritan, they immortalized a mirror reflection of themselves, of their unfulfilled though still vivid ambitions for that mastery over historicity for which they craved and sometimes – against odds – credited themselves with possessing.

Indeed, the notorious 'elective affinity' idea was not a product of the cool and detached scrutiny of empirical evidence, and no amount of historical research is likely to make it one. It was constructed retrospectively, from the vantage point of the 'iron cage' of a thoroughly rational world in which we allegedly lived or in which we would live tomorrow; it was this iron cage which served as a prototype for the 'light cloak' once lying on saintly shoulders. Not a

Calvin, nor a Baxter, nor a Franklin were the true heroes of Weber's myth, but precisely this 'elective affinity', the unbreakable link between the rational world and the passion for perfection, for a righteous life, for hard work, for the taming of instincts and emotions, for the delay of satisfaction, for a 'lifework of virtue', for control over both human body and fate. Weber's tale is not and never was an account of a historical event. As with all myths, it is placed outside historical time. It is the text of a mystery play which we all write and in which we are written, the scenario of an endless, but always complete, drama of modernity.

The 'capitalism' of the 'elective affinity' stood for the 'rationally organized society' (of which the 'rational pursuit of profit', Weber's tribute to the currently fashionable intellectual model of historicity, was just one, however central, aspect). The Puritan stood for this 'inner-directed', self-controlled man which the intellectuals, from the perspective of their own mode of life, construed as the central actor of a reason-guided society and the product of such a society. Between themselves, the Puritan and the 'rational pursuit of profit' represented the design, and the feasibility, of the intellectual project: their marriage gave sense, and confidence, to the intellectual thrust for the world made in their image. To paraphrase Voltaire – were there no Puritans, they would have to be invented.

It is perhaps a rule that the need for an aetiological and extra-temporal myth is felt most strongly when a particular type of social reality experiences the first prodromal symptoms of the approaching end. More probably still, the intensity with which the myth is recanted gathers force with the decline of this reality's 'obviousness' and self-confidence. Weber's tale had to wait to be rediscovered, properly appreciated and brought into the very centre of intellectual attention. The search for the Puritan, for his unique characteristic, for his formidable historical accomplishment, started in earnest when the thinkers pondering the direction their society had been taking first sensed, then loudly proclaimed that it had veered away from the original plan, that it was taking a wrong turn, that something of vital importance was missing or about to disappear. It was as if the Puritan grew more fascinating the more poignantly his absence was felt. Ostensibly, Weber constructed his modern version of the Promethean myth to explain the *origin* of modernity. Recently, the Puritan has mostly been examined to explain its *demise*.

It is not certain, to be sure, that a premonition of the imminent end to the world in which perfection took the shape of rationality (or of the futility of hope for such a world) did not play an important part in Weber's original decision to codify the precepts of the Puritan ethics. At the time when Weber was immersed in his study, the intellectual climate of Europe was already rife with prophecies of doom and warnings that the survival of a society built on reason and high cultural ideals is in question. The Puritan was not yet born, or the news of his birth had not yet reached the writers of the Apocalypse, but still – each one from his own starting-point – they all groped towards something uncannily similar to Weber's model; this yet unnamed Puritan stood behind the grandeur of modern civilization, while his withdrawal or eviction spelled the trouble to come.

And so Nietzsche bewailed his contemporaries' passion for the ephemeral and the momentary, their submission to the three plagues of the *Moment, Meinungen* (opinions) and *Moden* (fashions); the disintegration of their lives into a succession of fleeting experiences, excitements and titillations, without plan or design; their conspicuous lack of any capacity for long-term, purposeful effort or self-sacrifice in the name of worthy project (one would wish to say: the Puritan readiness to delay gratification).[1] Gustave leBon proclaimed the coming age as 'an era of the crowds', defining the crowd as a social setting in which individuality, defined in its turn as an ability for rational judgement, is effaced. The rule of the crowd is the end of civilization, as all civilized life must be grounded in moral forces, assuring a drive towards self-perfection and a life of reason.[2] Civilization is made out of a certain mental constitution and has its foundation in the characters of its people.[3] The popular mentality, which now takes over from the rational one, is prominent for its credulity, naïvety, submission to the guidance of others and incapacity for self-control or self-monitored action (one would wish to say: the popular mentality, in the ascendancy, has lost the Puritan qualities).[4] Ortega y Gasset's dystopia appeared somewhat later, but it only sharpened up the hunches and insights of his numerous predecessors; and, above all, it had become an instant classic and inflamed the European imagination well before Weber's tale was brought back into the limelight. The diagnosis of imminent doom was focused in Ortega on our existence 'from hand to mouth', our craving for a life exempt from all restrictions, our psychology 'of a spoilt child', our satisfaction with what we are and unwillingness to make it better, while a truly noble life must be 'synonymous with a life of effort' (one would wish to say: what is missing in us is precisely the Puritan thrust for self-constraint and self-perfection).[5]

There were many Virgils and Ovids who anticipated the Gospel. The Gospel gave a name and focus to this something they sought and tried to pinpoint: the Puritan, the maker of a world ruled by reason, and subsequently its anticipated product; a product which, however, failed to materialize.

Not all the writers who explore the legacy of the Puritan have only unqualified praise for this evasive herald of modernity. Richard Sennett is perhaps a most conspicuous example of an analyst who decodes the ills of jaded modernity as the posthumous vengeance of the Puritan, as the surfacing of the 'most corrosive' aspects of the Puritan personality: an excessive concern with self-authentication, a righteous life, self-denial, 'inwardness' resulting in contemporary narcissism, an obsession with self, dissipation of the ability to play a role or lead public life, the degeneration of privacy into intimacy, of sociality into an endless game oriented towards self-enhancement.[6] This devastating critique of the historical transmogrification of the Protestant ethic, though exposing the unsuspected dangers intrinsic to the hero as painted by Weber, does not necessarily deny the value of the Puritan in his idealized form. It only declares its unreality.

The dominant tune is one of opposition: the Puritan has passed away or is about to pass on, and a totally different personality has taken his place. A personality all the more odious as it is directly opposite to the one *les philosophes* dreamed of shaping, and one singularly unreceptive to the kind of services the descendants of *les philosophes* have the skills, and feel destined, to offer.

In what has been arguably the most passionate assertion of the demise of the Puritan and its dire consequences, John Carroll announces the advent of a 'remissive culture', producing, and pro-duced by, the 'remissive personality'.

> The remissive culture is prescriptively anti-moralist. In a moralist culture, like the Puritan, conflicts are resolved between society's demands and an individual's desire by the enforcement of prohib-itions; undisputed norms governing the conduct act as palliatives for panic and despair. The remissive-hedonist's one conscious norm is to be anti-Puritan, to abide by a symbolic of anarchist moral demands – slack commands to disregard norms – to doubt all inherited values,

to deny the primacy of any particular organization and personality. This state is one of 'permanent cultural revolution', with the proviso that too vigorous an assault on the old structures of order is neurotic, symptomatic of taking those orders too seriously, not being adequately emancipated from them . . .

But this anarchism represents the remissive's view of himself rather than any reality. A remissive style is necessarily normative, approving of spontaneity, intimacy, hedonist release, emotional openness, disapproving of authority and control, reproachful of the stance of reproach . . .

At the moral level, remission represents forgiveness of all sins; at the institutional level, release from all controls . . . Objective grounds for guilt are being abolished; no one and nothing is to blame, the only responsibility borne by the individual is that he choose his pleasures successfully.

Carroll's 'remissive man' is an exact opposite and in no way a progeny, legitimate or not, of the Puritan: '[E]conomic man was renunciative, anally-retentive and Puritan, whereas remissive man is appetitive, orally-indulgent and in many ways Catholic.' The Puritan's '[i]nner authority depends on commitment to a constraining structure of self, and in turn the primacy of ethos; but, for remissive-hedonist man, ego in this sense finally reveals itself as a cage, serving no purpose but to limit his pleasures.' And, to sum it all up, '[t]he pursuit of beauty, and in particular the quest for an image of perfection, bears the lineaments of Puritanism . . . Entertainment, by contrast, serves entirely as a means of release.'[7]

In Carroll's trenchant, deliberately exaggerated and provocative juxtaposition, the meaning of the 'death of the Puritan' flurry is revealed: the Puritan serves as a shorthand for the acceptance of constraint and supra-individual authority, for the willing effort to repress emotional drives and subordinate them to the precepts of reason, for the belief in an ideal of perfection and objective grounds of moral, aesthetic and social superiority, for self-restraint and self-improvement. In other words, the Puritan – of the 'death of the Puritan' debate – stands as the denizen of the selfsame world that the intellectuals of the Enlightenment set about constructing. He stands, simultaneously, for the society ruled by Reason and imposing constraints in its name, and its anticipated products – men who have interiorized its rules and serve as collaborating hosts to the 'garrisons in the conquered cities'. 'Death of the Puritan' stands for the feeling that such hopes have been irretrievably dashed. What seems now, in retrospect, to have been the 'project' of modernity, clearly has not worked. Neither culture as a whole, nor its individual members, seem to be amenable any more (if they ever were) to the kind of civilizing treatment *les philosophes* braced themselves for, and their heirs trained themselves to accomplish. With no bridge to the reality of daily life, with no hold on the bodies or spirits of ordinary men and women, the legislative ambitions bequeathed by *les philosophes* and institutionalized as the collective constitutive memory of the intellectuals seem to be hopelessly enclosed in the ivory tower of theory and ineffective criticism; at best, they may now serve as a formula for one among many (however noble and however richly gratifying) specialized and compartmentalized intellectual activities; an activity which has only its own continuation as its purpose.

The hopes were once, indeed, breath-taking. The enlightened, the learned, the intellectual believed they had something of great importance to offer to ailing and *waiting* humanity; they believed that humanities, once passed over and absorbed, would humanize; that they would reshape the life of humans, their relations, their society. Culture, the collective product and cherished possession of the intellectuals, was seen as the only chance humanity had to stave off the combined dangers of social anarchy, individual selfishness and the one-sided, maiming and disfiguring development of the self. Culture was to be a guided, but enthusiastically and universally shared, effort to reach perfection. No one expressed this hope more poignantly than Matthew Arnold:

Culture, which is the study of perfection, leads us . . . to conceive of true human perfection as a *harmonious* perfection, developing all sides of our humanity; and as a *general* perfection, developing all parts of our society . . . The idea of perfection as an *inward* condition of the mind and spirit is at variance with the mechanical and material civilization in esteem with us . . . The idea of perfection as a *general* expansion of the human family is at variance with our strong individualism, our hatred of all limits to the unrestrained swing of the individual's personality, our maxim of 'every man for himself'. Above all the idea of perfection as a *harmonious* expression of human nature is at variance with our want of flexibility, with our inaptitude for seeing more than one side of a thing, with our intense energetic absorption in the particular pursuit we happen to be following . . .

Culture indefatigably tries not to make what each raw person may like, the rule by which he fashions himself; but to draw ever nearer to a sense of what is indeed beautiful, graceful, and becoming, and to get the raw person to like that.[8]

Nowhere did Arnold spell out the rules by which one can recognize what is 'indeed' beautiful, graceful and becoming. It does not prevent his manifesto exuding an air of certainty and self-confidence. Arnold *knew*, knew for sure, what is beautiful and becoming, what is 'sweetness and light'; and he knew for sure that given the chance, everybody would have to agree with him. This self-confidence was not based on a methodical convention; it was not grounded in institutional agreement about the procedural rules. Arnold's certainty drew its strength from the firmest of possible foundations – the undisputed hierarchy of values, standing for an undisputed hierarchy of authority. What people perched on the pinnacle of civilization *saw* as graceful and deserving, was *indeed* graceful and deserving. There were no other yardsticks with which to measure beauty and worthiness.

One can see George Steiner's two essays entitled 'In a postculture' as, in more than one sense, Arnold's *Culture and Anarchy* revisited.[9] Not to know what we know today, Steiner says, was Arnold's or Voltaire's privilege; ignorance gave confidence. We know, what they did not: that humanities do not humanize – or at least not necessarily. From the heights of what legitimately passed at the time for the peak of civilization, it seemed obvious that there was a pre-ordained 'congruence between the cultivation of the individual mind through formal knowledge and a melioration of the commending qualities of life'. It does not seem obvious at all to us; worse still, we would find it very difficult to make a case for something being a 'melioration', as we have abandoned the axiom of progress, lost the technique of 'forward dreaming', stopped being 'animated by ontological utopia' and have with all that lost the ability to tell 'the better' from 'the worse'. Our time has brought an end to the agreed (one would rather say: the dominating) hierarchic value structure and a rejection of all the 'binary cuts which represented the domination of the cultural over the natural code', like the cuts between West and the rest, learned and untutored, upper and lower strata. The superiority of Western culture no longer seems self-evident; with this, we have lost the 'confident centre', without which there is no culture. Ours, indeed, is the time of 'post-culture'. Culture, Steiner insists, must be elitist and evaluating. With these two traits in dispute and under attack, the future of our civilization is 'almost unforeseeable'. One is tempted to sum up: Arnold's dichotomy was apt, the choice always was between culture and anarchy. But Arnold did not know which way the choice would be made.

Not all sociologists studying modern culture would go all the way with Steiner's apocalyptic forebodings, but most would agree with the substance of his diagnosis: the once uncontested hierarchy of cultural values has crumbled, and the most conspicuous feature of Western culture today is an absence of grounds on which authoritative judgements of value can be made. Naturally, sociologists are interested in the social processes which have led to such an outcome. Why did the thrust of the Enlightenment stop far short of the 'general' and 'harmonious' perfection of society and its members? Why did the hoped for congruence between formal knowledge and commending qualities of life fail to materialize? What went wrong? Did it have to go wrong?

One of the most common answers to such questions is the self-propelling and unstoppable splitting of human knowledge into a plethora of narrowly circumscribed, partial, only loosely connected specialisms. The topic is debated widely and incessantly, but the seminal formulation of the link between the fate of culture and the development of technology and sciences guided solely by the logic of the tools and productive capacities they had brought into being, offered by Georg Simmel more than 70 years ago, remains unsurpassed. Simmel's is a modern version of the sorcerer's apprentice story: tools emancipated from the human purposes they originally served, become their own purposes, dictating the pace and the direction of their own movement.

What drives forth the products of the spirit is the cultural and not the natural scientific logic of the objects. Herein lies the fatefully immanent drive of all technology, as soon as it has moved beyond the range of immediate consumption. Thus the industrial production of a variety of products generates a series of closely related by-products for which, properly speaking, there is no need. It is only the compulsion for full utilization of the created equipment that calls for it. The technological process demands that it be completed by links which are not required by the psychic process. The vast supplies of products come into existence which call forth an artificial demand that is senseless from the perspective of the subject's culture. In several branches of the sciences it is no different. On one hand, for example, philological techniques have developed to an unsurpassable finesse and methodological precision. On the other hand, the study of subject matter which could be of genuine interest to intellectual culture does not replenish itself as quickly. Thus, the philological effort frequently turns into micrology, pedantic efforts, and an elaboration of the unessential into a method that runs on for its own sake, an extension of substantive norms whose independent path no longer coincides with that of culture as a completion of life . . .

There is no reason why it should not be multiplied in the direction of the infinite, why not book should be added to book, work of art to work of art, or invention to invention. The form of objectivity as such possesses a boundless capacity for fulfillment. This voracious capacity for accumulation is most deeply incompatible with the forms of personal life.[10]

'The tragedy of culture', for Simmel, consists in the fact that science, technology, arts, all spawned by the thrust of the human spirit towards melioration and perfection, become increasingly irrelevant to their creator and their initial purpose, and this because of their very success. Humanities do not humanize, because their ramified, profuse and thriving offsprings ceased to be 'humanities' in the first place. 'The Creator' does not recognize himself any more in his creations. They appear to him as strange, objective beings, threatening, by their unfamiliarity and their 'outsidedness', the Creator's realm of control.

To put it in a different way, Simmel's vision is one of the progressive 'tapering' of the location where the civilizing intentions of the Enlightenment may retain their impetus. 'The intellectual' becomes now a concept which separates the carriers of culture not just from the untutored, ignorant, primitive or otherwise uncultured, but also from many a scientist, technician and artist. No wonder Simmel toyed with the idea of the intellectual as a stranger – a stranger in a world saturated with science, technology and arts. In such a world, the intellectual, in his traditional role of a cultural legislator, must be a tragic, homeless wanderer. His tragedy is exacerbated by the realization that no one of the many specialized enclaves of Reason is likely to welcome him back as its wrongfully neglected leader; most will not remember him even as their venerable – if out-of-date – ancestor. No one needs his guidance any more – except for a few other strangers like himself.

The sorcerer's apprentice's feeling of having lost control over his own product and heritage can perhaps be traced back to the fact that the discourses of truth, judgement and taste, which seemed to be fully administered by intellectuals (and in which only the intellectuals were the rightful participants), are now controlled by forces over which the intellectuals, the meta-specialists in the validation of truth, judgement and taste, have little, if any, control. Control has been taken over by other forces – by autonomous institutions of specialized research and learning, needing no validation but that constantly replenished by their own, institutionally supported procedural rules, or by equally autonomous institutions of commodity production, needing no validation other than the productive potential of their own technology. And over this institutionally fragmented world towers the new validating meta-authority: the market, with price and 'effective demand' holding the power of distinguishing between true and false, good and bad, beautiful and ugly.

Simmel's and Steiner's were arguably the most valliant, yet rearguard battles fought by the already defeated intellectual legislator. Other rearguard skirmishes were staged by the theorists of 'mass culture', horrified by the trends in which their successors – reconciled to the post-modern condition – would rejoice. In those other skirmishes the market became the prime target. It has been accused of unlawfully appropriating the right to decide on those matters on which only the cultural elite was a trustworthy judge. Having subordinated validation of culture to the practical judgement of quantifiable demand, the market reduced the cultural elite to one of the many 'taste interest groups' vying with each other for the benevolent attention of the consumer. Ostentatiously and self-consciously minority bound, always deriving a sense of its own superior value from its inaccessibility to the ordinary people, the 'high-culture' taste was singularly ill-prepared for such a competition and was bound to fare badly. It could not, therefore, accept the legitimacy of a court where the market sat as the presiding judge and the jury at the same time.

In a different context, David Joravsky once wrote on the 'dependence of intellectual freedom on the modern politicians' disdainful indifference to the world of the intellect'.[11] We have already discussed the seminal change in the foundations of the state power that followed the development of the panoptic techniques of control and increasing capillarization of social power; developments that led to the gradual displacement of ideological legitimations and in the end of rendering them virtually irrelevant to the reproduction of systemic integration. Seen from the opposite side, the same process may be described as a gradual emancipation of intellectual work from the political constraints of the state; freedom and irrelevance being only too closely related to each other. Their closeness prevents the intellectuals from viewing the process with untainted satisfaction; or, rather, it leads to a deep split among the once unified (in self-definition, if not in praxis) educated elite. The many-faceted specialisms noted by Simmel enjoy their freedom and make the best out of their localized, partial relevance and spatially and functionally limited control. The hard core of the educated elite, continuing the meta-discourse of modernity, concerned with the traditional problematics of truth, judgement and taste and with the traditional task of validity legislation, knows of only one relevance: global in scale and political in function. This having been withdrawn, the meta-intellectual must feel himself dispossessed. It is the irrelevance side of the deal, rather than the associated freedom, that he feels most strongly.

Joravsky's comment has a wider bearing; it applies to the sphere of culture as a whole. Here, as in the field of the 'legitimation discourse', irrelevance spawns freedom. The advent of the modern state with its interest in extirpating local differentiation, the autonomous and self-propelling, community-based ways of life, and replacing them with a unified, society-wide pattern of discipline, needed a cultural crusade for its completion. The organizing ambitions of the 'gardening' state harmonized well with the globalizing ambition of intellectual proselytism. The politics of the state and the civilizing effort of the intellectuals seemed to work in the same direction, to feed and reinforce each other – and to depend on each other for their success. As in the case of the legitimating discourse, however, the modern state became progressively less dependent on the uniformizing sweep of cultural crusades. With its panoptic techniques fully deployed, the state thrives on bureaucratic divisions, separations, classifications. 'Où sont les croisades d'autant?' Why should the politicians need them? The educated elite has retained, to be sure, its superior social status; but the values it boasted to guard, and showed as the evidence of its collective importance, have lost their political relevance, and hence the obviousness of their superiority.

Freed of its legitimizing burden, culture could be – and has been – deployed in a new integrating role. Freedom emanating from the systemic irrelevance of culture has brought little benefit to the educated elite with its value-legislating ambitions. It was not they who moved into the place vacated by the politicians. Deprived of political support, efforts to launch further cultural crusades must have looked increasingly fanciful as ideas and farcical as practices. Much to the horror of the cultural legislators, the emancipation of culture from state control proved to be, inextricably, the emancipation of culture from their own power. Redundant in the realm of systemic integration, culture moved into the sphere of social integration, where it found itself in the company of all other, plentiful and minute, capillary powers and shared their lack of focus, diversity and diffuseness.

From the point of view of cultural history, this was not, however, a return to the original sphere which culture inhabited before being deployed – in early modern times – in the service of the systemic integration of the modern state. The sphere, functionally similar to its pre-modern equivalent, has assumed a post-modern institutional shape of a very different character and consequence. Communal bases of localized powers have been effectively destroyed in the course of the long march of the modern state; they were not available when culture, made redundant in systemic reproduction, returned to the subsystemic, social level. Other bases of localized power have, however, been waiting – and soon made culture the object of their administration. Those bases were located in the institutional network of the market; culture became a marketable commodity, subject like other commodities to the supreme court where profits and effective demand sat as the judges.

It was the realization that the political freedom of culture brings about the powerlessness of cultural legislators, that stood behind the outraged condemnations of the theorists of 'mass culture'. Dwight Macdonald alerted his readers to the dangers immanent in the new situation: 'There is slowly emerging a tepid, flaccid Middle-brow Culture that threatens to engulf everything in its spreading ooze.' Perceptively, Macdonald located the roots of the frightening tendency in the very lack of discrimination which inevitably accompanies freedom and democracy: 'Mass Culture is very, very democratic: it absolutely refuses to discriminate against, or between, anything or anybody.' What must have seemed most abhorrent, of course, was the fact that the lack of discrimination meant in practice the downgrading of 'high culture', putting it on an equal footing with all other cultural choices, and the refusal to listen seriously to its priests' validating verdicts. Macdonald made no bones that his rage was directed against those who, under the cover of freedom, made (and 'imposed') choices, thereby flying in the face of the prerogatives only the cultural elite could claim of right – not against the 'people' who accept (or are 'forced' to accept) these choices. He went out of his way to distinguish sharply between the 'mass', the helpless victim of the violence of cultural manipulators, and true 'people', whom the cultural manipulators had destroyed as autonomous carriers of culture. Mass culture, Macdonald would stress over and over again, is not another version of 'Folk culture' ('A folk or a people . . . is a community, i.e., a group of individuals linked to each other by common interest, work, traditions, values and sentiments'), but 'an expression of *masses*, a very different thing'.[12] Macdonald conveniently forgot the role of intellectuals in the very destruction of 'folk culture' and the communities in which it used to be embedded. Exempt from elitist cultural control, the descendants of the yesterday ignorant, superstitious primitives, suddenly became the carriers of value to be defended against 'mediocre' culture in a way they were never defended against the encroachments of the elitist *Kulturträgers* and educators. On the 'special relationship' between the intellectuals and the 'raw', culturally uninitiated, 'ordinary' people, Pierre Bourdieu commented that the artist

> prefers naivety to 'pretentiousness'. The essential merit of the 'common people' is that they have none of the pretentions to art (or power) which inspire the ambitions of the 'petit-bourgeois'. Their indifference tacitly acknowledges the monopoly. That is why, in the mythology of artists and intellectuals, whose outflanking and double-negating strategies sometimes lead them back to 'popular' tastes and opinions, the 'people' so often play a role not unlike that of the peasantry in the conservative ideologies of the declining aristocracy.[13]

In this otherwise perceptive and well-pointed observation, Bourdieu fails to note the true import of the comparison: it was the *declining* aristocracy that idealized 'the peasant'; it is the *declining* 'cultural legislators' that idealize 'the people'. The hunters of yesterday defend 'the people', their legitimate cultural game, against the poachers.

As to the content of mass culture criticism – we find here the same themes we have discovered in the 'death of the Puritan' discourse; only this time they are organized around the notion of culture, now as before understood as the teaching process, as 'doing something to somebody'. As in the case of reciprocal validations of the concept of 'good artist' and 'good art', so in the mass culture criticism the ideas of 'doing wrong things' and 'those who do such things are wrong persons' mutually validate each other. Condemnation of contemporary (non-intellectual) culture administrators needs a proof that their products are of inferior quality; but the inferiority of the products cannot be proved but by invoking the lack of credentials of those who vouch for their quality.

Thus mass culture is accused, first and foremost, of promoting the cult of effortlessness. Macdonald's middle-brow culture was 'tepid and flaccid' mostly because it was limited to things easily understandable and rejected things which demanded of their consumer hard work and expert training. Supreme effort to reach the mysterious and the truly worthy was always an indispensable part of the intellectuals' self-legitimating mythology (see chapter 1). The supposition that one can be 'cultivated' without effort, sacrifice and suffering, cuts at the very roots of intellectual superiority. 'If education and cultivation are gradual, progressive, orderly processes', wrote Bernard Rosenberg, 'then popular culture is its opposite. For what makes mass culture so tantalising is the implication of effortlessness.'[14] The effects have been summed up by Ernest van den Haag: 'Culture becomes largely spectator sport.'[15]

The Rosenberg and White volume and the mass culture debate it triggered off in the 1950s and 1960s were perhaps the parting shots in the history of the 'declining aristocracy' of spirit. C. W. Mills wrote at the same time that the mass communication media should be withdrawn from the control of market forces and repossessed by the intellectuals to whom they rightfully belonged. It still seemed at that time that the direction culture took once it had been disentangled from its old legitimizing function within the system could be reverted; that the legislating role could be restored to the hard core of intellectual elite, the latter-day descendants of *les philosophes*. Such hopes progressively faded over the years, and with them the mass culture debate petered out. The hopes, and the debate, could continue as long as the irreversible political irrelevance of the cultural–artistic sphere inside the late-modern state remained overlooked. And overlooked it was – both by detractors and the few admirers of mass culture. Among the second category Edward Shils saw in the new phenomenon of 'mass society' a truly praiseworthy development: bringing the masses, previously condemned to the 'periphery', closer to the 'centre' of society, that is, its central institutions and central value systems.[16] Like the critics of mass culture, Shils saw culture in its old and already lost function. Contrary to his opinion, 'central institutions' reached indeed the 'periphery' better than before (though through their panoptic tentacles rather than any missionary outposts), but 'central value systems' remained the concern of the intellectuals alone, as they lost their usefulness, and hence their significance, to anybody else.

In more recent years it has become increasingly clear that the absorption of culture by market forces has reached the point of no return. Accordingly, the focus of cultural debate has been slowly but clearly shifting. One hears less of the revindication claims of the high culture spokesmen; expectedly, with the claims less and less realistic, the horrified accounts of the morbid and degrading impact of market-distributed cultural goods give way slowly to more sober and detached studies of diverse 'taste systems', consumer choices, cultural fashions and the institutional network backing all this. The theory of post-modernist culture is a culmination of this trend. In it, the legislative role of the intellectuals is finally discarded and the outlines of the new role, that of the interpreter, are gradually put together.

The changes of the last couple of decades can perhaps be ascribed to the discovery of the self-perpetuating and self-reproducing mechanism of what has now become known as consumer culture. This mechanism has been by now widely described and there is no need here for its detailed analysis. We can confine ourselves to an inventory of some of its major points.

Arguably the most important point is the ability of the consumer market to make the consumer dependent on itself. In Wolfgang Fritz Haug's apt formulation, '[f]irst new commodities make the necessary chores that much easier, and then the chores become too difficult to do unaided . . . The private car, together with the running down of public transport, carves up the towns no less effectively than saturation bombing, and creates distances that can no longer be crossed without a car.'[17] The first sentence is true because of the destruction of skills which the introduction of new products brings in its wake; the second is true because of the restructuring of the environment which the acceptance of the new product requires. In both cases, new commodities make themselves indispensable; they create their own necessity – which sometimes has been expressed by the analysts as the ability of the market to create 'artificial' needs (it would be much better to express the phenomenon in terms of the capacity of the market to render new needs practically indistinguishable from the 'natural' ones; given the plan of most contemporary American cities, and the contemporary space relation between residence, work and leisure, it would be futile indeed to argue that the need for a car, or any other vehicle of personal mobility, is an 'artificial', or worse still – a 'false' need).

Market dependence also arises from the progressive destruction of social skills – the ability and willingness of men and women to enter social relations, maintain them, and repair them in case of conflicts. Richard Sennett's penetrating analysis of the transformation of 'privacy' into 'intimacy', and 'eroticism' into 'sexuality' is well known; the transformation leads, in Sennett's view, to the establishment of a 'destructive *Gemeinschaft*' – the kind of setting in which the creation of stable relations, complete with rights and obligations, is avoided for lack of social skills in the participants; in which 'the other' serves solely as a tool in the never-ending (because lacking in definable purpose) struggle for individual authenticity; and in which the accumulation of social skill is impossible because of the brittleness and fragility of all temporary and 'until further notice' interhuman bonds. This is the 'social void' easily filled by the market. Unable to cope with the challenges and problems arising from their mutual relations, men and women turn to marketable goods, services and expert counsel; they need factory-produced tools to imbue their bodies with socially meaningful 'personalities', medical or psychiatric advice to heal the wounds left by previous – and future – defeats, travel services to escape into unfamiliar settings which it is hoped will provide better surroundings for the solution of familiar problems, or simply factory-produced noise (literal and metaphorical) to 'suspend' social time and eliminate the need to negotiate social relations.

Dependence on marketable goods and services generated by the absence of social skills quickly turns into market dependency. Goods and services introduce themselves as the solutions to genuine human problems: a liquid softener as a cure for the lack of attention of the family to the not-that-young-and-attractive-any-more wife and mother; a new brand of perfume as a means of attracting the services of the opposite sex without really trying ('on impulse'); a new brand of wine to make the party guests well disposed and interesting to each other. The cumulative effect is the conviction that for every human problem there is a solution waiting somewhere in the shop, and that the one skill men and women need more than anything else is the ability to find it. This conviction makes consumers still more attentive to the goods and their promises, so that dependency may perpetuate and deepen. Shopping becomes the skill to deputize for all other skills, redundant or extinct.

Since the goods promise more than they can deliver, and consumers are bound to discover sooner or later the lack of correspondence between the ostensible and the genuine use–value of each individual product, conviction must be galvanized continuously by 'new' and 'improved' promises and their material embodiments. Hence the well-described phenomenon of 'in-built obsolescence' – first thought to be of a physical, technological nature, but now seen above all as the function of the 'crowding out' technique of marketing. The role of new products consists mainly in outdating the products of yesterday; together with 'old' goods disappears the memory of their unfulfilled promises. Hope is never fully frustrated; it is held instead in a state of continuous excitement, with interest always on the move, shifting to ever new objects. Jean Baudrillard said of fashion that it 'embodies a compromise between the need to innovate and the other need to change nothing in the fundamental order'.[18] We would rather shift the emphasis: fashion seems to be the mechanism through which the 'fundamental order' (market dependency) is maintained by a never ending chain of innovations; the very perpetuity of innovations renders their individual (and inevitable) failures irrelevant and harmless to the order.

Consumers depend on the market not only for coping with the problems they would handle with their own technical and social skills and abilities of forward dreaming if only they possessed them; consumers also need the market as the foundation of their certainty and self-confidence. With the skill of shopping paramount, the certainty which counts most and promises to compensate for all other (absent) certainties, is one related to buying choices. Fashion, supported by the statistics of other people's choices, offers such certainty; one buys 'Whiskas' with less fear of personal inadequacy once one knows that out of ten cats six prefer it to all other food. The pride of being 'rational' in goods selection (if only in the sense of going with the majority) fills the place left vacant by the absent, and no longer available, gratifying self-assessment based on the display of technical or social skills. The housewife may now boast the wisdom of buying the right washing powder instead of priding herself on the excellence of her laundry skills.

Market dependency has been exacerbated by the colonization of a growing volume of needs. Among such needs, one can include the need for a life-project; this is now organized around a time series of intended purchases. Or the need for entertainment; on top of the ever growing quantity of toys and time-killers the market offers, it offers itself as supreme entertainment. Shopping means not only acting in order to satisfy one's craving for lost skills, certainty, purpose of life; it is also excellent fun, an inexhaustible treasury of sensual stimuli, and – being shared by everybody else – the ultimate social occasion. It provides as well the contemporary equivalent of adventure, exploration of exotic lands, exposing oneself to mild titillating dangers, the displaying of prowess and risk-taking.

Supported by the market as the pivotal institution of contemporary Western society – an institution which renders its own position unassailable through its ability to produce and reproduce a total dependency on itself – 'consumer culture' becomes, in most analysts' view, an irremoveable attribute of our times. Consumer culture is a culture of men and women integrated into society as, above all, consumers. Features of the consumer culture explicable solely in terms of the logic of the market, where they originate, spill over all other aspects of contemporary life – if there are any other aspects, unaffected by market mechanism, left. Thus every item of culture becomes a commodity and becomes subordinated to the logic of the market either through a direct, economic mechanism or an indirect, psychological one. All perceptions and expectations, as well as life-rhythm, qualities of memory, attention, motivational and topical relevances are trained and moulded inside the new 'foundational' institution – that of the market. According to the same analysts, one needs therefore to refer to that market logic to understand contemporary art or politics.

Consumer culture creates its own, self-sustained and self-sufficient world, complete with its own heroes and pace-setters

- people in the limelight, brought there by selling many tapes, breaking box-office records, winning in the pools, guessing the 'right price' of a currently fashionable commodity, and otherwise excelling in consumer virtues, untainted by embarrassing memories of puritan hard work and self-denial. This world is densely populated – heroes replace each other with lightning speed, to stave off all chances of disenchantment, with a few 'supergreats' kept in the audience memory to embody the timelessness and continuity of the consumer way of life. The crowded world of consumer heroes leaves little room for all the others; in a news broadcast, time devoted to sport, entertainment and 'people' (a considerably expanded 'gossip column') occupies most of the space and draws most of the viewer's or reader's attention. Tightly squeezed by the consumer heroes, politicians must behave like them – or perish. Political information must be served in a way to which the consumer market has prepared the audience: 'news' is mostly a tool of forgetting, a way of crowding out yesterday's headlines from the audience consciousness. The result is a narrative equivalent of Stockhausen's score: a chain of items subject to no syntagmatic order, with no determination of later information by the preceding one, and hence a complete randomness of succession; structures of expectations are not allowed to gel and thus the freedom of the composer remains unfettered.

It is obvious that within the context of consumer culture no room has been left for the intellectual as legislator. In the market, there is no one centre of power, nor any aspiration to create one (the alternative would be a political 'dictatorship over needs', an equally unattractive proposition for the intellectuals with legislative ambitions). There is no site from which authoritative pronouncements could be made, and no power resources concentrated and exclusive enough to serve as the levers of a massive proselytizing campaign. With that, the traditional, real or hoped for, means of 'intellectual legislation' are absent. Intellectuals (like anybody else) have no control over market forces and cannot realistically expect to acquire any. Consumer culture means a kind of society very different from one where the tradition of *les philosophes*, the historical foundation of the living memory of intellectual legislation, was born and to which it was geared.

One of the most profound analysts of culture in its consumer phase, Pierre Bourdieu, suggests that the enthronement of the latter means a substantive change in the mode of domination central to social integration. The new mode of domination distinguishes itself

by the substitution of seduction for repression, public relations
for policing, advertising for authority, needs-creation for norm-
imposition. What ties individuals to society today is their activity
as consumers, their life organized around consumption. Individuals
do not need, therefore, to be repressed in their natural drives and
tendency to subordinate their behaviour to the pleasure principle;
they do not need to be invigilated and policed. (This function has
been taken over by the market – through making information technology the object of private consumption, a 'surveilling' society has
been replaced, as Jacques Attali suggests, by an 'auto-surveillance'
society.)[19] Individuals willingly submit to the prestige of advertising,
and thus need no 'legitimation' beliefs. Their conduct is made
manageable, predictable and hence non-threatening, by a multiplication of needs rather than by a tightening of norms.

Bourdieu's concept is a product of a curiously narrowed vision;
one which leaves out a considerable part of contemporary society,
and, for all we know, an indispensable, unavoidable and irreducible
part of it. This part may be easily overlooked, to be sure, in model-
ling a theory of society dominated by the market, as it is precisely the
domination of the market which makes it irrelevant, marginal, and
theoretically 'alien', 'residual' or 'not-yet-eliminated' (much in the
same way as the capital-centred social theory treated the 'non-
capitalist' forms of life, the Enlightenment-originated theory treated
the 'uneducated', or the state-centred theory of communism viewed
'non-socialist' aspects of human character). However, this other
part of society, which does not fit Bourdieu's description, is as equally
inevitably produced by the market as the one which does. It constitutes the 'other side of the coin', the other pole of the magnet. The
two parts can exist only together – and only together can they be
eliminated. As one can read out from Bourdieu's own analysis,
seduction is so tremendously effective because repression is its alternative; and '[w]hat the competitive struggle makes everlasting is not
different conditions, but the difference between conditions'.[20] The
difference between conditions is one between freedom and necessity,
each deriving its meaning from the presence of the other. And
money is what makes the difference. The market is a democratic
institution; it is open to everybody, like the Ritz Hotel. It does not
require internal passports or special permits. The only thing men
and women need to enter it is money. Without this thing, however,
they must remain outside – and there they find a world of an entirely

different character. What makes money so terribly attractive and prompts people to try so hard to obtain it, is exactly the possibility of buying one's way out of this second world. Against that world, the market economy glitters as the kingdom of freedom, and the embodiment of liberation.

More than a century ago, Disraeli made one of the most memorable statements of modern times: 'I was told that the Privileged and the People formed Two Nations.'

What Disraeli meant, one would guess, was two nations of employers and employees, the exploiters and the exploited. Our society consists again of two nations. Only ours are nations of the seduced and the repressed; of those free to follow their needs and those forced to comply with the norms. Without the second of the two nations, the picture of the post-modern world is fatally incomplete.

11

Two nations, mark two: the repressed

Lev Trotsky once remarked of the Russian 'intelligentsia', '[d]eprived of any independent significance in social production, small in numbers, economically dependent, . . . rightly conscious of its own powerlessness, [it] keeps looking for a massive social class upon which it can lean'.[1] Looking for a massive class was arguably keener and more intense in Russia than in any Western European country, and hence easier to observe. The way the Russian intellectual circles had been brought into being in the course of the nineteenth century (see the excellent analysis of Robert J. Brym),[2] a century after the patterns for the intellectual mission had already been firmly set in the West, left but the tiniest of room for any hope of transforming the Tsars into enlightened despots, and the state they ruled into an organizational framework for the progress of Reason. No wonder the Russian intelligentsia had to be radical in order to remain faithful to the role it assumed; no wonder it looked around for a 'massive class' likely to be, by its nature, more inclined to create the setting the intellectuals needed to carry out their mission.

The unique circumstances of Russia only sharpened, however, a situation of a much wider import. What united the intellectuals throughout the modern history of Europe, in Russia as much as elsewhere, was the urge for the rational organization of the social world, and an image of the end-product of such an organization as a kind of a permanent 'teach-in' session; as was to be expected, intellectuals moulded the vision of the ideal society out of their own collective mode of life, and, equally to be expected, one attribute they never failed to ascribe to such an ideal was the high authority accorded to Reason and its spokesmen. The extant types of societies tended to be evaluated from the same point of view; they were judged by the degree of approximation to the kingdom of Reason model, and by the likelihood that they would advance, on their own, to a full implementation of such a model.

This was the element of unity; all the rest divided the intellectuals into mutually hostile camps, often engaged in a war more bitter and unscrupulous than the enmity manifested against any other part of society or social category. Among the most divisive factors were the strategies that various sections of the intellectual stratum proposed to employ in the effort to promote the rationalization of their society; and the powers they proposed to enlist to carry out the task. We have seen above (in chapters 3 and 4) that the task itself had been first conceived in the context of the ascendant absolutist monarchy, and its demand for the techniques of social administration on a scale never known before. It was only natural that the enlightened despot, and his virtually unlimited potential to change social reality by decree, emerged as the obvious power and strategy. He could not, however, last long in this role. The Russian Catherine or the Prussian Frederick were not exactly what the Voltaires, Diderots, D'Alemberts or Rousseaus of this early optimist era hoped them to be, or to become. None of the descendants of Louis XIV shone as brightly in the philosophers' sky as the 'Sun King', the unforgettable protector of arts and science.

From then on, the intellectuals were to remain divided. First of all, the process of 'hiving off' gathered in force: areas of interest and inquiry branching out from the common stem developed an ever growing distance from the original rationalization project. Various specialized offsprings of *les philosophes* colonized, or constructed areas within society which they controlled to their satisfaction, or inside which they enjoyed a high degree of autonomy – all this becoming only obliquely and tenuously related to the fate of the original project. The other effect of this process was the progressive tapering of the hard core of general intellectuals, still bent on performing a role which inevitably brought them in touch, or in conflict, with the political powers of the state. There is a widespread consensus among sociologists that the two sides of the process have been inversely related in their intensity. The more successful were partial intellectuals, the more welcoming and absorptive were their specialized enclaves for the successive newcomers to the ranks of the educated elite. The less prominent was the presence of the general intellectuals, the less pronounced was their involvement in conflict politics (and, of course, vice versa). Bearing this in mind, let us concentrate, however, on whatever remained of the general intellectuals, the guardians and practitioners of the patterns preserved in the collective memory of the hopes, accomplishments and frustrations of the Age of Reason. It is their own internal divisions which will interest us here.

There is one feature common to all classes and strata of modern society. Their collective portraits are always painted by the same artists: the intellectuals. In painting such portraits, the intellectuals have inevitably applied their own standards of beauty or ugliness. Criteria of beauty have remained strikingly the same throughout the modern era: an intimate affinity with progress, understood as the widening of the scope for Reason at the expense of whatever opposed it; an appreciation of the value of rationality and a strongly pronounced need for enlightenment; a cult of truth, and respect for those who know it and can separate it from error; and the willingness to give Reason the ultimate authority in shaping and administering the society and the life of its members. Criteria of ugliness have remained no less uniform: opposition to the precepts of rationalization; a tendency to suppress inconvenient truths; an inclination to cling to ideas which the experts on truth declare irrational, prejudicial or mythical; and putting 'partial' (because at odds with the universality of Reason) interests above the 'general' (because dictated by universal Reason) needs of society and its members.

With the standards of beauty and ugliness constant, the portraits differed and changed over time, recording successive intellectual hopes and their frustrations. The gallery of portraits could best be made sense of as a history of unconsummated romances and unrequited loves. There are many modern heroes in the gallery, and each of them has accumulated over the years flattering as well as degrading likenesses.

The pioneer of industry, the tamer of Nature, the conqueror of virgin lands and the tapper of man's unused creative powers, was lovingly painted by Saint-Simon as the flawless, fearless knight of Reason. Unlike the nobility, which tried to tie his hands for fear of the progress his deeds heralded, Saint-Simon's heroic industrialist was curious, inquisitive, open-minded, in love with the man of science, whom he respected and to whose advice he listened. Such industrialists had to create a world made to the measure of the most daring intellectual dreams. The trouble with such a likeness was that (had he ever bothered to examine it) the unaware sitter would not have recognized it as his own. More trouble was to come; other intellectuals stared at the portrait incomprehensibly, knowing its putative object as a coarse, ignorant creature, suspicious of high-flown ideas and of those who – unsuccessfully – tried to peddle them; as somebody who likes 'rationality' but only inside his own property, and who would not bother with the devastation it brings to everything on the other side of the fence. And thus Marx initiated the critique of industrial tycoons for the absence of the selfsame virtues that Saint-Simon had credited them with.

There were other heroes in the gallery as well. Democratically elected politicians, for example, who, bound by their dependence on 'reasons of state', or the 'general interest', would have to impose constraints on everything selfish, private, parochial, partial. They were the latter-day carriers of the enlightened despot mantle. Burdened with the task of administering the complex machinery of the modern state, they were in urgent need of a sound theory of political action, of a purpose acceptable to all for its universality, of a lot of experts and plenty of educated people to communicate the purpose to the nation and administer its attainment. Or, once the politicians proved to be mostly interested in 'party' politics and more in need of catching slogans than of theories and purposes and concerned with finding ways out of the successive mess rather than with designs for a distant future, many an intellectual pondered the possibility that he had only himself and people like him to rely on; that the artist, the man of letters, the philosopher would have to carry the burden of progress on his own shoulders, hoping that his own ideas would become material forces powerful enough to outweigh the extant earthly powers.

Among all the heroes, however, one occupied a particularly notorious role: the 'proletariat', the 'wretched of the earth', those who suffer too much to agree to take it anymore, those who bear the brunt of the delay in the coming of the rational society and for this reason would not fail to rally under the banners of progress the moment they see the truth of their penury. These could be the peasants of the Russian populist intelligentsia or their latter-day suc-cessors – African or Latin-American radicals. First and foremost, however, it was the industrial workers who sat, usually unknowingly, for their portraits as the proletarian standard-bearers of Reason.

More than any other class of modern society the workers seemed to resemble the idealized portrait of the collective hero about to lead mankind to the promised land of Reason. First of all, they were un- tried, and hence, unlike more fortunate classes of society, uncom- promised: their hopes had no reality yet to be tested against and so discarded. The ancient name stuck to them by their history- conscious admirers notwithstanding, modern workers had no exact equivalent in any of the preceding ages of mankind. They were a true novelty, and for that reason could carry a promise of the future uncontaminated by the bitter memories of the past. Unlike other suffering classes of the past, they were condensed and thus visible, they were fast growing in numbers, they – like tribal blacksmiths – performed magical rites making nature tame and malleable, and for this reason they were expected to develop endurance and physical strength their admirers could not help but be impressed with.

But there were yet more important grounds for fixing the search for 'historical class' on the workers and proclaiming them the pro- letariat of the modern era. They showed signs of being conscious of the commonality of their fate, and of a determination to do some- thing about it; they were stubborn, militant, they took to the streets, rioted, built barricades. In retrospect, we know that their militancy reached its peak in the vain attempt to arrest 'the progress of Reason', that is, the substitution of factory confinement for what memory held alive as the freedom of the petty producer.[3] At the time, however, no such wisdom was available and it was easy to naturalize the historically occasioned militancy and impute to the restless and backward-looking factory hands the interests they did not possess. Violent resistance to being transformed into a disciplined and closely surveilled class of 'rational', capitalist society, could be taken as proof that 'class in itself' was already turning into the 'class for itself'; the workers were accredited with a degree of 'settledness' in the 'rationalizing' society similar to that which came naturally to their intellectual mythologists.

Perhaps the most important of reasons for focusing the forward- dreaming of the intellectuals on industrial workers was that here, at last, the spokesmen of Reason came across a category of population unlikely to question, now or ever after, their authority. Indeed, here was a class virtually destined to serve as a prototype to the vision of 'organic intellectuals' – intellectuals who instead of trying hard to make themselves useful, had their usefulness literally forced upon them by the 'historic interest' of a class. The workers were clearly in need of improvement and self-perfection: they were uneducated, ignorant, incapable of grasping great and complex ideas, of tying their personal suffering into the majestic march of history. In view of the nature of their deprivation, they could be improved and perfected only in the way which the intellectuals were the experts in supervising: by being taught. They cast the intellectuals, so to speak, in the role of a collective Pygmalion (that of Bernard Shaw's version). Workers gave the intellectuals the force they needed, but this force was to be formed and controlled by the powers intellectuals, and only they, had. Even when they denigrated their own ineffective, tepid intellectuality, comparing it with the 'class instinct' and 'natural power' of the workers, intellectuals merely did what proud parents so often do: contrasting their own mediocrity to their children's prodigality. In the project of bringing together 'those, who suffer' and 'these, who think', the sufferers were assumed not to be thinking on their own, and the thinkers were accorded the task of bringing together.

This motif perseveres throughout the stormy history of the intellectual romance with the 'proletariat' of modern factories. It is audible clearly in Marx's vision of the passage from 'class in itself' to 'class for itself' – a passage accomplished by the acquisition of the theory of society and of history. It is clear in his insistence that the latter can be attained only by scientific study, that is, by what professional intellectuals have the habit, and skills, of doing; in his caustic comments on the trade-union proclivity to fall under the charm of 'bourgeois respectability', if left to their own intellectual resources; and, last but not least, in his treatment of the 'critique of ideology', or 'critique of political economy', those supremely intellectual tasks of the highest sophistication, as the royal road to the ultimate 'rationalization' of modern society, which the toppling of capitalism by a proletarian revolution would finally bring about. The same motif sounds in the visions of many, and various, of Marx's followers. Kautsky viewed socialism as a marriage between the working-class movement (spontaneity, natural inclinations, class instinct, etc.) and a socialist party (an organized carrier of scientific theory). With all his heresies as to what scientific theory has to say about the shape a socialist version of rational society would take, Bernstein would agree on that point. Lenin embraced Kautsky's formula whole-heartedly, adding that on their own, workers could reach, at the utmost, a 'trade-union' mentality (that is, the inferior mentality of the ignorant, concocting images of reality out of a localized, parochial experience, and incapable of lifting itself to the level of universality which only scientific knowledge can reach). Looking for the best expression of the already axiomatically accepted relationship, Gramsci called the party a 'collective intellectual'. Lukacs took great pains to prove the superiority of 'class consciousness' – a product of intellectual analysis – over the 'consciousness of class', that is, the opinions the workers merely hold: the latter, he proved, was inescapably a 'false' consciousness, one in need of being corrected, one waiting for the good tidings only a thorough analysis of historical process can bring. Althusser elevated ideas – the world in which the intellectuals live and consider their own – to the status of a reality in its own right, and for all practical intents and purposes located in it the roots and the initiative of societal change. Increasingly fissiparous and increasingly critical of Marx, the sects and grouplets of the left today are preoccupied (in the time left free from in-fighting) with 'bringing consciousness' to the people, and 'making people understand'. They do it prompted by historical memory rather than by the present collective experience of the 'general' (not to mention the 'partial') intellectuals.

All this is not meant to imply that the marriage which a considerable section of the intellectuals sought with the working class was dictated solely by reasons of calculated convenience. In the passionate self-identification with the proletarian cause there was in most cases quite a powerful ingredient of genuine humane compassion and concern with the lot of the deprived and the suffering. In some cases this factor itself prompted people to act (as the instances of Mayhew, Booth or Riis testify) without the support of any historiosophical interests; sometimes compassion, originally aroused by the latter, turned from a means into the end of action (arguably, a pattern best exemplified by Blanqui). The suffering was, indeed, an inseparable part in all intellectual theorization of the working-class plight and anticipated role. Never on its own, however, was the poverty of the factory workers seen as a factor which could alone make the workers the prime agent of historical rationalization. For the latter to be proclaimed, compassion had to meet with the attribution of situational and intrinsic qualities, which factory workers, for reasons spelled out above, seemed to justify.

It is the recognition of the absence, or erosion, of such justification that is manifested in the loss of interest in the working classes among contemporary intellectuals. Interrupted only by sporadic resuscitations of old hopes, triggered off by the 'symptomatically interpreted outbursts' of short-lived workers' militancy (in 1968 in France, in the strike epidemic of the early 1970s in Britain), the present-day general intellectuals (or, rather, the part of this category still faithful to the traditional, legislative definition of their role) are, in Alvin Gouldner's famous phrase, 'shopping for an historical agent' again.[4] They obviously do not believe any more that the industrial working class will do in the future what it has demonstrably failed to do thus far: deliver on the (imputed) promise. Books, articles, manifestoes abound carrying titles like 'farewell to the proletariat' and messages of embourgeoisement, privatization, incorporation or enslavement by the Ideological State Apparatuses which have allegedly put industrial workers once and for all outside the reach of the historical role they were supposed (rightly at the time, or erroneously from the start) to play. At the same time, the present-day poor, who are not embourgeoised, privatized or incorporated, are not trusted with the inheritance of historical agency; indeed, they have not been offered one; suffering does not make one necessarily an agent of rationality. With all other painted heroes having been proved to be what they were from the start – *painted* heroes – two strategies only seem to remain open. One: for the painter to stop hiding behind his paintings, admit – like postmodern artists – that the painting represents nothing but himself and his technical art, and to proclaim himself as the prime agent of the coming rational society (as Gouldner implied, when he called the intellectuals the 'best chance we have', or as Daniel Bell suggested in the *Coming of Post-Industrial Society*, only to put his own suggestions in question in the *Cultural Contradictions of Capitalism*). Second: to abandon legislative ambitions altogether, admit that the rationality of the world does not seem to grow, but proclaim that this does not matter anyhow, as the major human need is not truth but understanding and what people need is a good interpretation rather than legislation – something which does not, fortunately, require a historical agent and could be perfectly well done by the intellectuals themselves.

But why did the working class lose its attraction for the intellectuals? And why did the 'new poor' not have it from the start?

There is almost universal agreement between students of current economic trends, that the numbers of industrial workers have already passed their peak and will continue to shrink until they are reduced to a relatively small minority of the population. Indeed, the opinion is gaining ground that industrial manufacture is going through a process similar to the one that took place in the agriculture of the nineteenth century. A general increase in global agricultural production was then accompanied by the decimation of the agricultural labour force; 40 per cent of the population was employed in food production at the beginning of the century, but only 3 per cent at the end. What happened in agriculture, is now happening in the production of industrial goods; by some computations, the total volume of products turned out by today's industry would require, in quarter of a century from now, only about 5 per cent of the total labour force. Manual workers are displaced in ever growing numbers by automation and robots, which have finally become cheaper than 'live' workers. The factory buildings of today bear little resemblance to the huge and ugly 'concentration camps' of yesteryear, inside which proletarian wrath seethed and revolutionary impetus was forged – or so it seemed to the outsiders.

The total number of the employed does not shrink with the same speed as its industrial core. It undergoes, however, considerable restructuring, with one overwhelming effect: a rapidly growing distance between the real attributes of employed labour and those once ascribed to the proletariat, radicalized by its working conditions. The new structure of the labour force is marked above all, in André Gorz's words, by 'a dualistic division of the active population: on one side, acting as the repository of industrialism's traditional values, an elite of permanent, secure, full-time members, attached to their work and their social status; on the other, a mass of unemployed and precarious casual workers, without qualifications or status, performing menial tasks'.[5] The 'meniality' of the tasks performed is, of course, an effect of the denial of status by the withdrawal of trade-union protection; a by-product of the 'closure by exclusion' tactics of entrenched, unionized labour. It seems that the analysts attempting to explain the erosion of trade-union radicalism by changes occurring in certain categories of workers considered separately from the overall restructuring of the labour force, were on a wrong track. As in the third quarter of the nineteenth century in Britain, the division inside labour occupies pride of place in trade-union concerns, providing a major determinant of their strategy and directing the edge of the 'jobs for the boys' policy against the casual, part-time, non-unionized, formally unskilled and low-paid labour. Challenged with a new technological revolution, trade-union organizations have responded so far with digging trenches around the accumulated privileges of the thinning ranks of traditional, skilled, full-time workers. Theirs is, to be sure, a rearguard battle with little chance of success. According to all available computations, for the first time in modern history the investment of capital today means a decrease in the number of jobs (at least in the sense galvanized by trade-unionist practice). The working class – in the form idealized by the intellectuals 'shopping for a historical agent' and institutionalized by trade-union organizational practices – is on the way out. One can only debate its role as a historical agent in terms of unfulfilled promises and lost chances.

This leaves out the 'mass of unemployed and precarious casual workers'; the new poor, the true proletariat in the ancient Roman sense of the word; the growing millions of those who rely on supplementary or welfare payments for their physical survival; impoverished, handicapped, deskilled drop-outs or rejects whom the latest technological revolution, the ultimate triumph of rationality, has deprived (some think permanently) of an economic role. They suffer. Intellectuals feel and express their pity, but somehow refrain from proposing to marry their thought with this particular variety of suffering. They theorize the reasons for their reluctance. Habermas would say that the new poor are not a revolutionary force because they are not exploited. Offe would add that they are politically ineffective, as, having no labour to withdraw, they are deprived of bargaining power. All in all, pity takes the place of compassion: the new poor need help on humane grounds; they are unfit for grooming as the future remakers of the world. With historiosophical indifference comes disenchantment with poverty. Being poor once again seems unromantic. It contains no mission, it does not gestate future glory. Psychologically, if not logically nor historically, it appears residual, marginal, alien.

Marginality, which makes the present-day poverty 'new', seems to be in the last account a product of the emancipation of capital from labour. Today, capital does not engage the rest of society in the role of productive labour; more precisely, the number of people it does so engage becomes ever smaller and less significant. Instead, capital engages the rest of society in the role of consumers. More precisely, the number of people it does so engage becomes ever bigger and more significant. These are the people who, to recall Bourdieu's observation, are seduced rather than repressed, guided by needs rather than constrained by norms; people to whom public relations techniques and advertising, replacing police and ideology, are addressed. Above all, these are the people on whom the reproduction of capital primarily depends, and with it the perpetuation of the social system organized around capital and the market. Before emancipation of capital from labour, the poor were first and foremost, 'the reserve army of labour'; they kept capital growth options open, and helped to keep the capital–labour conflict off the limit where they would jeopardize the reproduction of the system. The poor were, therefore, not just an unavoidable, but an indispensable part of the system – in no way an alien body. After the emancipation of capital from labour, the poor could play a similar 'inner-systemic' role only if they could be seriously considered as 'the reserve army of consumption'. But could they be so considered?

Repression, policing, regimentation by authority and enforceable norms formed at the early stage of modernity the dominant cluster of integrating mechanisms from which none but a very few privileged and very rich were exempt. The cluster served well the human management prerequisites of the factory – the most crucial institution of a society where the domination of capital rested on constituting the rest of society as a real or potential labour force. With the economization of the conflict over control, more and more members of society were given the chance to buy personal exemption from the cluster. Such chances grew more profuse together with the advances of capital on its road towards emancipation from labour: for an increasing number of people, whose consumer skills counted now more than their productive potential, the old cluster became increasingly counter-productive (or, rather, 'counter-consumptive'?) and, above all, irrelevant. These people were now effectively and efficiently integrated (in a way resonant with their actual role in the reproduction of capital) through a new cluster of mechanisms – seduction, public relations, advertising, growing needs. Not all people, however, passed the borderline dividing the two worlds.

The new poor are those who did not. They are not consumers; or, rather, their consumption does not matter much for the successful reproduction of the capital (what they consume is mostly excluded from market circulation anyway). They are not, therefore, members of the consumer society. They have to be disciplined by the combined action of repression, policing, authority and normative regulation. Not for them is Bourdieu's 'cultural game'. If, stupidly, they think otherwise, Jeremy Seabrook can tell the consequences:

> I think of Michelle. At fifteen her hair was one day red, the next blonde, then jet-black, then teased into Afro kinks and after that rat-tails, then plaited, and then cropped so that it glistened close to the skull. She wore a nose-stud, and then her ears were pierced; in the bright feathers, rhinestones or ceramic or silver. Her lips were scarlet, then purple, then black. Her face was ghost-white and then peach-coloured, then bronze as if it were cast in metal. Pursued by dreams of flight, she left home at sixteen to be with her boyfriend, who was twenty-six. If they took her home, she said, she would kill herself. 'But I have always let you do what you want', her mother protested. 'This is what I want'. At eighteen she returned to her mother, with two children, after she had been badly beaten by her man. She sat in the bedroom which she had fled three years earlier; the faded photos of yesterday's pop stars still stared down from the walls. She said she felt a hundred years old. She felt weary. She'd tried all that life could offer. Nothing else was left.[6]

The consumer paradise has its own portative hell: for illegitimate visitors.

The market provides the acid test of eligibility for membership of the consumer society. The appeals of the latter are thoroughly democratic: they are aimed indiscriminately at everybody who would listen, and everybody is encouraged to listen or forced to hear. So, potentially, everybody is seduced or seducible. Once seduced, however, Michelle and her ilk soon discover that the goods they covet, apart from being attractive to everybody, bring happiness only to some; or so Michelle guesses, as the only thing she knows for sure is that she herself is not among those 'some'. The commodity game does not bring rewards; the game itself is the only reward, offering as it does the ever renewed hope of winning. But to reap this kind of a reward, one must be able to go on playing without end, so that hope is never allowed to die and defeat always means losing a battle, not the war. Once you stop playing, the hope disappears, and you know that you have lost, and that there will be no next battle to recoup your losses. To the temple of hope, only those who can play have the legitimate entry. Michelle knows now she is illegitimate: there is no place for her at the other people's party. She was given a chance; she failed. She must be humble now.

And humble she is, the recipient of state administered 'charity' in the form of welfare payments or supplementary benefits. Of her and others like her Hilary Rose wrote: 'The "gift relationship" which exists in Supplementary Benefit is one of an exchange of public cash for personal humiliation . . . [T]he applicant must adopt a suppliant role, like a mediaeval leper exhibiting his sores.'[7] In the practice of means tested welfare, no trace has been left of the high hopes of the prophets of the welfare state. As Sir John Walley reminds us, in the Beveridge Report

> [t]he hope was rooted in the assurance that the resulting payments would be made as of right without any enquiry into means or character and would, in the contingencies provided for, be themselves sufficient to avoid having to apply for help as a poor person. *All* citizens – not merely the better off – would thus become free to save and embark on plans for their own future advantage or that of their families, without the fear that all might be swept away in one of the misfortunes now to be covered by social insurance.

Beveridge's ideas had been conceived within the world of the producers – or shaped by the vivid memory of such a world: falling out of the game in such a world was still a temporary mishap, and those who found themselves on the margin had the duty to come back inside, while the state was there to help them (as Klaus Offe would say, to 'recommodify labour'). There was no reason to treat them, therefore, in a radically different way from the rest. Beveridge's ideas were already out of date the moment they were conceived. The ensuing practice proved them so. In virtually every field of social insurance, payments of right have been displaced and replaced by means tests, which 'affect the dignity of the recipient', and are intrinsically 'socially divisive'.[8] And divisive they are meant to be, dividing being the paramount benefit they bring to the society of consumers. In D. V. Donnison's words, British supplementary benefits have become 'a stigmatised second-class service for stigmatised second-class citizens'.[9] It is the deliberately maintained second-class nature of the services that constitutes the clients as second-class citizens, or at least serves as a badge warning the others around that this is exactly what the clients are.

Those who proved to be inappropriate objects for seduction can expect nothing but the old and trusty repression. Advertising will leave them blind or, worse still, make them furious (as smashing and burning the shops during inner-city riots showed); armed authority needs to pick up the pieces. New needs may only augur trouble to come; norms are needed to make sure that the poor stick to the old ones. All in all, repression is needed to undo the harm to social order caused by indiscriminate seduction. Repression and norms are not, of course, news for the poor. But now they are in addition a means of discrimination; they come to the new poor at a time when a growing number of other people are buying their way out of repression, authority or normative regulation. The poor must hence be constituted, by law and by practice, as a separate category, to which different rules apply. The city manager of Newburgh, New York, Joseph Mitchell, spoke for those who found it cosy on this side of the consumer society fence, when he declared:

> We challenged the right of social parasites to breed illegitimate children at the taxpayer's expense. We challenged the right of moral chiselers and loafers to squat on the relief rolls forever. We challenged the right of cheaters to make more on relief than when working. We challenged the right of those on relief to loaf by State and Federal edict. We challenged the right of people to quit jobs at will and go on relief like spoiled children. We challenged the right of citizens to migrate for the purpose of becoming or continuing as public charges.

Behind this morally elevating manifesto there is a practice of humiliation. According to Joe R. Feagin's findings,

> not only have welfare agencies [in the USA] often watched over the marital and sex lives of recipients, but they have supervised other aspects of their lives. Caseworkers may go uninvited into their homes to scrutinize their housekeeping methods and their child-rearing practices. Another example of state interference in the lives of recipients has been in the form of extreme birth control pressure. In the early 1970s a number of news stories probed the fact that local welfare boards had participated in the forced sterilization of welfare mothers.[10]

Another American study has shown that with the present system of public relief the poor need a 'great amount of patience (as when welfare officials refuse to make appointments and keep recipients waiting interminably), high tolerance for rudeness and insult (as when indigent users of hospital emergency rooms find that no one even notices that they are trying to ask questions), and unusual readiness to make their private lives public (as when one is questioned in an open cubicle of a welfare office about one's sex life)'. This is how the poor are being taught their bureaucratically assigned roles, their new and segregating social definitions:

> [T]he impecunious find it necessary to learn to play out scripts attached to such bureacratic categories as 'recipient of Aid for Dependent Children' or 'participant in a work-training programme'. One prob-lem with such roles is that they carry with them newly devised social labels by which the poor persons become known to agencies and, at times, to the public (e.g., 'ADC mother'). Once attached, such labels can be difficult to remove; the poor person may find that no matter what he does to improve his financial situation, he still is known prin-cipally by his poverty label – often an injurious, dispiriting, and stigmatising one.

Classification is meant to be self-perpetuating; the bureaucratic prac-tice has discarded all pretences to rehabilitation – it wants instead to brand, to separate, to enforce permanence on its products. Assign-ment and 'successful' learning of poverty roles 'may undo the per-son's will toward positive action. He may learn, for example, to adopt as dependent and fawning a manner toward public officials as bureaucratic procedures would seem to require; or he may come to accept as true a stigmatising label, thus losing self-respect or reac-ting with self-defeating anger.'[11] Everything is done to assure that the roles are learned, embraced, identified with – and that they stay that way. As Joel F. Handler and Ellen Jane Hollingsworth discovered:

> The laws and regulations governing the intake process and the means test delegate extremely wide powers of inquiry to the intake workers. Almost everything about the welfare client can be the official concern of the agency. In determining need, not only are all resources to be considered, but the agency is authorised to work out plans in order that 'resources may be fully utilised' . . . [A]lthough the means test functions as a gatekeeper, its application is not restricted to the intake

stage. Its administration extends from the time of the application until the recipient leaves the programme. At any time, resources and needs can change and eligibility can be lost . . . Disclosing assets and resources, revealing names of one's friends and associates, submitting to investigations and questioning accounting for expenditures and social behaviour – these are the price of receiving welfare.[12]

The overall effect of welfare legislation and practice is to disempower the poor. Disempowering means also preventing the recipient of welfare from rejoining the ranks of the legitimate members of the consumer society. Indeed, there is nothing in the welfare institutions meant to facilitate such a rejoining, as the case studies conducted by Edythe Shewbridge,[13] and other similar investigations have vividly demonstrated. On the contrary, welfare practice focuses on the 'unlearning' of skills that membership of the consumer society requires; the recipients are not allowed now to make their own 'buying choices'; those are made for them.

The formidable mixture of inhumanity, malice and sheer cruelty in the welfare state's relation to its 'beneficiaries', and above all the antipathy and suspicion with which the welfare recipients are treated by a very large part of the population, has often been explained away by the allegedly dysfunctional character of welfare: based on secondary transfers, unrelated to labour contracts and exempt from the rule of the market, it appears to undermine the 'work ethic', indispensable for the reproduction of capital–labour relations. But who needs the poor to undermine the work ethic? Credit cards were introduced in Britain under the slogan 'take the waiting out of wanting'. The work ethic has an ever diminishing relevance to the reproduction of capital, whose profits now depend much more on the manipulation of the market than on the exploitation of its labour force, and which needs a society where the motives of spending and consuming dominate those of earning and saving. The work ethic is anathema to the consumer market. In the mythology necessary to keep the consumer game going, there is only a humble place left (if at all) for the 'lifetime of work' commandment. As Jeremy Seabrook observed, the young of the consumer society are being raised 'to a vast luxuriance of fantasy'; 'They have grown up to think of money not allied to work, but as something mysteriously as likely to be found through a big win or a break-in or a talent for disco-dancing or a Bingo jackpot, as it is from selling their labour.'[14] This thinking does not arise out of experience of being on welfare. It comes from the best authority – this self-advertising of the consumer market, this post-modern ideology to put paid to all ideologies.

It is also being said that the welfare system limits the power of the market and hence is a 'decommodifying' factor; in this capacity it is bound to be seen, rightly, as an alien element of the society of consumers, the elimination of which, or at least radical reduction, is something the joint interest of consumers needs. What is functional to the consumer market is in fact this very belief. 'Denaturalization' of the poor as welfare recipients is an indispensable condition of the 'naturalization' of consumerism. The maintenance of the self-identity of consumers needs the constitution of non-consumers as its repugnant and detestable opposition – and a threat to be vigilant against. Were there no poor, they would have to be invented. They bring into relief what it means not to be a consumer in a consumer society. Their plight makes the tensions and the frustrations of consumer life seem innocuous and utterly tolerable by comparison. That is, on condition that they are treated as they indeed are: they are living embodiments of the only alternative to the consumer market the latter agrees, and indeed is willing, to discuss and publicly demonstrate. Made visible as the horrifying alternative, they are supposed to make all other alternatives, the very 'alternativeness' as such, horrifying. Clive Jenkins and Barrie Sherman commented on present-day British society: 'The British have always prided themselves on being a caring, tolerant, civilised society, one in which it is possible to live a decent upright life with the minimum of social and political disorder. Up to a point this is true, provided that you are white, are a male, in employment, financially solvent or (preferably) wealthy, but not old, disabled or mentally handicapped.'[15] To be acknowledged as civilized, the consumer society needs the uncivilized alternative against which its attainment can be daily measured. In order to remain tolerant towards its members, it needs the members' intolerance of anything which is not itself.

The new poor are, in fact, a product of the consumer market. Not of its 'malfunctioning' (as once was said of the poor marginalized by the production-oriented capitalist economy), but of its way of existence and reproduction. Consumer society creates its own poor by setting the rich, the ostentatious consumer, not as a boss, an exploiter, a member of a different class, an enemy – but as a pattern-setter, an example to be followed, a target to be reached, overcome and left behind; as a pioneer on the road everyone must aspire to follow, and a confirmation that aspiring is realistic. To quote Seabrook again:

> [o]ur poverty has been redefined in such a way that all attempts to determine how much would be needed to lift people out of want appear inconclusive and unattainable, are hopelessly, menacingly costly; and this is because poverty has been set not against need, but against an unlimited capacity to produce and sell. In this way, it has become an insoluble problem; or, rather, its solution lies not in remedial action to compensate the poor but with the rich, in whose image the poor have been remade.[16]

The 'tragedy' of consumer society is that it cannot reproduce itself without reproducing inequalities on an ever rising level and without insisting that all 'social problems' must be translated into individual needs satisfiable through the individual consumption of marketable commodities; by so doing, it daily generates its own handicapped, whose needs cannot be met through the market and who therefore undermine the very condition of its reproduction. In a truly dialectical manner, consumer society cannot cure the ills it generates except by taking them to its own grave.

Whatever the reasons, the fact remains that the repressed and the normatively regulated are tangibly present inside the consumer society, however prosperous – and are likely to remain there for the whole length of the consumer-market life. It is therefore a most striking and crucial feature of consumer society that it deploys two distinct systems of social control; two radically different mechanisms through which members of a society organized around consumption are integrated. No model of social order or of the process of societal reproduction can be complete without giving its due to this duality.

This is not, however, what the theorizing of contemporary society as a 'consumer society' usually does. In unison with the self-image of consumer society, it treats the repressed as a marginal phenomenon, only tangentially related to the society it describes; as an element either transitory or alien, but in both cases removable without changing the validity of the essential model; and as a phenomenon requiring a different set of factors for its explanation than that of the attributes of the consumer society itself.

12

Conclusions: one too many

Conclusion, modern style

In the last chapters, we have tried to trace the convoluted story of the (thus far) failed, or at least incomplete, rationalization project of modernity. We have seen that the rationalization process has brought in its wake an extreme fragmentation of the sites of authority; in each site, availability of rational technology permits an ever increasing measure of autonomy from the system, leaving the market as the only link between the sites. Thus rationalization of fragments of the system does not lead to the rationality of the system as a totality. On the contrary, rendering the market indispensable as the major mechanism of societal reproduction, it is bound to produce an ever increasing volume of irrational waste. Not dependent any more on systemically upheld goals and principles, fragments cannot account for their own activity but in terms of the potential contained in the technological means and methods at their disposal. The system, on the other hand, has an ever increasing difficulty with generating, and making plausible, a legitimation capable of presenting the working of the system as something else than a quasi-natural and uncontrolled process. As a mechanism of systemic integration, the market tends to subordinate and subsume all conceivable legitimations of the system. The role of the state is reduced to the employment of political means in the service of perpetuating the conditions for the domination of the market. The state is, first and foremost, an instrument of re-commodification.

In the absence of systemic legitimation, the market becomes as well the principal mechanism of social integration. This role of the market promotes radical individualization of the members of society; they are constituted as individuals by the market-generated translation of systemic needs into private consumption. This feature of individuality constitution is in its turn responsible for individuality being defined in terms of consumption. The market transforms members of society into individual consumers. This eases the pressure on systemic legitimation, as the irrationality of the system is dealt with by an increased individual consumption. The tensions associated with the absence of a global rational plan are thus dislocated. Instead of generating the necessary pressure on a discursive redemption of the rational values and purposes of modern society, they result in an urge to intensify private consumption and the supply of commodities the latter requires. The modern project of individual autonomy has been subordinated and subsumed by the market-defined and market-oriented freedom of consumer choice.

For the individual as a consumer, the conditions created by the failure of the modernity project mean above all a never relenting urge to increase the appropriation of commodities. Individual needs of personal autonomy, self-definition, authentic life or personal perfection are all translated into the need to possess, and consume, market-offered goods. This translation, however, pertains to the appearance of use–value of such goods, rather than to the use–value itself; as such, it is intrinsically inadequate and ultimately self-defeating, leading to momentary assuagement of desires and lasting frustration of needs. Frustration of needs may be temporarily mollified only by the generation of still more novel desires and the hopes pinned to their satisfaction. Individual needs of autonomy and the good life are not satisfied, but the translation of their frustration into systemic concerns (like the questioning of systemic legitimacy) is infinitely postponed, while conditions for the domination of market exchange are infinitely perpetuated. The gap between human needs and individual desires is produced by market domination; this gap is, at the same time, a condition of its reproduction. The market feeds on the unhappiness it generates: the fears, anxieties and the sufferings of personal inadequacy it induces release the consumer behaviour indispensable to its continuation.

Identification of the satisfaction of human needs with private consumption has also this consequence, that the needs which cannot be channelled into private consumption must be either laid fallow or repressed. One manifestation of this consequence is Galbraith's rule of 'private affluence, public squalor': the needs which are 'non-marketable' (or non-redeemable through the market), are not provided for, and the satisfaction of needs not yet privatized (or still beyond the purchasing power of the bulk of the population) lags behind the prompt and ever more sophisticated servicing of such private desires as are related to private consumption goods. The neglect of public consumption (that is, inadequate prevention of pollution, insufficient medical provision for the most common of ailments, erosion of public transport, starvation of public housing and schooling, etc.) can only be compensated for by the purchase of individual exemptions, which further strengthens the identification of needs satisfaction with private consumption, thereby reinforcing the grip of Galbraith's rule. Another manifestation of the previously mentioned consequence is the transformation of the welfare service into the instrument of the repression of the needs of those individuals who for one reason or another are incapable of seeking their redress through the commodities supplied from the market. Big or small, or smaller still, the 'secondary transfer' means of survival made available to the recipients of welfare are exempt from the market, and as such addressed directly to 'genuine needs' (this is perhaps the only context in which the existence of 'genuine', as distinct from 'artificial', needs, is admitted in the market-dominated society), unmediated by market-prompted desires. In a market-dominated society, deprivation is socially defined as the prevention of needs from being translated into a desire for commodities and the hope of attaining the 'authentic life', autonomy or self-perfection that the latter monopolize.

In the case of consumers, coming to grips with the task of personal autonomy or self-identity is effectively postponed, indeed removed from the agenda, by the endless chase for the appearances of use-value in which the commodities are wrapped. In the case of non-consumers or 'flawed' consumers, even the appearances are not available as a substitution, and hence the task of personal autonomy or authentic life is administratively suppressed. In both cases, the bridge linking individual needs to systemic rationality – one which figured so prominently in the project of modernity – has been either made invisible or destroyed. This has brought in its wake the growing privatization of individual concerns, a decrease in participation in public affairs and a gradual, but consistent fading of the 'legitimation discourse'. The petty rationalities of personal or sectional pursuits have been 'uncoupled' from the overall project of a rational society.

The project of modernity, in other words, has failed. Or, rather, its implementation took a wrong turn. It does not mean necessarily that the project itself was abortive or doomed to failure. The needs to which it had been a response are as vivid today as they were in the past, and the tasks the project of modernity put on the agenda of guided, purposeful societal development remain fully in force. The strategies suggested for the implementation of the tasks have not been fully put to the test and hence cannot be declared discredited. The potential of modernity is still untapped, and the promise of modernity needs to be redeemed.

The needed redemption requires, first of all, the separation of the paramount values of autonomy, self-perfection and authenticity from the renderings forced upon them by the domination of the market in the current, consumer version of modern society. The first and necessary (though perhaps not sufficient) condition of redemption is to return those values to where they belong – to the realm of public discourse; their practical redemption must start from their discursive redemption, in which the unbreakable link between the enhancement of person-oriented values and the construction of the rational society is once more brought into relief and made visible. Another, closely associated work the discursive redemption must accomplish is to dispose of the pretensions of the commodification process to provide an adequate means to person-oriented ends; and, on the way, to expose the limitations of instrumental reason and thus restore the autonomy of human communication and meaning-creation guided by practical reason.

The urgency of discursive redemption, if anything, adds to the importance of the role intellectuals are called to play. Discursive redemption is unmistakably their duty. The project of modernity had been deposited and still resides in the cultural tradition the intellectuals perpetuate and develop. As before, the intellectuals must initiate and guide a process of enlightenment, through supplying an adequate theory (of history, of social system, or communicative action) which reveals the possibility of redemption contained in the form modern society has currently assumed, and points out realistic strategies of redemptive practice; and, secondly, through promoting genuine democracy by involving ever wider sections of society in the redemptive debate.

The legitimation of the social system must again be made a matter of public debate; once this happens, the pressure upon the social system to legitimize itself in terms of person-oriented values rather than achievements of commodification, in terms of practical rather than instrumental reason, will necessarily follow; and thus conditions for emancipation, promised by the project of modernity, will be created.

In its actual history, as distinct from its original project, modernity has subordinated such individual autonomy and democratic tolerance as it promoted to the functional prerequisites of instrumental reason of industry and commodity production. The fullness of subordination has made the historically created relation seem natural and immutable. The task of the redemptive theory is to expose the contingency of the relation; the task of redemptive action is to break it.

As long as the task remains unfulfilled, modernity is not yet over. It is alive through, and together with, the cultural tradition of the West, and the collective practice of its intellectual carriers. The discovery of truth, moral right and the aesthetic criteria of beauty still lie ahead, having lost nothing of their urgency, importance and realism. Obituaries written by the heralds of the post-modern condition are, to say the least, slightly premature. Viewed from the perspective of the modernity project, the post-modern condition does not bring anything qualitatively new, as long as the tasks of modern intellectuals are still to be performed and hence cannot be seen as redundant. The age of modernity (that is, the age marked by the presence of the dual values of personal autonomy and societal rationality) cannot end; it can only be consummated. It has not yet been. It still remains the function of the intellectuals to bring the project of modernity toward its fulfilment.

Conclusion, post-modern style

In the last chapters, we have tried to trace the convoluted story of what seems today, looking backwards, the failed romance with the Puritan. Whether for his own original sin, or because of the conspiracy of some other forces, the Puritan has turned into the consumer – in every detail his opposite; a type guided by neither the 'pleasure' nor the 'reality' principle, but a 'principle of comfort' of sorts: a type who would not stretch himself even in the name of pleasure, who would neither love strongly nor hate passionately.

Because the Puritan loomed large in intellectuals' plans and strategies for the better, rational society, the calling of this particular bluff has been experienced by many contemporary intellectuals as the most important event on the road from modernity to post-modernity; after all, behind every 'carrier of rationality' the intellectuals appointed, the Puritan was lurking, and the recognition of his disappearance made all further painting of likenesses gratuitous. Hence the most popular description/interpretation of the post-modern condition is that of the 'consumer society'; a description which pinpoints, as the paramount feature of the new historical period, the advent and the (at least numerical) dominance of the consumer.

The demise of the Puritan has changed also the intellectual perspective on the poor and the oppressed. The poor lost their attraction – they are most unlikely 'carriers of rationality', whoever might be to blame for it. In a world theorized as the dominion of the consumer they are not any more the collective *alter ego* of the Puritan, the Prometheus in chains waiting only to be unchained to bring truth, light and happiness to tormented society. They are rather construed as bleak copies of the ruling consumer, his inept imitations, sometimes tragic, sometimes grotesque; if 'liberated', they would waste no time to 'outconsume the consumer'. The poor who 'attack each other, fire the ghettos, mutilate others and damage themselves with drugs and alcohol', are as unprepossessing as the 'consumer in distress' may be; rummaging the shops instead of firing them, and damaging themselves with more exquisite and expensive drugs is seen as their only 'untapped potential'.

Thus the rich have all the freedom and autonomy they can imagine; they bought it with their money and they cherish it; the fringe whispering of 'real' freedom and 'genuine' autonomy sounds all but incomprehensible to them; if they listen at all, they cannot ascribe to such whispers any other meaning but more goods and still less trouble. The poor, on the other hand, cannot imagine freedom and autonomy in any other form but becoming rich themselves, which the lucky few among them who do strike gold (for example, winning the pools) convincingly demonstrate.

This has been, of course, a caricature of reality. A caricature, yet not a joke. It does represent the ultimate product of theorizing society in terms of the rationalizing process; a product of the legislative ambitions institutionalized in the historically formed role of the intellectuals, it transforms past hopes into present frustrations. It is this picture, which in somewhat less blatantly caricatural, but nevertheless clearly recognizable form, stands behind the talk of the 'absence of historical agent', and of the present-day historical stage as an empty space still to be occupied by the yet unknown actor.

Indeed, no social group or category of the post-industrial world seems to be fit for the role set aside by the history-as-rationalization theory for the 'agent of Reason'. In practical terms, this means that no social group or category, either dominating or struggling for domination, seems to have any overwhelming demand for the kind of authoritiative versions of truth, judgement or taste the intellectuals are capable of providing; or, rather, no social group is likely to make such versions authoritative by endorsing them with its own domin-ation. This is, perhaps, the ultimate meaning of that uneasiness and feeling of bankruptcy of the traditional role which is captured today in the concept of the post-modern condition.

The sense that rationalization is today a project without an agent to supervise its implementation, makes suddenly all old and pro-spective blueprints for a 'good society' seem embarrassingly unreal and naïve. The result is what has been described as the 'loss of nerve' or the loss of the 'capacity for forward dreaming'. Ours is, decisively, not an age of utopias. The age of utopias is an age when utopias seem practical and realistic; ours is an age when the pro-grammes intended as practical seem utopian. We are angry when a scholar, having thoroughly and cogently criticized the shortcomings of our condition, fails to end up with a prescription for improving it. But if he or she does come up with such a prescription, we meet it incredu-lously and deride it as another utopia. The very activity of prescription-writing has been discredited, not just the individual prescriptions. Throughout the modern age, forward dreaming was respectable as it was aimed at one or another, but invariably powerful agent, hoped to be able and willing to carry out the rational measures the images of rational society suggested. With the aim no longer visible, forward dreaming is just this: dreaming. Or so it seems to be.

Contemporary intellectual strategies may be interpreted as responses to the novelty of this situation. Some insist, hoping against hope, that a historical agent in the traditional sense, that is, a would-be dominant force interested in constructing a rationally organized society, must be found; moreover, that it must exist somewhere, unknown to others and to itself. It must exist in an inchoate form, more a potential than a reality, waiting to be discovered, or rather to be helped to discover its own possibility; an agent who does not have yet the ability to rise over his partial vision, who has to be taught his own globality. This is what Touraine, and in a somewhat different form Castells, propose; or, in his inimitable style, Seabrook: 'These processes can be resisted only by a joint project of rich and poor together; a liberation movement that dares to recognise common ground between them; perhaps a version of liberation theology in the West which will unite and inform those generous but still discrete impulses that underlie the feminist, Peace and Green movements.'[1] It could be the feminists, the CNDs and the Greens yesterday; it may be someone else who will hit the headlines tomorrow. What will remain constant for some time at least, is the conviction that the 'agent in itself' has been already born and the task is to locate the stable and the cradle and to talk him into becoming an 'agent for itself' and for us. This is, indeed, what the 'intervening method' of Touraine calls us to do.

Some other strategies call for the abandonment of global projects altogether. They wish to draw their courage from despair; they consider despair as the ultimate intellectual courage. Hope for the world, but no hope in the world; the world having been corrupted beyond repair, with rationality itself turned into the technique of oppression, Reason cannot hope to find its home out there. The critical spirit of the intellectuals is its last harbour. The philosophers' wisdom may be only polluted by coming in touch with the world outside; it should be guarded against such contacts, preserved in its purity, cultivated for its own sake, as there is nothing outside it which can keep alive the hope of human emancipation. In their very dissimilar ways, Husserl or the Frankfurt theorists in their exile period (this being essentially a strategy of exile, it was helped tremendously by the exile of the strategists) are the most prominent representatives of this response. The trouble with this response, as it has frequently been pointed out, is that the questions, to which it was intended to be an answer, tend to be forgotten; and that those who ask will not recognize the questions in the answers. Once having separated itself from human practice, theory will not find its way back. The decision to keep the enlightenment project alive results in its ultimate surrender.

There is a strategy of recoiling upon the territory considered to remain relatively safe, as the claims to legislative authority are unlikely to be challenged there. Thus the realm of the legislative domination in the name of Reason and rationality is confined to the domain of the spirit proper: science and art, to be precise. The legislative model of the intellectual role is translated as, say, deciding on conditions under which truth or 'good art' may be recognized, and authoritatively accepted, as such. This is a programme of a sort of meta-science or meta-aesthetics. Its purpose is to provide foundations, justifications, legitimations – this time not for earthly powers, but for intellectual activity itself. Thus Popper's philosophy concentrated on the business of falsifying – an activity which hopefully will keep sciences permanently dependent on something which stands above it and which they themselves cannot replace. Habermas would castigate 'positive sciences' for not being interested in accounting for themselves and providing grounds for the acceptance of their own procedures and findings. Artists would be preached to on the need for an aesthetic theory to justify the artistic nature of their work. This strategy is self-centred and self-concerned, and as such it is well supported by the general intellectual atmosphere of the time when comedians make jokes mostly about other comedians, novelists love to write novels about writing novels, pastiche – essays on other people's images – become the most popular form of artistic imagery, and artists consider the flatness of their canvas and the colours of their paints the main subject-matter of their painting. At the same time, the strategy is a recipe for frustration. The numerous areas of intellectual activity which have branched off the original stem have either been successfully colonized by other powers, or have developed their own institutional bases of authority; in both cases they acquire a high degree of autonomy – virtually, full independence – in relation to the legislative or foundational offers of meta-scientists or meta-aestheticians. They are now kept in motion and legitimized by other factors, over which the general intellectuals have no control, and hence may safely disregard the foundational discourse as totally irrelevant to the work they are doing – and doing, by their own institutionalized criteria, well. Thus the offer hangs very much in the air; the helpful hand is stretched, but few want to shake it.

With the three strategies named thus far not fully gratifying, no wonder a fourth one is recently gaining in popularity. This is a strategy which abandons the legislative ambitions altogether, and with them the long attachment to the legitimizing and foundational discourses. Perhaps 'altogether' is going a bit too far; the fourth strategy does contain a form of legislating intent, but this is now aimed at the authority of interpretation. The idea of interpretation assumes the meaning-constituting authority to reside elsewhere – in the author, or in the text; the role of the interpreter boils down to reading out the meaning. The good interpreter is one who reads the meaning properly – and there is a need (or so one may hope) for somebody to vouch for the rules which guided the reading of the meaning and thus made the interpretation valid or authoritative; somebody who would sieve good interpretations from bad ones. But the strategy of interpretation does differ from all strategies of legislation in one fundamental way: it does abandon overtly, or put aside as irrelevant to the task at hand, the assumption of the universality of truth, judgement or taste; it refuses to differentiate between communities which produce meanings; it accepts those communities' ownership rights, and the ownership rights as the only foundation the communally grounded meanings may need. What remains for the intellectuals to do, is to interpret such meanings for the benefit of those who are not of the community which stands behind the meanings; to mediate the communication between 'finite provinces' or 'communities of meaning'. Not a menial task, to be sure, given the incurable split of the human world into a plethora of fully or partially autonomous, institutionally entrenched traditions and 'meaning factories'; and given the apparently undeniable need of mutual communication and understanding between them. Gadamer's proposition seems therefore eminently attractive (particularly if supplemented with what Betti asked to be done – the grounding of the legislative authority, adjusted to the conditions of the world seen first and foremost as a communication-and-interpretation process). The old doubts do not go away, however. The best of interpretations must still find its way back to those whose understanding it wants to enhance. Would they accept it? Would the intellectual guarantee of validity be sufficient to make them accept? Making people accept a correct translation instead of a misleading one is also, after all, a form of proselytism. Can the conversion be carried out on the strength of the intellectual expertise alone?

So there is also Rorty – with the most radical of all possible responses to the post-modern condition. (Though he refuses to admit that his philosophy is such a response, which he must do, as long as he insists on the ultimate freedom of philosophers to philosophize gained through Western history, and since then unconstrained by conditions of time and place.) His is a strategy to put an end to all strategies, one which declares the search for *the* strategy a waste of effort, a misaimed concern. The intellectual activity draws its legitimacy from the intellectuals' own moral conviction as to the value of their work and as to the worthiness of the discourse they are keeping alive and guarding against being stifled or numbed in the cacophony of communal traditions. With such a strategy adopted, the fact that others do not care for the legitimations we offer is no longer a problem. We simply do not offer legitimations. We do not do any more what we believed, and made others believe, since Descartes, Locke or Kant, was our job. That is, if we ever did this job at all.

Rorty's anti-strategy seems to fit very well the autonomy and the institutionally encouraged concern of academic philosophy with its own self-reproduction. Until further cuts, that is.

Notes

Notes to chapter 1

1 Paul Radin, *Primitive Religion, Its Nature and Origin*, Hamilton, London 1938, p. 14.
2 Ibid., p. 23.
3 Ibid., pp. 24-5.
4 Ibid., p. 18.
5 W. Ross Ashby, 'The Application of Cybernetics to Psychiatry', in Alfred G. Smith (ed.), *Communication and Culture*, Harcourt, Brace and World, New York 1966, p. 376.
6 Radin, *Primitive Religion*, pp. 131-2.
7 Paul Radin, *Primitive Man as a Philosopher*, Appleton, New York 1927, pp. 231-3.
8 Kurt Goldstein, 'Concerning the Concept of "Primitivity"', in Stanley Diamond (ed.), *Culture in History*, essays in honour of Paul Radin, New York 1960, pp. 111-12.

Notes to chapter 2

1 Richard J. Bernstein (ed.), *Habermas and Modernity*, Polity Press, Oxford 1985, p. 192.
2 Leonard Krieger, *Kings and Philosophers 1689-1789*, Weidenfeld and Nicolson, London 1971, p. 174.
3 Alexis de Tocqueville, *The Ancient Regime and the French Revolution*, transl. by Stuart Gilbert, Collins, New York 1976, pp. 69, 88, 89.
4 Cf. John Passmore, *The Perfectibility of Man*, Duckworth, London 1972, p. 173.
5 Cf. *Enlightened Absolutism, A Documentary Sourcebook*, by A. Lentin, Avero, Newcastle 1985, p. 15.

6 de Tocqueville, *The Ancient Regime*, p. 60.

7 Ellery Schalk, *From Valor to Pedigree, Ideas of Nobility in France in the Sixteenth and Seventeenth Centuries*, Princeton University Press, 1986, p. xiv.

8 Ibid., pp. 57–8, 60–1, 73, 79.

9 Ibid., pp. 181, 192.

10 Augustin Cochin, *Les sociétés de pensée et la démocratie moderne*, Plon, Paris 1921, p. 14.

11 François Furet, *Penser la Révolution Française*, Gallimard, Paris 1978.

12 de Tocqueville, *The Ancient Regime*, p. 164.

13 Ibid., p. 161.

14 Furet, *Penser la Révolution Française*, p. 59.

15 Cf. Richard H. Popkin, *The History of Scepticism from Erasmus to Spinoza*, University of California Press, 1979, pp. 104 ff.

16 Augustin Cochin, *Le révolution et la libre pensée*, Plon, Paris 1924, p. xxxvi.

17 Furet, *Penser la Révolution Française*, p. 223.

18 Cochin, *Les sociétés de pensée*, p. 8.

19 Ludwig Wittgenstein, *Culture and Values*, Basil Blackwell, Oxford 1980, p. 10.

Notes to chapter 3

1 Lucien Fébvre, *Le problème de l'incroyance au XVIe siècle*, Paris 1968, p. 380.

2 Robert Muchembled, *Culture populaire et culture des élites dans la France moderne (XVe–XVIIIe siècles)*, Flammarion, Paris 1978, pp. 45, 52.

3 Fletcher, Anthony and Stevenson, John (eds), *Order and Disorder in Early Modern England*, Cambridge University Press, Cambridge 1985, p. 36.

4 Antony Black, *Guilds and Civil Society in European Political Thought from the Twelfth Century to the Present*, Methuen, London 1984, p. 153.

5 A. L. Beier, *Masterless Men, The Vagrancy Problem in England 1560–1640*, Methuen, London 1985, p. 146.

6 Ibid., p. 12.

7 Alan Forrest, *The French Revolution and the Poor*, Basil Blackwell, Oxford 1981, p. 19.

8 Cf. Beier, *Masterless Men*, p. 86.

9 Michel Foucault, *Power/Knowledge*, ed. Colin Gordon, Harvester Press, Brighton 1980.

10 Olin H. Hufton, *Europe: Privilege and Protest 1730–1789*, Harvester Press, Brighton 1980, p. 37.

11 Beier, *Masterless Men*, pp. 159–60.

12 Foucault, *Power/Knowledge*, p. 148.

Notes to chapter 4

1 Ernest Gellner, *Nations and Nationalism*, Basil Blackwell, Oxford 1983, p. 50.
2 Albert O. Hirschman, *The Passions and the Interests*, Princeton University Press, 1977.
3 Baruch Spinoza, *Ethics*, transl. by N. H. White, Oxford University Press, Oxford 1927, part iv, prop. 14.
4 F. W. Nietzsche, *The Genealogy of Morals*, transl. by Francis Gotfrey, Doubleday, New York 1956, pp. 160–2.
5 Jacques Revel, 'Forms of Expertise; Intellectuals and the "popular" culture in France (1650–1800)', in *Understanding Popular Culture, Europe from the Middle Ages to the Nineteenth Century*, ed. by Steven L. Kaplan, Mouton, London 1984, pp. 262–4.
6 Ibid., p. 265.
7 David Hall, 'Introduction', in *Understanding Popular Culture*, p. 6.
8 Günther Lotte, 'Popular Culture and the Early Modern State', in *Understanding Popular Culture*, pp. 167, 162.
9 Robert Muchembled, *Culture populaire et culture des élites dans la France moderne (XVe–XVIIIe siècles)*, Flammarion, Paris 1978, pp. 230, 229, 226.
10 Ibid., pp. 341–2.
11 Jacques Revel, 'Forms of Expertise', pp. 257–8.
12 Yves-Maine Bercé, *Fête et révolte, Des mentalités populaires du XVIe au XVIIIe siècle*, Hachette, Paris 1976.
13 Ibid., p. 154.
14 Ibid., pp. 117–18.
15 Ibid., p. 117.
16 R. Malcolmson, in *Popular Culture: Past and Present*, ed. by B. Waites, T. Bennett and J. Martin, Croom Helm, London 1982, p. 41.
17 Anthony Delves, 'Popular Recreations and Social Conflict in Derby, 1800–1850', in Eileen and Stephen Yeo, *Popular Culture and Class Conflict 1590–1914: Explorations in the History of Labour and Leisure*, Harvester, Brighton 1981, pp. 90, 95.
18 Ibid., p. 98.
19 Vic Gammon, ' "Babylonian performances": the Rise and Suppression of Popular Church Music', in *Popular Culture*, pp. 77, 78, 83.
20 Eileen and Stephen Yeo, 'Ways of Seeing: Control and Leisure versus Class and Struggle', in *Popular Culture*, pp. 129, 134, 136.

Notes to chapter 5

1 'Rapport et projet de decrét sur l'instruction publique presenté à l'Assemblée Nationale le 20 et le 21 avril 1792', in *Une éducation pour la*

démocratie, Textes et projets de l'époque révolutionnaire, ed. by B. Baczko, Garnier Frères, Paris 1982.

2 Ibid., p. 20.

3 'Plan d'éducation nationale présenté à la Convention Nationale par Maximillien Robespierre le 13 juillet 1793', in *Une éducation*, pp. 377 ff.

4 'Rapport sur l'éducation révolutionnaire et républicaine, le 13 prairial, an II', in *Une éducation*, pp. 440–1.

5 Quoted from Harry C. Payne, *The Philosophers and the People*, Yale University Press, 1976, p. 155.

6 *Ancient Regime and the French Revolution*, transl. by Stuart Gilbert, Collins, New York 1976, p. 140.

7 Quoted from *The Philosophers and the People*, p. 29; Harvey Chisick, *The Limits of Reform in the Enlightenment, Attitudes towards the Education of the Lower Classes in Eighteenth Century France*, Princeton University Press, 1981, pp. 70, 251; John Passmore, *The Perfectibility of Man*, Duckworth, London 1972, p. 173.

8 *Œuvres complètes*, Gallimard, Paris 1959, vol. ii, p. 567.

9 Ibid., vol. iv, p. 267.

10 Chisick, *The Limits of Reform*, pp. 263–5, 274.

11 Ibid., p. 67.

Notes to chapter 6

1 Margaret T. Hogden, *Early Anthropology in the Sixteenth and Seventeenth Centuries*, Philadelphia 1946.

2 In J. S. Slotkin, *Readings in Early Anthropology*, Methuen, London 1965.

3 Richard H. Popkin, *The History of Scepticism from Erasmus to Spinoza*, University of California Press, 1979.

4 Michel Montaigne, *Essays*, The Modern Library, London 1930.

5 In *Civilisation, le mot et l'idée*, exposés par Lucien Febvre et al., La Renaissance du Livre, Paris 1930.

6 Cf. Z. Bauman, *Culture as Praxis*, Routledge, Kegan and Paul, London 1972.

7 Philippe Bénéton, *Histoire de mots culture et civilisation*, Presses de la fondation nationale des sciences politiques, Paris 1975, pp. 23 ff.

8 Ibid., p. 92.

Notes to chapter 7

1 Fr. Picavet, *Les idéologues*, reprinted Burt Franklin, New York 1971, pp. 305, 78.

2 Theodore Olsen, *Millenarianism, Utopianism, and Progress*, University of Toronto Press, 1982, p. 282.
3 Picavet, *Les idéologues*, p. 21.
4 *Destutt de Tracy and the Origins of 'Ideology'*, The American Philosophical Society, Philadelphia 1978, p. 47.
5 Picavet, *Les idéologues*, p. 122.
6 Destutt de Tracy, *Traité de la volonté et ces effets*, Librairie philosophique J. Vrin, Paris 1970 (from the second edition of 1818), p. 448.
7 Destutt de Tracy, *Éléments d'idéologie*, vol. i. 'Idéologie proprement dite', Librairie philosophique J. Vrin, Paris 1970, pp. 299–300.
8 Picavet, *Les idéologues*, p. 110.
9 Ibid., pp. 203, 211.
10 Ibid., p. 331.
11 Ibid., p. 583.
12 Positive Polity, vol. iv, 1822.
13 *Destutt de Tracy and the Origins of 'Ideology'*, pp. 75, 213.

Notes to chapter 8

1 Cf. Günther S. Stent, *The Coming of the Golden Age, A View of the End of Progress*, National History Press, New York 1969.
2 Ian Miles and John Irvine, *The Poverty of Progress; Changing Ways of Life in Industrial Societies*, Pergamon Press, 1982, p. 2.
3 Richard C. Rubenstein, 'The Elect and the Preterite', in *Modernisation, the Humanist Response to its Promise and Problems*, ed. by Richard L. Rubenstein, Paragon House, Washington DC 1982, p. 183.
4 Michel de Certeau, *The Practice of Everyday Life*, transl. by Steven F. Rendell, University of California Press, 1984, p. 179.
5 Stanley Cohen, *Visions of Social Control: Crime, Punishment and Classification*, Polity Press, Oxford 1985, p. 185.
6 David Carrier, 'Art and its Market', in Richard Hertz, *Theories of Contemporary Art*, Prentice Hall, Englewood Cliffs 1985, pp. 202, 204.
7 Georg Simmel, 'The Conflict in Modern Culture', in *The Conflict in Modern Culture and Other Essays*, transl. by K. Peter Etzkorn, Teachers College Press, New York 1968, p. 15.

Notes to chapter 9

1 Jürgen Habermas, 'Questions and Counterquestions', in *Habermas and Modernity*, ed. by Richard J. Bernstein, Polity Press, Oxford 1985, p. 192.

2 Connie D. Kliever, 'Authority in a Pluralist World', in *Modernisation, the Humanist Response to its Promise and Problems*, ed. by Richard L. Rubenstein, Paragon House, Washington DC 1982, pp. 81 ff.

3 Matei Calinescu, *Faces of Modernity: Avant-Garde, Decadence, Kitsch*, Indiana University Press, 1977, pp. 146–7.

4 Francis Picabia, *Dadas on Art*, ed. by Lucy R. Lippard, Prentice Hall, Englewood Cliffs 1971, p. 168.

5 Frederic Jameson, 'Postmodernism and Consumer Society', in *The Anti-Aesthetic, Essays on Postmodern Culture*, ed. by Hal Foster, Bay Press, Port Townsend 1983.

6 Peter Bürger, *Theory of Avant-Garde*, transl. by Michael Shaw, Manchester University Press, Manchester 1984, pp. 63, 87.

7 Picabia, *Dadas on Art*, p. 143.

8 Cf. Suzanne Gablik, *Has Modernism Failed?*, Thames and Hudson, London 1984.

9 Bürger, *Theory of Avant-Garde*, pp. 52, 53.

10 Kim Lewin, 'Farewell to Modernism', in Richard Hertz, *Theories of Contemporary Art*, Prentice Hall, Englewood Cliffs 1985, pp. 2, 7.

11 Rosalind E. Kraus, *The Originality of the Avant-Garde and other Modernist Myths*, MIT Press, Boston 1985, p. 22.

12 Howard S. Becker, *Art Worlds*, University of California Press, 1982, p. 137.

13 I. Gombrich, *Meditations on the Hobby Horse*, Phaidon, London 1963, pp. 17–18.

14 P. Bourdieu, *Distinction, a Social Critique of the Judgment of Taste*, transl. by Richard Nice, Routledge and Kegan Paul, London 1984, p. 327.

15 Wylie Sypher, *Rococo to Cubism in Art and Literature*, Vintage Books, New York 1960, p. 104.

16 *Baudelaire as a Literary Critic, Selected Essays*, transl. New York by Lois Boe Hylsop and Francis E. Hylsop, Pennsylvania State University Press, 1964, p. 298.

17 Calinescu, *Faces of Modernity*, p. 142.

18 Becker, *Art Worlds*, pp. 352–3, 360, 151, 155.

19 Marcia Muelder Baton, *Art and Non-Art*, Associated University Press, 1983, pp. 118, 107, 158.

20 Ernest Gellner, 'Tractatus Sociologico-Philosophicus', in *Objectivity and Cultural Divergence*, ed. by S. L. Brown, Royal Institute of Philosophy Lecture Series, 17, 1984, p. 258.

21 Richard J. Bernstein, *Philosophical Profiles*, Polity Press, Cambridge, 1986.

22 Ernest Gellner, *Nations and Nationalism*, Basil Blackwell, Oxford 1983, pp. 48–9, 55.

Notes to chapter 10

1 David Frisby, *Fragments of Modernity, Themes of Modernity in the Work of Simmel, Kracauer and Benjamin*, Polity Press, Oxford 1985, pp. 28–32.
2 Gustave leBon, *Psychologie des foules*, Alcan, Paris 1907 (12th edition), pp. 3, 51, 55–6.
3 *Lois psychologiques et l'évolution des peuples*, Alcan, Paris 1906 (7th edition), pp. 64–5, 117.
4 *La psychologie politique*, Flammarion, Paris 1916, pp. 124, 136.
5 Jose Ortega y Gasset, *Revolt of the Masses*.
6 Richard Sennett, *The Fall of the Public Man*, Vintage Books, 1978, pp. 11–12, 333–5; 'Destructive Gemeinschaft', in *Beyond the Crisis*, ed. by Norman Birnbaum, Oxford University Press, Oxford 1977, pp. 171 ff.
7 John Carroll, *Puritan, Paranoid, Remissive, a Sociology of Modern Culture*, Routledge and Kegan Paul, London 1977, pp. 17–19, 21, 45, 56.
8 Matthew Arnold, *Culture and Anarchy*, Cambridge University Press, Cambridge 1963 (orig. 1869), pp. 11, 49, 50.
9 George Steiner, in *Extraterritorial*, Atheneum, London 1976.
10 George Simmel, 'On the Concept and the Tragedy of Culture', in *The Conflict in Modern Culture and other Essays*, transl. by K. Peter Etzkorn, Teachers College Press, New York 1968, pp. 42–4.
11 David Joravsky, 'The Construction of the Stalinist Psyche', in *Cultural Revolution in Russia 1928–1931*, ed. by Sheila Fitzpatrick, Indiana University Press, 1978, p. 121.
12 Dwight Macdonald, 'A Theory of Mass Culture', in *Mass Culture, The Popular Arts in America*, ed. by Bernard Rosenberg and David Manning White, Free Press, Glencoe, Ill. 1957, pp. 63, 62, 69.
13 Pierre Bourdieu, *Distinction, a Social Critique of the Judgment of Taste*, transl. by Richard Nice, Routledge and Kegan Paul, London 1984, p. 62.
14 Bernard Rosenberg, 'Mass Culture in America', in *Mass Culture*, p. 5.
15 Ernest van den Haas, 'A Dissent from the Consensual Society', in *Mass Culture Revisited*, ed. by Bernard Rosenberg and David Manning White, Van Nostrand, New York 1971, p. 91.
16 Edward Shils, 'Mass Society and Its Culture', in *Mass Culture Revisited*, p. 61.
17 Wolfgang Fritz Haug, *Critique of Commodity Aesthetics*, transl. by Robert Bock, Polity Press, Oxford 1986, pp. 53, 54.
18 Jean Baudrillard, *For a Critique of the Political Economy of the Sign*, transl. by Charles Lewin, Telos Press, New York 1981, p. 51.
19 Jacques Attali, *Les trois mondes*, Fayard, Paris 1981, pp. 283–9.
20 Bourdieu, *Distinction*, pp. 154, 164.

Notes to chapter 11

1 Lev Trotsky, *1905*, transl. by A. Bostock, Penguin, Harmondsworth 1971, p. 58.
2 Robert J. Brym, *The Jewish Intelligentsia and Russian Marxism, A Sociological Study of Intellectual Radicalism and Ideological Divergence*, Macmillan, London 1978, chapter 2.
3 Cf. Z. Bauman, *Memories of Class*, Routledge and Kegan Paul, London 1982.
4 Alvin Gouldner, 'Prologue to a Theory of Revolutionary Intellectuals', *Telos*, London 1975, 26, p. 8.
5 André Gorz, *Paths to Paradise, On the Liberation from Work*, Pluto Press, London 1985, p. 35.
6 Jeremy Seabrook, *Landscapes of Poverty*, Basil Blackwell, Oxford 1985, p. 59.
7 Hilary Rose, 'Who can Delabel the Claimant?', in *Justice, Discrimination, and Poverty*, ed. by M. Adler and A. Bradley, Professional Books, New York 1971, p. 152.
8 Klaus Offe, *Social Security – Another British Failure?*, Charles Knight, London 1972, pp. 73, 108.
9 Cf. Paul Spicker, *Stigma and Social Welfare*, Croom Helm, London 1984, p. 37.
10 Joe R. Feagin, *Subordinating the Poor, Welfare and American Beliefs*, Prentice Hall, Englewood Cliffs 1975, pp. 3, 73.
11 Hristen Grønbjerg, David Street and Gereld D. Suttles, *Poverty and Social Change*, University of Chicago Press, 1978, pp. 142, 133, 134.
12 Joel F. Handler and Ellen J. Hollingsworth, *The 'Deserving Poor'*, Markham Publishing Company, 1971, pp. 77, 79, 165.
13 Edythe Shewbridge, *Portraits of Poverty*, W. W. Norton, 1972.
14 Seabrooke, *Landscapes of Poverty*, p. 94.
15 Clive Jenkins and Barrie Sherman, *The Leisure Shock*, Methuen, London 1981, p. 105.
16 Seabrook, *Landscapes of Poverty*, p. 87.

Notes to chapter 12

1 Jeremy Seabrook, *Landscapes of Poverty*, Basil Blackwell, Oxford 1985, p. 175.

Index

Lightning Source UK Ltd.
Milton Keynes UK
UKOW041529110313

207455UK00002B/599/A